Superhero Blockbusters

Screen Serialities

Series editors: Claire Perkins and Constantine Verevis

Series advisory board: Kim Akass, Glen Creeber, Shane Denson, Jennifer Forrest, Jonathan Gray, Julie Grossman, Daniel Herbert, Carolyn Jess-Cooke, Frank Kelleter, Amanda Ann Klein, Kathleen Loock, Jason Mittell, Sean O'Sullivan, Barton Palmer, Alisa Perren, Dana Polan, Iain Robert Smith, Shannon Wells-Lassagne, Linda Williams

Screen Serialities provides a forum for introducing, analysing and theorising a broad spectrum of serial screen formats – including franchises, series, serials, sequels and remakes.

Over and above individual texts that happen to be serialised, the book series takes a guiding focus on seriality as an aesthetic and industrial principle that has shaped the narrative logic, socio-cultural function and economic identity of screen texts across more than a century of cinema, television and 'new' media.

Titles in this series include:

Film Reboots
Edited by Daniel Herbert and Constantine Verevis

Reanimated: The Contemporary American Horror Remake
By Laura Mee

Gender and Seriality: Practices and Politics of Contemporary US Television
By Maria Sulimma

European Film Remakes
Edited by Eduard Cuelenaere, Gertjan Willems and Stijn Joye

Superhero Blockbusters: Seriality and Politics
By Felix Brinker

Superhero Blockbusters

Seriality and Politics

Felix Brinker

University Press

Edinburgh University Press is one of the leading university presses in the UK. We publish academic books and journals in our selected subject areas across the humanities and social sciences, combining cutting-edge scholarship with high editorial and production values to produce academic works of lasting importance. For more information visit our website: edinburghuniversitypress.com

© Felix Brinker, 2022, 2024

Edinburgh University Press Ltd
The Tun – Holyrood Road
12(2f) Jackson's Entry
Edinburgh EH8 8PJ

First published in hardback by Edinburgh University Press 2022

Typeset in 11/13 Ehrhardt MT
by Manila Typesetting Company, and
printed and bound by CPI Group (UK) Ltd,
Croydon, CR0 4YY

A CIP record for this book is available from the British Library

ISBN 978 1 4744 8518 0 (hardback)
ISBN 978 1 4744 8519 7 (paperback)
ISBN 978 1 4744 8520 3 (webready PDF)
ISBN 978 1 4744 8521 0 (epub)

The right of Felix Brinker to be identified as the author of this work has been asserted in accordance with the Copyright, Designs and Patents Act 1988, and the Copyright and Related Rights Regulations 2003 (SI No. 2498).

Contents

List of Figures	vi
Acknowledgements	viii
Introduction: Superhero Blockbusters, Seriality, and the Politics of Audience Engagement	1

Part I Seriality

1	Seriality, Culture Industry, and Digital-Era Popular Culture	23
2	Superhero Narratives between Seriality and Political Meaning	59

Part II Politics of Audience Engagement

3	The Hyper-Referential Style of Storytelling	81
4	The Superhero Blockbuster as Fan Management	121
5	Cinematic Populism and the Political Superhero Blockbuster	149
	Conclusion: Superhero Blockbusters as Entertainment for the Age of Cognitive Capitalism	181
Works Cited		191
Index		217

Figures

0.1 Christopher Reeve stars as the titular hero in Richard Donner's *Superman* (1978), the first superhero blockbuster. Screengrab from Amazon Prime Video — 5

0.2 Three live-action Spider-Men exemplify the genre's penchant for reboots: From top to bottom, Tobey Maguire in *Spider-Man 2* (2004), Andrew Garfield in *The Amazing Spider-Man* (2012), and Tom Holland in *Spider-Man: Far from Home* (2019). Screengrabs from Amazon Prime Video — 8

3.1 The title sequence of 2008's *The Incredible Hulk* reimagines the opening credits of the eponymous 1978 television show for a twenty-first-century audience. Screengrab from Amazon Prime Video — 82

3.2 Michael Keaton stars in 1992's *Batman Returns* (top image); 1995's *Batman Forever* recasts Val Kilmer (bottom) in the title role and thereby produces a rupture in series continuity. Screengrabs from Amazon Prime Video — 88

3.3 The opening scene of *X2* (2002) ends with a shot the composition of which echoes the aesthetics of superhero comics. Screengrab from Amazon Prime Video — 95

3.4 *Marvel's The Avengers* (2012) assembles the heroes of the *Marvel Cinematic Universe* for a shared adventure. Screengrab from Disney+ — 103

3.5	Batman (Ben Affleck), Superman (Henry Cavill), and Wonder Woman (Gal Gadot) team up in 2018's *Justice League*. Screengrab from Amazon Prime Video	109
4.1	In 2017's *Logan*, Wolverine (Hugh Jackman) finds an *X-Men* comic book – a moment that self-reflexively addresses fans' investment in the conventions of the genre. Screengrab from Amazon Prime Video	122
4.2	The title sequence of 2016's *Deadpool* ends on a digitally rendered tableau that evokes the imagery of superhero comics. Screengrab from Amazon Prime Video	134
4.3	In 2016's *Suicide Squad*, a flashback sequence narrates part of the Joker's (Jared Leto) and Harley Quinn's (Margot Robbie) backstory – a scene that directs narrative momentum away from the film's central plotline. Screengrab from Amazon Prime Video	141
5.1	Early in *Captain America: The Winter Soldier* (2014), Steve (Chris Evans) and Sam (Anthony Mackie) work out in front of Washington DC's Capitol building and other political landmarks. Screengrab from Amazon Prime Video	161
5.2	*Captain America: Civil War* ends with a showdown between Captain America (Chris Evans) and Iron Man (Robert Downey Jr). Screengrab from Amazon Prime Video	168
5.3	With his last words, Killmonger (Michael B. Jordan) situates his actions within a longer history of African-American struggle. Screengrab from Amazon Prime Video	172

Acknowledgements

From the very first notes jotted down in the summer of 2012 to its publication, this book has been almost ten years in the making. Along the way, I benefited tremendously from the support of many others who deserve none of the blame for the content of the following pages but are directly responsible for most of the good ideas that ended up in this book (and in the doctoral thesis on which it is based). Among them were my teachers Ruth Mayer and Shane Denson who, early in the process, suggested that my dissertation, which set out to articulate a grand theory of everything serial and digital, might focus on superhero movies instead. Over the following years, Ruth Mayer's unwavering support continued to be crucial: From my first sketches to chapter drafts and the finished dissertation, Ruth read everything and provided invaluable feedback – and also wrote letters of recommendation, provided me with jobs that paid my bills, offered encouragement when I was ready to throw in the towel, and did many, many other things that helped me get this project over the finishing line. Frank Kelleter, who eventually ended up as the lead advisor of my dissertation project, offered equally crucial support. This book lifts many of its best ideas directly from Frank's work and from (now probably long forgotten) off-the-cuff remarks made in various academic settings. It could not have been written without his insights, patience, and ability to look past the flaws of hastily thrown-together project presentations, progress reports, and dissertation drafts.

The dissertation on which this book is based was generously supported by funding from several institutions. The early phases of my research were financed by a start-up grant from Leibniz Universität Hannover's Graduate Academy. Afterwards, my doctoral studies at Freie Universität Berlin (2013–18) were funded by a full-time PhD scholarship from the John F. Kennedy

Institute's Graduate School of North American Studies. Finally, in the fall of 2015, a travel grant by the German Academic Exchange Service (DAAD) provided funding for a research trip to the United States.

In addition, my work over the years has profited immensely from my participation in the American Studies colloquium at Leibniz University and the always constructive feedback of its members who, led by Ruth Mayer, helped to turn my thoughts into a meaningfully structured text – among them are Ilka Brasch, Bettina Soller, Florian Groß, Christina Mayer, Anna-Lena Oldehus, Abby Fagan, Svenja Fehlhaber, Jatin Wagle, and Annabel Friedrichs. I am also thankful to the other members of the Graduate School of North American Studies' 2013 doctoral cohort – Talel Ben Jemia, Mathias Großklaus, Nikolas Keßels, Siofra McSherry, Katharina Metz, Koen Potgieter, Sophie Spieler, and Min Kyung Yoo – whose hard work and general put-togetherness provided models of academic work when I needed them. At the Kennedy Institute, I furthermore profited from my participation in the Culture Department's research colloquium (led by Frank Kelleter) and the helpful comments of Martin Lüthe, Simon Schleusener, Birte Wege, Maria Sulimma, Alexander Starre, Kathleen Loock, Andreas Sudmann, Julia Leyda, and Daniel Stein. Of the former, Martin, Birte, and Kathleen deserve special thanks because they also served as members of the committee for my doctoral defense. The ideas articulated in this book are furthermore strongly indebted to the work of the now-defunct research unit "Popular Seriality – Aesthetics and Practice" (2010–16), of which I was an associated member. In this context, I also benefited from a series of workshops organized by Maria Sulimma, which allowed me to discuss some of my ideas with scholars Constantine Verevis, William Urrichio, Rita Felski, Robyn Warhol, Sean O'Sullivan, and Jason Mittell.

Finally, I want to thank my parents, Anne and Heinz Brinker, for their unflagging support over all these years. I also wish to thank Benjamin Brune, who has been a true friend and always knew exactly what else to watch, read, or listen to when I got tired of superheroes. In Berlin, Meret Matthes, Matthias Clausen, and Nils Kumkar offered refuge and shelter from the stress of graduate school life. Above all, however, I thank my wife Caroline and our children, Frederik and Carla, who, over the past few years, had to share me with my work on this project. This book is dedicated to them.

For Caro, Frederik, and Carla

Introduction: Superhero Blockbusters, Seriality, and the Politics of Audience Engagement

Born from the pages of American comic books in the late 1930s, superheroes made the jump to the silver screen early and have never really left the cinema since. But over the past two decades, the popularity of superhero movies has risen to unprecedented heights. Between early 2000 and the end of 2020, Hollywood released no fewer than seventy-four films about the exploits of iconic figures such as Superman or Wonder Woman, super-teams such as the Fantastic Four or the X-Men, or lesser known characters such as Harley Quinn or Venom.[1] Several of these movies count among the most profitable Hollywood productions of the last decades, with films such as *The Dark Knight* (2008), *Iron Man 3* (2013), or *Avengers: Endgame* (2019) grossing more than a billion US Dollars during their respective theatrical runs alone ("All Time"). Considering such commercial successes, Dan Hassler-Forest has rightly identified "the superhero movie" as "the dominant genre in 21st-century Hollywood cinema" (*Capitalist Superheroes* 3). This dominance also expresses itself in the wealth of cultural activity that clusters around new releases. As privileged objects for the overlapping media publics of the early twenty-first century, superhero blockbusters garner the attention of interested observers who incessantly discuss, dismiss, or promote them. This conversation occurs not only offline, but also in online fan forums, in the mainstream press, and on news websites with a focus on popular culture, as well as in topical publications by professional critics. The discourse about superhero movies fills the gaps between releases with a constant coverage of production news, speculation about upcoming films, and the celebration or critical dissection of earlier ones. It also includes commentary and analyses that trace references to source materials or decipher deeper levels of meaning, fan fiction in various forms and guises, and scholarly treatises (such as this one) that seek to explain the genre's popularity. Beyond their status as cinematic entertainments, superhero movies thus are fulcra for an ongoing, multi-faceted discussion that creates a significant part of the genre's cultural visibility.

This book sets out to explain the current prominence of superhero blockbuster films by examining their interactions with the cultural environment that sustains them. To this end, it scrutinizes the narrative, thematic, and film-aesthetic means by which these productions address their consumers, explores why these films resonate with the members of a vocal fan culture, and examines how they prompt discussion within the discourses that surrounds them. Very generally put, this book considers what superhero blockbusters do to attain and maintain their popularity. But it also advances an argument about the politics of this type of film and its relationship to a larger regime of capitalist popular culture. In this regard, it suggests that twenty-first-century superhero blockbuster films pursue a project of cultural mobilization that contributes to processes of capital accumulation, participates in a micro-political organization of consumers' free time, and actively intervenes in the shaping of audience discourses. This project manifests itself in what I call the genre's politics of audience engagement, a concept that refers to a set of carefully calibrated narrative, thematic, and film-aesthetic tools that superhero blockbuster films employ to mobilize consumers and interact with their cultural and medial environment. These tools include the ways in which recent superhero movies tell their stories, the themes they negotiate, and the cinematic attractions they offer. The means and devices that make up the genre's politics of engagement can be grouped into three broad categories: a hyper-referential style of storytelling that indexes related narratives and materials in other media, textual and extratextual practices of fan management that intervene in the discourses of online fandom, and a cinematic populism that seeks to pre-structure superhero movies' critical reception. I suggest that the contemporary popularity of the genre results, to a significant extent, from the deployment of these tools, which endow films of the genre with a remarkable ability to set audiences and discourses in motion. This mobilizing power is, in turn, inextricably connected to superhero movies' seriality and status as parts of larger storytelling frameworks that also encompass comic book source materials, sequels, spin-offs, and other forms of continuation, as well as previous film adaptations of the same properties and related superhero narratives in a variety of media. This study thus considers recent superhero blockbusters as prime examples of a type of serialized commercial entertainment that becomes successful precisely because it manages to enroll different groups of recipients – from average consumers and a hard core of dedicated fans to specialized professionals who write about popular culture for living – into the service of its own promotion.

This book furthermore suggests that superhero blockbuster cinema's politics of engagement is paradigmatic for a culture-industrial formation that more generally governs the operations of commercial popular culture today. This digital-era culture industry has replaced the once-prominent idea of the passive consumer with an ideology that – like the academic discourse on "participatory culture" – frames culturally productive and socially networked media users as the most important recipients of commercial entertainment. Within this ideological framework, movie-goers figure not only as consumers whose purchases allow producers to realize a surplus of economic value, but also as potential collaborators who can help to increase the cultural visibility of commodities by engaging in practices of collective "decipherment, speculation, and elaboration," as Henry Jenkins puts it in his study *Convergence Culture* (95). Arguing that this view of the audience is an expression of digital-era capitalism, this book suggests that the commercial success of popular entertainments today hinges on their ability to (1) address their consumers repeatedly via a variety of media; (2) encourage recipients to engage in communicational, textual or (more broadly put) cultural production related to said entertainments; and (3) harness this productivity for promotional gain.

The same imperatives also inform the aesthetics of superhero blockbuster cinema, which has found particularly effective ways to solicit the cultural production of media audiences. The political significance of contemporary superhero blockbuster films thus manifests itself on several interlocking levels. As commodified products of a profit-driven industry, superhero blockbusters contribute to the perpetuation of a capitalist mode of production by circulating through markets and realizing their surplus value in exchange for money. As popular entertainments, they are furthermore consumed as part of everyday recreational practices and make demands on the time and attention of viewers. In doing so, superhero movies participate in the structuring of consumers' free time. In addition, the collective engagement with superhero movies provides a foundation for the emergence of fan-oriented media publics whose discourses are at least potentially political as well. Finally, superhero movies' status as blockbuster films endows them with an ability to put ideas and images into cultural circulation, to prompt follow-up conversations and, thereby, to participate in ongoing cultural and political debates. All these dimensions come together in the genre's politics of audience engagement, which turns superhero blockbusters into highly effective instruments of an entertainment industry that seeks to capitalize on consumers' digitally mediated cultural practices.

To make this case, the following chapters consider the medial, politico-economic, ideological, and narrative foundations of the genre's politics of engagement and the workings of its three core components – hyper-referential style, practices of fan management, cinematic populism – in greater detail. First, however, the rest of this chapter elaborates on the kind of argument that I want to advance and introduces concepts that are central to my inquiry. To begin, the next section defines what I mean by the term "superhero blockbuster" and addresses the inherent seriality of the genre. Afterwards, I elaborate further on the idea of a politics of audience engagement, consider the non-human agency of serial narratives, and discuss superhero blockbuster's role for capitalist reproduction. Lastly, this introduction offers an overview of the following chapters.

SUPERHERO MOVIES, BLOCKBUSTER CINEMA, SERIAL STORYTELLING

This book focuses on superhero movies based on properties by DC and Marvel Comics, the United States' two biggest comics publishers. More precisely, it examines DC- and Marvel-based superhero films that have been widely released in US-American theaters, distributed internationally, and produced or released under the umbrella of one of the big conglomerate-owned Hollywood film studios or one of their mini-major competitors.[2] These movies are part of a larger genre of superhero film that also includes animated features, adaptations of DC or Marvel properties without a wide theatrical release, films based on titles by other publishers, releases not explicitly based on comics sources, and movies that operate in the modes of parody or pastiche, all of which fall outside of the scope of this study.[3]

As superhero movies, most of the films considered here are, as Hassler-Forest notes in his own book on the genre, ...

> ... clearly identifiable [. . .] on three basic levels: semantically (by the appearance of costumes, masks, superhuman powers, etc.), syntactically (narratives in which heroes save cities/worlds/communities from destruction by evil), and pragmatically (texts that are written and talked about as part of an existing superhero genre) (*Capitalist Superheroes* 8).

As adaptations of DC or Marvel comics properties, the films discussed in this book furthermore center on pre-established characters that possess significant histories in other media. Finally, the movies examined here are part of blockbuster cinema, which is to say that they are, in one way or another, bigger than other kinds of film – in terms of production costs, profits, or cinematic attractions, for example. Along similar lines, Julian Stringer observes that the term blockbuster is commonly applied to a type of big-budget spectacle that "flaunt[s] its assets [. . .] and creates audience awareness" through "ever-increasing levels of audio-visual intemperance" (5). The films discussed here, in other words, present themselves as emphatically cinematic spectacles that foreground the allure of state-of-the-art special effects as well as the "pace, excitement, [and] exhilaration" of elaborate action sequences (Tasker 5). Moreover, the films discussed in this book are part of a specifically American tradition of blockbuster cinema that originates in the New Hollywood of the 1970s and is often associated with films like *Jaws* (1975) and *Star Wars* (1977) (see Kuhn and Westwell, "New Hollywood"; Shone; Cucco; Schatz). Blockbuster cinema in this sense refers to a type of big-budget filmmaking that operates in conjunction with large-scale marketing campaigns, seeks to turn the theatrical exhibition of feature films into widely publicized "social events" (Stringer 3) and frequently connects to practices of cross-promotion that are meant to further the sale of soundtrack albums, tie-in toys, and other film-related merchandise (see Cucco; Meehan; Wyatt). This book uses the terms superhero blockbuster, superhero blockbuster genre, superhero movie, or similar constructions to refer to films based on DC or Marvel Comics properties that follow the model of the New Hollywood blockbuster.

Superhero blockbusters in this narrow sense emerged at the tail end of the 1970s with the back-to-back production of Warner Bros.' *Superman* (1978; Figure 0.1) and its sequel *Superman II* (1980). The following decades saw the release of additional *Superman* sequels and other high-grossing superhero movies (such as 1989's *Batman* and its sequels, for example). But the genre exploded in the late 1990s and early 2000s, when the release of the highly profitable *Blade* (New Line Cinema, 1998), *X-Men* (Fox, 2000), and *Spider-Man* (Sony/Columbia, 2002) set off a proliferation of similar films that went on to dominate the domestic American box office charts during the following years. I discuss the history of the genre in more detail in Chapter 3, but I want to emphasize here that superhero blockbusters eventually came to occupy a central position within the Hollywood economy. By the mid-2000s, entries of

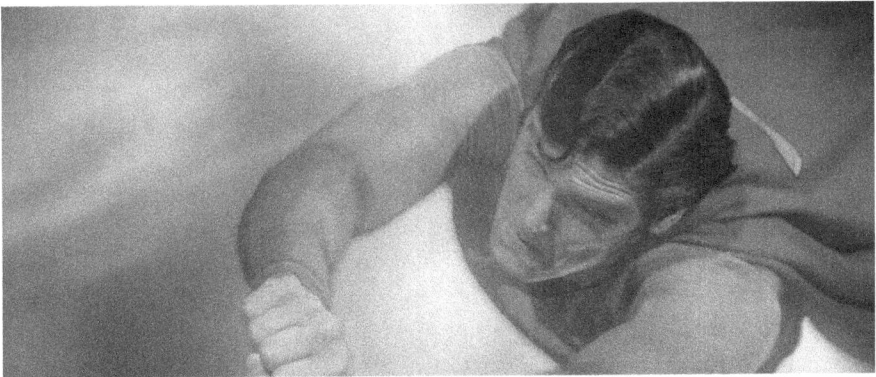

Figure 0.1 Christopher Reeve stars as the titular hero in Richard Donner's *Superman* (1978), the first superhero blockbuster. Screengrab from Amazon Prime Video.

the genre regularly counted among the industry's most reliable "tentpole" pictures and thus among a class of films whose expected profitability was meant to offset the risks created by studios' overall production slates (see Balio 25–28). As such, superhero blockbusters were not only profitable, but generated returns that made the production of other, smaller films possible. Furthermore, their success secured or elevated the status of film studios and production companies, as well as the careers of producers, directors, screenwriters, and stars. At the time of writing in the summer of 2021, superhero movies based on DC or Marvel properties have held this special status for more than two decades. And while the COVID-19 pandemic and the resulting shutdowns of film production and theatrical exhibition have rendered the genre's immediate future somewhat uncertain, Hollywood's big studios seem determined to continue this success story for quite some time.

Superhero blockbusters also exemplify another important tendency of New Hollywood blockbuster cinema: its repeated attempts to replicate earlier successes through the production of sequels, spin-offs, and other forms of cinematic continuation. This tendency already informed Warner's *Superman* films and played a crucial role in the genre's subsequent rise to prominence. But, generally, twenty-first-century blockbusters have embraced serialization practices more strongly than earlier examples of the format. This trend manifests itself, for instance, in the commercial successes of the many other successful blockbuster series that were launched during the early years of the new millennium. These include George Lucas's three *Star Wars* prequels (1999, 2002, 2005; five additional films since 2015), the *Fast and the Furious* films (ten releases since 2001), and movie franchises built around adaptations of pre-existing media properties, such as Disney's *Pirates of the Caribbean* amusement park ride (five films since 2003), Tolkien's *Lord of the Rings* and *The Hobbit* books (six films since 2001), the *Harry Potter/Fantastic Beasts* novels (ten films since 2001), or the *Transformers* toys and cartoons (six films since 2007) (see Balio 25–33; Brinker, "On the Political Economy").

The rise of superhero blockbuster cinema figures centrally in this embrace of blockbuster serialization, and the genre today includes some of Hollywood's longest-running film series. The *X-Men* series, for instance, began with a trilogy of feature films based on the eponymous Marvel's comics title (*X-Men*; *X2: X-Men United*, 2003; *X-Men: The Last Stand*, 2006) but has since grown to encompass thirteen installments. These include a second trilogy of films about the character Wolverine (*X-Men Origins: Wolverine*, 2009; *The Wolverine*, 2013; and *Logan*, 2017), a series of prequel films featuring younger versions of the main characters (*X-Men: First Class*, 2011; *X-Men: Days of Future Past*, 2014; *X-Men: Apocalypse*, 2016; *Dark Phoenix*, 2019), two films about the antihero Deadpool (*Deadpool*, 2016; *Deadpool 2*, 2018), and the spin-off *The New Mutants* (2020). While each entry tells a self-contained story about a conflict between super-powered heroes and villains, all of them share a narrative continuity that allows the main characters – such as Hugh Jackman's Wolverine or X-Men leader Professor X (portrayed by Patrick Stewart and, after *First Class*, also by James McAvoy) – to cross over from one film to the next. Plot elements of earlier installments are referenced again in later films as well; likewise, deaths and shifting relationships between characters leave a lasting impact on the narrative world of the series. In addition, almost all *X-Men* films end with scenes that hint at the possibility of further adventures. Produced and financed by 20th Century Fox but made by different filmmakers, the *X-Men* films thus are a close match for Frank Kelleter's definition of serial narratives as "heavily schematized, mass-addressed continuing narratives with a constant set of characters that are produced according to rules of economic standardization (that is, with a specialized division of labor and by industrial means)" ("Einführung" 18; translation mine).

But the *X-Men* series' complicated order of interconnected sub-series and spin-offs is just one example of the seemingly interminable drive to continue and expand that is so obviously on display in contemporary blockbuster cinema. The same drive also comes to the fore in the frequent reboots of ongoing series. Hollywood rarely abandons underperforming superhero properties – instead, it restarts them with new directors, casts, and narrative continuities.[4] In this manner, the Michael Keaton-led *Batman* and *Batman Returns* (1992) were followed by *Batman Forever* (1995) starring Val Kilmer, who was replaced by *Batman & Robin*'s George Clooney two years later – only to be succeeded by the Christian Bale-Batman of Nolan's *Dark Knight*-trilogy (2005, 2008, 2012) and subsequent incarnations of the character portrayed by Ben Affleck (multiple films since 2016) and Robert Pattinson (*The Batman*, 2022). Likewise, Ang Lee's *Hulk* (Universal, 2003; starring Eric Bana) was followed by Louis Leterrier's *The Incredible Hulk* (Universal, 2008; starring Edward Norton); Bryan Singer's *Superman Returns* (Warner, 2006; starring Brandon Routh) gave way to Zack Snyder's *Man of Steel* (2013; starring Henry Cavill); and the hero of Sam Raimi's *Spider-Man* trilogy (Sony, 2002, 2004, 2007; played by Tobey Maguire) was succeeded by the protagonist of Marc Webb's two *The Amazing Spider-Man* films (Sony, 2012 and 2014; portrayed by Andrew Garfield) and a third incarnation of the figure portrayed by Tom Holland (who appears in several entries of Disney's *Marvel Cinematic Universe*; see Figure 0.2).

These examples demonstrate that serialization does not necessarily involve the construction of an unbroken narrative continuity. Making a similar point, Umberto Eco notes that serial fictions often foreground the "the enjoyment of a scheme" that is reiterated (with significant variation) by each new installment ("Innovation and Repetition," 162). To illustrate this aspect, Eco points to the authors of classic serial detective fictions – such as Arthur Conan Doyle and his series of Sherlock Holmes stories, for example – who "invent[ed] a 'new'

Figure 0.2 Three live-action Spider-Men exemplify the genre's penchant for reboots: From top to bottom, Tobey Maguire in *Spider-Man 2* (2004), Andrew Garfield in *The Amazing Spider-Man* (2012) and Tom Holland in *Spider-Man: Far From Home* (2019). Screengrabs from Amazon Prime Video.

crime and 'new' secondary characters" for each adventure, but also made sure to "reconfirm the permanence of a fixed repertoire of *topoi*" (such as Holmes's tics or Watson's supporting role) ("Innovation and Repetition," 164). Likewise, Kelleter argues that telling "the same again, but in a new way" is one of the key challenges of serial narration ("Einführung," 27; translation mine). Since serial narratives unfold over extended periods of time, the ability to do so is invariably bound to "extranarrative realms" that might pose unforeseen problems, including "failed contract negotiations" with actors and intellectual property rights holders or poor critical reception, fan-backlash, and sudden shifts in "the world of geopolitics," for example (Kelleter, "Five Ways" 17). Series reboots and narratively convoluted series such as Fox' *X-Men* franchise navigate such contingencies in different ways: by starting over from scratch, or by branching out into new directions.

Finally, superhero film series are part of larger media franchises whose expansion can also be understood as a serial proliferation (see Johnson, "Learning to Share" 9–19). Reaching well beyond the cinema, these franchises reiterate the narrative patterns, central characters, and iconographies of superhero comics properties for a variety of formats and products, from films, television series and digital games to toys, clothes, and other merchandising articles. Superhero franchises thus are particularly visible examples of a widespread practice of pop-cultural "multiplication and replication" that, as Derek Johnson notes, is often framed as "monstrously homogenized, self-determining, and childish" and understood as a threat to the commercial viability of ostensibly more original works (*Media Franchising* 2, 1). Cautioning against such easy dismissals, Johnson points to the long history of media franchising practices, which he sees as rooted in a general "push towards deregulated consolidation and post-Fordist flexibility" within the entertainment industries that began in the late 1970s and early 1980s (*Media Franchising* 4). The emergence of the heavily cross-promoted New Hollywood blockbuster needs to be understood within the same context. In fact, Donner's *Superman* is an early example for franchising practices that would, in subsequent decades, become a norm in blockbuster cinema. In the late 1970s, both Warner Bros. (the studio which made Donner's film) and DC Comics (which owned the intellectual property on which the film was based) were part of the Warner Communications conglomerate (WCI), which, in turn, also held subsidiaries in magazine and book publishing, recorded music, and television production (among other things). For WCI, the production and release of *Superman* thus presented itself as an opportunity to cross-promote other *Superman* content – such as ABC's animated television series *Super Friends* [1973–86], or DC's ongoing *Superman* and *Action Comics* titles – and to bring a variety of new products (such as a soundtrack album, a tie-in novel, and a *Superman* game for the Atari 2600) to market. As a result, Donner's film, whose 1978 release was timed to roughly coincide with the fortieth anniversary of the Superman character, did double-duty as the first installment of a film series and as an outsize advertisement for an array of closely related commodities. Similar franchising and cross-promotion strategies have been at work in superhero blockbuster cinema ever since, turning entries of the genre into, as Eileen Meehan has argued with reference to 1989's

Batman, "commercial intertext[s]" that alert viewers to the existence of all kinds of related products (70).

Filmic serialization, rebooting, media franchising – in the context of this book, these and other practices of continuation, retelling, and proliferation are understood as different, but closely related modes of popular seriality.[5] Adopting a similar perspective, Shane Denson suggests that "seriality" can generally be understood as "a formal property and/or organizational principle that is commonly associated with ongoing narratives, recurring patterns, and periodic publication schedules" ("Seriality" 684). The two-fold character of this definition is important here: on the one hand, seriality can be identified as an intrinsic feature of narratives that are told in installments or re-told for new audiences. On the other hand, seriality denotes an organizational principle that more generally informs the production, circulation, and consumption of commercial entertainment. Capitalist popular culture has always balanced the old and the new, as well as reiterated established success formulae to make its products profitable; similarly, recurring patterns and regular schedules are not a unique feature of serial narratives, but intrinsic to modern commercial entertainment in general. Finally, commercially operated mass media such as broadcast television or radio have always attempted to capture audiences' attention over longer periods of time, even when their contents are not explicitly serialized (which they often are). Commercial popular culture is thus always latently serial. Serial narratives capitalize on this latent seriality, make it explicit, and turn it into a tool for an ongoing audience mobilization. Understood this way, seriality is not simply a feature of some narrative texts, but a label for a set of closely related practices of commercial cultural production, distribution, and consumption that endow serial narratives with their characteristic ability to continue and multiply, to attract and re-attract viewers, and to inspire attendant cultural production.

Analogously, cinematic serialization can be understood as a socially interactive practice that not only connects individual texts to each other, but also involves film studios, filmmakers, and stars, technological infrastructures and media platforms, diverse audiences, intellectual property rights, merchandising products, fictional characters and their stories, online discourses, and more. In this book, the notion of seriality thus refers to a dynamic principle of profit-oriented cultural production that is at work in different types of serial narrative, that brings together a variety of different actors and agencies, and that produces lasting cultural, social, and medial effects (for a similar view, see Mayer, *Fu Manchu* 6–7). I will elaborate on this understanding of seriality below and in the following chapters. But first, I would like to discuss three issues that are central to this book's interests: serial narratives' politics of audience engagement, their agency to shape their cultural environments, and their contribution to the reproduction of capitalist orders.

POLITICS OF ENGAGEMENT, SERIAL AGENCY, CAPITALIST REPRODUCTION

Much of this book focuses on how superhero blockbuster films encourage a serialized reception of ongoing film series and larger media franchises, as well as closely related, culturally and economically productive audience activity. In pursuing this interest, I take some inspiration from television studies, where the concept of "audience engagement" has long been used to refer to viewers' dedication to cult programming and the fan practices inspired by shows such as *The X-Files* (Fox, 1993–2002, 2016–18) or *Lost* (ABC, 2004–10) (see Reeves, Rodgers, and Epstein; Sconce; Mittell, "Narrative Complexity"; for a history of the term, see Evans 1–7). In that context, a useful definition has been offered by Ivan Askwith, who uses the term as shorthand for "the range of possible investments (financial, emotional, psychological, social, intellectual, etc.) that a viewer can make in a media object" (49). Elizabeth Evans notes that "engagement" in this broad sense has become "a buzzword within both the screen industries and screen-related scholarship" in the first decade of the twenty-first century (2). On the one hand, the increased interest in the concept is informed by the entertainment industries' attempts to capture the attention of an increasingly fragmented audience; on the other hand, it stems from media scholars' interest in new modes of media consumption. Askwith's definition is thus part of a broader engagement discourse that not only unfolds within television and media studies, but also encompasses work in the fields of "sociology, political science, media psychology, education and branding and marketing studies" (Evans 6). Trying to come to terms with the rise of the Internet and the digitization of consumer electronics, much of this discourse focuses on the behavior of audiences who are "willing to pursue content across multiple channels" and actively participate in online discourses about popular entertainments (Jenkins, Ford, and Green 116; see also Evans 7–9; Jenkins, *Convergence Culture* 64–8). The engagement discourse overlaps with a diverse body of scholarly work that considers the online activities of media audiences as expressions of a "participatory culture" (see Jenkins's *Textual Poachers*; *Convergence Culture*; *Fans, Bloggers, and Gamers*; Delwiche and Henderson), as a form of "produsage" that blurs the line between production and consumption (Bruns), or as a type of unpaid "free labor" that might be exploited by profit-oriented corporations (Terranova; De Kosnik; Stanfill; for an overview, see Bolin). Attempting to synthesize these perspectives, Henry Jenkins, Sam Ford, and Joshua Green have suggested that digital-era popular culture operates under an "engagement-based paradigm" that "see[s] the audience as a collective of active agents whose labor may generate alternative forms of market value" (116; compare Stanfill pos. 100–13). Under this paradigm, so Jenkins et al. suggest, the commercial success of cultural commodities is predicated on their ability to encourage strong engagements and solicit enough audience activity to become centerpieces of highly visible cultural phenomena.

This book also considers the concept of engagement to be of central importance to the operations of contemporary popular culture. However, rather than uncritically accepting the notion of an engagement-based paradigm, I suggest that the concept of engagement is more adequately understood as the centerpiece of an influential ideological framework that orients much of commercial entertainment (and much of the scholarship about it) today. This ideology – which I will discuss in more detail in the next chapter – justifies and legitimizes corporate attempts to capitalize on the activities of media audiences, but also orients commercial cultural production on a practical level. The aesthetics of contemporary superhero blockbuster cinema, I suggest, are purposely configured to maximize engagement in the sense described above. What I call superhero blockbusters' politics of engagement refers to the means they employ towards this end, that is, to the tools on which these films rely to engage viewers over longer periods of time, prefigure their own reception, and set off larger cultural mobilizations.

Superhero movies do not have a monopoly on the politics of audience engagement, as serial narratives of all periods and media work towards involving their audiences across time. Similarly, many popular series have found ways to encourage debates among recipients.[6] Accordingly, what I call politics of engagement more generally refers to the devices that serial narratives employ to shape their cultural environment. Perhaps the most basic of such devices is the cliffhanger ending, the sudden suspension of narration during a moment of heightened dramatic tension at the end of an installment. Cliffhangers encourage recipients to return for the next part of the story, but they can also yield powerful publicity effects, as they often inspire lively discussions about future plot developments within segments of the media public. What Kristen Thompson calls "dispersed exposition" – expository dialogue that thematizes past events, established character constellations, or simmering conflicts for the benefit of the audience – is another such device (*Storytelling* 65; see also Brinker, "Formal Politics" 51), as is the "previously on . . ." segment that appears at the beginning of many broadcast television series. In today's media environment, these devices of serial storytelling often work in conjunction with a variety of online promotional materials (such as trailers, clips, or social media posts) that similarly seek to encourage a serialized reception, while also addressing new viewers and serving to bolster series' overall cultural visibility. In summary, a series' politics of engagement includes all textual and paratextual means that are employed to engage consumers and generate public attention. These means are always historically and medially specific, shaped by the concrete conditions under which serial narratives operate, and inflected by the aesthetic means they have at their disposal.

The tools that blockbuster film series employ to engage viewers and stage themselves as social events thus differ from the televisual means of engagement mentioned above. They are not only a matter of narrative unfolding, either. As examples of blockbuster cinema, superhero movies foreground the spectacular and sensational aspects of the film experience as much as their narrative dimension. Emphasizing this point, Dick Tomasovic discusses superhero films as a contemporary "cinema of attractions" that integrates narrative appeals with the visceral pleasures of kinetic action scenes and spectacular special effects (309–11). In films of the gerne, such cinematic attractions are furthermore bound up with the mechanics of serial storytelling, as newer entries of ongoing series generally try to offer spectacles that are at least on par with (but ideally more impressive than) those of preceding films. Both dimensions also cannot be disconnected from the content level of films, as the narrative mechanics, cinematic spectacles, and thematic resonances of superhero blockbusters are closely intertwined. Any given entry of the genre thus presents itself as a complex bundle of storytelling strategies, audiovisual attractions, and ideologically charged contents.

To untangle these appeals, this book suggests that the genre's politics of engagement encompasses three core components. The first of these components is a hyper-referential style of storytelling that invites viewers to continue their engagement elsewhere and to watch sequels and spin-offs, read many-decade-old source materials and newly released superhero comics, or peruse paratextual materials online, for example. Recent superhero blockbusters connect this style of storytelling to practices of fan management that seek to enroll the support of online fandom. These fan management efforts are at work both within superhero movies – which often demonstrate a conspicuous familiarity with fan-cultural discourses – and in sophisticated niche marketing campaigns that seek to position these films prominently within a fan-oriented media public. Finally, the genre's politics of engagement includes a cinematic populism that governs the ways in which superhero movies negotiate political subject-matter. This populism combines a narrative framework that conceives the world as a sphere of violent, Manichean conflicts with an affectively powerful cinematic presentation, a combination that invites allegorizing readings on the part of reviewers and critics. By relying on these means, superhero blockbusters interfere with the media consumption practices of viewers, participate in the organization of their free time, intervene in audience discourses, and attempt to harness viewers' cultural productivity for commercial gain.

In making this case, I understand superhero blockbuster films as media objects that interact with and actively shape the world around them. This perspective follows in the footsteps of recent cultural and media studies work that conceptualizes serial narratives as recursive and dynamic systems which develop over extended periods of time and bring together different actors and agencies. Along these lines, Frank Kelleter and Daniel Stein have discussed serial narratives as Actor-Networks in the sense of Bruno Latour's Actor-Network Theory (ANT) (Kelleter and Stein 260; see also Kelleter, "Five Ways" and "Einführung"; on ANT, see Latour, *Reassembling*). Similarly, Ruth Mayer has invoked the Deleuzian notion of the "machine" to consider the fictional Chinese supervillain Fu Manchu – who, like the protagonists of superhero movies, has been reincarnated in serial narratives of various media – as "a contraption or ensemble that conjoins living beings and technological apparatuses into intricately layered arrangements of interaction" (Mayer, *Fu Manchu* 7). The dynamic and interactional character of serial narratives is saliently on display in their interplay with the activities of their audiences. Since the production of contemporary superhero blockbusters occurs while preceding entries of the genre are still playing in theaters or circulating through ancillary markets for home video, viewers' reactions – mediated through box office returns, reviews, fan discussion, and chatter on social media – can feed back into the production process and inform the decisions of studio executives, filmmakers, and marketers. Superhero blockbuster series thus are "evolving narratives" that respond to their own reception (Kelleter, "Five Ways" 12). Like other serial narratives, they furthermore exhibit an "immanent tendency" to "release creative practices on the part of their recipients" (Kelleter and Stein 259; translation mine). This tendency comes to the fore in the countless fan activities that they inspire, which include discussions on fan sites, events such as fan conventions, practices such as cosplay, and more. In encouraging such activities, superhero movies contribute to the shaping of a cultural environment that can sustain their further serial unfolding. As dynamic, recursive, and culturally productive forms, superhero blockbusters assume a modicum of agency to interfere with the practices of other actors and participate in the production of larger social and cultural phenomena.

The above view of serial narratives is based on an understanding of non-human agency that requires some elaboration. Serial narratives obviously do not coerce their viewers into acting out any specific kind of behavior, nor do they exert any kind of hidden influence that escapes the audience's attention, nor are the practices of their recipients somehow the mere result of film reception.[7] The claim that inanimate objects such as films possess an agency of their own makes more sense, however, if agency is understood as non-intentional and distributed. As Rita Felski puts it, . . .

> Non-human actors do not determine reality or single-handedly make things happen – let us steer clear of technological or textual determinism. [. . .] The "actor" in actor-network-theory is not a self-authorizing

subject, an independent agent who summons up actions and orchestrates events. Rather, actors become actors via their relations to other phenomena, as mediators and translators linked in extended constellations of cause and effect. (Felski 582–83; compare Latour, *Reassembling* 37–42, 63–86)

Likewise, superhero movies are not magic objects that completely determine the reception practices of their viewers, but entities that, because of their specific characteristics and relations to other actors, make a difference in the social interactions in which they participate. From a similar vantage point, Kelleter and Stein suggest that the agency of serial narratives is best understood as "*something which makes us do things*," as a potential to "create courses of action, intentional possibilities and identities for all participants" (Kelleter and Stein 260, my translation; see Kelleter, "Five Ways" 22–26). Informed by this understanding of agency, I consider superhero blockbusters as "mediators" (in the Latourian sense of the term) that leave their mark on the practices of audiences and orient these in specific ways.[8] In that way, superhero movies do not merely reflect the culture around them but participate in its operations.

But this book is not a work of applied Actor-Network-Theory. Instead, it combines an ANT-inspired understanding of serial narratives with a historical materialist perspective on commercial popular culture. The argument developed here situates itself within a tradition of scholarship that, as Jason Edwards puts it, is concerned with the "ongoing analysis of the current social and political conditions of contemporary capitalist societies, their embedded institutions and practices, and the contingent circumstances that serve to reproduce them [. . .] over time" (282). My work follows thus in the footsteps of a Marxist tradition of critical theory that emphasizes the complicity of commercial entertainments with processes of capital accumulation and insists on the political significance of mundane, everyday practices. While ANT is often discussed in opposition to Marxist approaches, this combination of perspectives is not as counterintuitive as it might seem. Josef Barla and Fabian Steinschaden have suggested that ANT and Marxist theory are substantially different, but not incompatible "sociologies of association" which both "consider 'the social' as something that needs to be explained before it can be used as a starting point for explanatory frameworks that try to make sense of social and physical reality" (367; my translation). Moreover, Marx and Latour both consider "things [. . .] not just as passive objects [. . .] but always as networked with human and non-human actors" (Barla and Steinschaden 367, my translation). This aspect is evident in the Marxian category of the commodity, for example, which is defined both by its use value (which is derived from material properties that are the outcome of specific production processes and concrete human labor) and by its status as a carrier for an abstract exchange value that is defined by a complex system of interdependent social relations (see Marx, *Capital* Vol. I, 125–77). Any given commodity is defined by properties that are both material and social, as commodities are always made for practical use and to function as media of social exchange – and the same is true for cultural commodities such as blockbuster movies.

From this vantage point, this book explores how the contemporary popularity of superhero blockbusters came about, what aesthetic practices sustain it and how it relates to a larger regime of digital-era capitalism. In doing so, it considers superhero movies as cultural commodities that contribute to the reproduction of capitalist orders in a number of ways: by realizing profits for the studios, production companies, distributors, and other companies involved in their making; by becoming objects of consumers' recreational media consumption practices and organizing their free time in socially acceptable ways; by figuring as the content of an ongoing discourse about the genre that helps to sustain an ecosystem of commercially operated fan sites, online publications, and social media platforms. The fact that superhero movies perform these operations is, in and of itself, unremarkable. Most commodified entertainments are nowadays similarly defined by their triple status as commercial products, recreational media objects, and topics of conversation within an online public. What is remarkable about recent superhero blockbusters, however, is that they perform these operations much more effectively than other forms of entertainment. This study examines why this is the case and suggests that the answer can be found in the efficacy of the genre's means of audience engagement, which are fine-tuned to operate within (and co-evolve with) a thoroughly networked, digitized, and commercialized media environment.

To make this case, it is important to acknowledge that superhero blockbuster cinema's politics of engagement not only targets people who engage with popular entertainment in their free time. As noted at the beginning of this chapter, recent superhero blockbusters are accompanied by a flurry of discursive activity, much of which is created by professionals who are paid for their work, including editors, journalists, and critics who work for online publications about popular culture, write reviews for news outlets, or produce other kinds of media coverage about the genre. Together with the unpaid activities of non-professional consumers, the contents produced by professional audiences constitute a discursive environment within which superhero blockbusters need to position themselves if they want to be profitable. Superhero blockbusters' politics of engagement can thus be understood as a two-pronged project. On the one hand, this project seeks to maximize the time, money, and attention that non-professional consumers dedicate to the consumption of serialized media content, to attendant consumption practices, and to a range of related cultural activities. On the other hand, superhero movies seek to enroll the support of professional consumers to generate publicity effects within a larger media public. These two objectives intersect in the generation of media buzz about individual releases – that is, in broader cultural mobilizations that include chatter on social media, attention by the mainstream press, and coverage by fan-oriented online publications. This buzz, in turn, increases the cultural visibility of individual titles and drives further media consumption (fostering the sale of tickets, home video releases, merchandise, and so on). Ultimately, superhero blockbusters' politics of engagement seeks to generate a perpetual busyness on the part of both professional and non-professional consumers.

This centrality of audience discourses has implications for the academic study of contemporary popular culture, as scholars who write about commercial entertainment might also contribute to the latter's popularity. The work conducted for this study, for instance, has already made a small, but not entirely negligible contribution to the profitability and visibility of superhero movies. While researching and writing this book, I came to approximate the ideal of the active, culturally productive consumer and spent considerable amounts of time and money on the consumption of superhero films, comics, and television series. I also bought pricey merchandising items and consulted countless paratextual materials about the genre, visited comic conventions on two different continents, and discussed the merits and faults of recently released films with colleagues, friends, and family members. My academic work likewise allowed me to circulate the products of my cognitive and textual labors in the form of social media posts, conference papers, university seminars, and scholarly publications. Ultimately, this book also makes a modest contribution to the already rich academic discourse about the genre. In different ways, all these activities contributed to the revenue streams and/or discursive flows that sustain the current prominence of superhero blockbuster cinema. Even critical approaches to the politics of superhero movies might thus end up promoting the objects that they discuss. In the digital media environment of the twenty-first century, such a promotion is perhaps unavoidable, as it no longer seems possible to observe popular culture from a safe distance. But scholars who ignore the various layers of cultural mediation and economic valorization involved in phenomena such as the superhero blockbuster are bound to miss something crucial about the object of their research: namely, that the popularity of commercial entertainment could not be sustained without the active support of consumers. In acknowledging these entanglements, this book advances an argument that differs significantly from the concerns of earlier book-length studies of the genre, which have focused on the formal aesthetics of comic book adaptations (see Morton; Burke) or on superhero movies' political themes (see Brown; Hassler-Forest; DiPaolo), but only rarely discussed both dimensions in close conjunction. Arguably, to understand superhero blockbusters' place within a larger regime of digital-era popular culture, a broader perspective is needed – one that bridges the gaps between narrative, aesthetic, political, media-infrastructural, and economic dimensions and pays close attention to the inherent seriality of the genre.

CHAPTER OVERVIEW

To offer this perspective, this book examines how superhero blockbuster films engage their viewers, how they position themselves within audience discourses and how they attempt to manage their own reception. It also discusses the larger politico-economic constellations, ideological beliefs, and media environments that orient the genre's aesthetic practices. As noted above, this study considers superhero blockbuster cinema's politics of engagement as paradigmatic for a larger regime of commercial entertainment that sustains itself by harnessing the productivity of its cultural environment. This type of popular culture emerges in response to transformations within the capitalist mode of production that include the ascent of a knowledge-based digital economy and the appearance of a "new spirit of capitalism" (as Luc Boltanski and Ève Chiapello have put it), which seeks to remodel business practices in response to the decline of Fordism and advancing digitization. In the late 1990s and early 2000s, these changes in the medial, economic, and ideological landscape began to leave their mark on the narrative, film-aesthetic, and thematic politics of superhero blockbusters. The latter now adopt operating principles and procedures that, eventually, also come to orient commercial popular culture more generally. The contemporary popularity of the genre is rooted in this period.

This book advances its arguments in two parts. The first part comprises Chapters 1 and 2 and articulates a theoretical and conceptual framework for my discussion of superhero blockbuster cinema's politics of engagement. This politics of engagement, in turn, is the main concern of the book's second part, which encompasses Chapters 3 through 5. Afterwards, a short conclusion ties the different strands of the argument together.

Chapter 1 begins this trajectory by situating the concept of seriality within a broader theory of commercial entertainment. To do so, the chapter develops a new reading of Max Horkheimer and Theodor W. Adorno's theory of the culture industry that can account for the centrality of serial repetition and variation within capitalist cultural production. The chapter then maps central tenets of the ideology of engagement that orients much of commercial screen entertainment today. For this purpose, it reads Jenkins's work on digital-era participatory culture against Boltanski and Chiapello's study of *The New Spirit of Capitalism*. The chapter then proceeds with a discussion of recent conceptualizations of digital-era capitalism which, I argue, can offer a much-needed qualification for some of Jenkins's claims about digital-era popular culture. The chapter ends by considering the relationship between superhero blockbusters' enduring popularity and the technological infrastructure of the digital era. Picking up this thread, Chapter 2 examines the narrative parameters of the superhero genre in greater detail. Drawing on work by Umberto Eco, Shane Denson, and others, it suggests that most superhero narratives combine linear and non-linear types of seriality. The chapter also argues that the genre's longevity is indebted to the adaptability and flexibility of its basic storytelling formula. Finally, it suggests that this formula – which is itself a serial principle rather than a fixed pattern – informs a shared political imaginary that enables and limits the kinds of messages that can be articulated within the genre.

Chapter 3 then considers the key elements, mobilizing power, and evolution of the hyper-referential storytelling style that is at work in films of the genre. Combining a high density of references to other superhero narratives with attempts to approximate the aesthetics of comic books, this style is already on display in Richard Donner's *Superman* (1978) and serves to locate feature films within larger networks of closely related narratives and media. Suggesting that this style evolves in response to larger cultural, medial, and industrial transformations, the chapter argues that more recent superhero blockbuster films have successively increased the frequency of their references to other narratives and media. To make this case, the chapter traces the evolution of the hyper-referential style across four waves of releases that began with Donner's *Superman* and came to an end in 2020, after the beginning of the COVID-19 pandemic. Afterwards, Chapter 4 considers the fan management practices that position superhero blockbusters within the discourses of online fandom. Building on the arguments of the preceding chapters and recent work by Mel Stanfill, Matt Hills and others, the chapter examines the 2016 films *Deadpool* and *Suicide Squad*, as well as accompanying marketing efforts, to show how corporate actors actively intervene in the discourses and practices of online fandom. Chapter 5 then shifts the focus to the political messages of the genre and its reception within a broader media public. More precisely, the chapter discusses three films – 2014's *Captain America: The Winter Soldier*, 2016's *Captain America: Civil War*, and 2018's *Black Panther* – which offer particularly clear articulations of a cinematic populism that is more generally at work in the genre. On the one hand, this populism foregrounds political themes that echo the central concerns of political populisms (such as the notion of a conflict between heroic leaders and morally corrupt elites, for example). On the other hand, it uses references to real-world events and discourses to project a sense of political relevance. Recent superhero blockbusters, so the chapter argues, rely on these means to generate publicity effects that increase their cultural visibility. Hence, these films reiterate a schematic worldview that resonates with a politically ambivalent tradition of populist thought which has recently returned to the center stage of American political life.

The volume ends with a brief conclusion that connects the claims of the preceding chapters and relates the practices of recent superhero blockbuster cinema to phenomena in other genres and media.

NOTES

1. This count includes films based on superhero properties published by either DC Comics or Marvel Comics only. In addition to the films released during the first two decades of the twenty-first century, superhero blockbuster cinema in this narrow sense includes ten additional movies released between 1978 and the end of 1999. For an overview, see Chapter 3.
2. Hollywood's conglomerate-owned film studios are Walt Disney Studios, Sony Pictures, Universal, Paramount, and Warner Bros. and their subsidiaries (20th Century Fox, the erstwhile sixth major in charge of the *X-Men* films, was absorbed by the Disney conglomerate in early 2020; Warner's subsidiary New Line Cinema has produced entries of the genre as well). Mini-majors are smaller film studios whose films compete directly with those of Hollywood's big five. On "conglomerate Hollywood," see Schatz.
3. The broader field of superhero films is part of an even bigger genre of comic book movies that also includes releases based on non-superhero comics properties; see Morton.
4. Reboots are not unique to the superhero blockbuster genre. Derek Johnson, for example, points to the 2009 relaunch of the *Star Trek* film series and SyFy's re-imagined *Battlestar Galactica* television series (2003–9) (*Media Franchising* 3). The many filmic incarnations of Ian Fleming's James Bond are another prominent example. For a discussion of the reboot as a form of cinematic remaking, see Kelleter and Loock.
5. On the concept of popular seriality, see Kelleter, "Einführung"; "Five Ways."
6. On the politics of engagement in twenty-first-century television drama series, see Brinker "NBC's *Hannibal*" and "Formal Politics." For a discussion of reader engagement in 1970s superhero comic books, see Brinker "Reader Mobilization"; for a comparison of recent comic book movies' and classic film serials' politics of engagement, see Brasch and Brinker.
7. Latour's notion of "irreductionism" suggests that "nothing can be reduced to anything else, nothing can be deduced from anything else, everything may be allied to everything else" (Latour, *Pasteurization* 163). Latour here cautions against the "reductionist" tendency to explain any social phenomenon simply as being derived from another force or agency. In this sense, audience responses of any kind are never simply an effect of film reception, but occur within, as Graham Harman puts it, "a cosmos of mutually irreducible actors" that align or disconnect their forces under contingent circumstances (Harman 39).
8. In *Reassembling the Social*, Latour introduces the terms "mediator" and "intermediary" to distinguish two types of actants that can serve as "means" to produce social groupings, movements and interactions: "An *intermediary* [. . .] transports meaning or force without transformation [. . .]. *Mediators*, on the other hand, [. . .] transform, translate, distort, and modify the meaning or the elements they are supposed to carry" (38–39; 37–42). In this sense, intermediaries are mere "relays" of force, while mediators shape social interactions in specific ways. See also Stein 135.

Part I
Seriality

CHAPTER I

Seriality, Culture Industry, and Digital-Era Popular Culture

From comic books to animated cartoon series, digital games, live-action television drama, and blockbuster cinema, to T-shirts, coffee mugs, and cereal boxes, the entertainment industries' licensing and franchising practices have turned superheroes such as Batman, Spider-Man, or the X-Men into fixtures of our media environment. Such proliferations have, in fact, gone on for quite some time. DC Comics' Superman, for instance, has appeared in numerous comic books, films, and TV series, inspiring the production of innumerable trinkets, toys, and other kinds of merchandise since his inception in the late 1930s (see Daniels 47–62). In the twenty-first century, superhero figures have entered more high-brow cultural and literary fields as well, turning up in pop-art and high fashion, in auteurist films such as Alejandro G. Iñarritu's *Birdman* (2014, Fox Searchlight) and acclaimed novels such as Michael Chabon's *The Amazing Adventures of Kavalier and Clay* (2000). This omnipresence attests to superheroes' remarkable cultural staying power and ability to adapt, transform, and change contexts. Other, older characters from the realm of anglophone mass culture have had similar careers: Mary Shelley's Frankenstein and his monstrous creation, Bram Stokers' Dracula, Sax Rohmer's Fu Manchu, or Ian Fleming's James Bond, for example, have also been reincarnated many times and proliferated across a variety of media. Ruth Mayer discusses such frequently re-invented characters as "serial figures" that "move across media and medial forms" and, in the process, become widely known "cultural icon[s]" (*Fu Manchu* 9; see Denson and Mayer; Denson, "Marvel Comics' Frankenstein"). The persistence of such figures, Mayer suggests, is linked to their formulaic "flatness" and status as amalgams of easily "recognizable images, [. . .] plots, phrases, and accessories that, once established, can be rearranged, reinterpreted, recombined, and invested with new significance" (*Fu Manchu* 10, 11). Likewise, iconic superheroes such as Superman or Spider-Man are "in constant flux and yet unchanging," continuously spreading out into new cultural territories and nonetheless staying recognizably the same (*Fu Manchu* 3).

This chapter engages with the culture-industrial processes of serial repetition and variation that undergird such proliferations, their place within a larger system of commercial entertainment, and the consequences of popular culture's digitization at the beginning of the twenty-first century. In the introduction to this book, I suggested that seriality is both a formal property of serial narratives and an organizing principle more generally at work in commercial popular culture. A significant part of this chapter focuses on the latter aspect and discusses the centrality of the serial principle for a larger system of capitalist entertainment; the modes of serial storytelling at work within the superhero genre will be explored in the next chapter. I separate the discussion of these two dimensions for analytical reasons. Not all capitalist entertainments are explicitly serialized, but the principle of seriality and practices of serial reiteration are nonetheless integral to large-scale, profit-oriented cultural production, even though individual commodities are often advertised as innovative, unique, and unprecedented. Like serial narratives, capitalist popular culture generally invites an ongoing engagement on the part of consumers, relies on established success formulae that are reiterated again and again, and presents its distractions as recurring occasions around which leisure time can be structured. Since it sensitizes us to the ongoing, repetitive, and practical aspects of commercial entertainment, the concept of seriality, I argue, can shed new light on the political-economic, ideological, and media-infrastructural basis of twenty-first-century popular culture.

To start making this case, this chapter reads Umberto Eco's essay on "Repetition and Innovation" against Max Horkheimer and Theodor W. Adorno's oft-maligned theory of the culture industry. Using key moments in the early history of the DC Comics character Superman as examples, I argue here that the concept of culture industry is best understood not as name for a monolithic power-bloc in charge of capitalist entertainment, but rather as shorthand for a dynamic, flexible, and evolving social system that organizes the free time of consumers through the serial production of cultural commodities. Subsequently, the chapter accounts for the fact that the culture-industrial system has undergone significant ideological, media-technological, and economic shifts since its description by Horkheimer and Adorno. Picking up on my discussion of audience engagement in the introduction to this book, the second half of this chapter returns to the idea that the digitized culture industry of the early twenty-first century addresses culturally productive media users whose activities are potential sources of surplus value. To gauge the implications of this change, I advance an ideology-critical reading of key works by media scholar Henry Jenkins, who has described digital-era commercial entertainments as centerpieces of a fundamentally democratic "participatory culture." Here, I suggest that Jenkins's work on the subject reiterates key talking points of a neoliberal ideology which legitimizes corporate attempts at exploiting the work of professional and non-professional consumers. The chapter then turns to recent conceptualizations of digital-era capitalism and explores what is at stake in such attempts to capitalize on user activity. Finally, the chapter's conclusion brings the different strands of my argument together and suggests that blockbuster films based on DC and Marvel Comics are particularly suited to operate within the digital-era cultural industry. This is so because superhero blockbusters can capitalize on the long-standing cross-medial diffusion of the properties on which they are based. Superhero movies, in other words, not only bring the defining features of established serial figures and their comics properties into innovative new constellations, but also reap the benefits of long histories of previous, culturally resonant serial unfolding.

SERIALITY AND THE CULTURE INDUSTRY

The idea that seriality is central to commercial entertainment is hardly new. Already in 1985, Umberto Eco's article on "Innovation and Repetition" argued that "mass-media products" generally combine practices of "repetition, iteration, [and] obedience to a pre-established schema" with formal innovation and thematic variation (162). On the one hand, Eco notes that popular narratives frequently rely on well-established tropes, motifs, and narrative formula that can, in the case of commercial success, be easily reiterated. On the other hand, he stresses that the same narratives often include innovative twists, tweaks, and revisions to their formulae to accommodate the expertise of "smart" consumers who are well-versed in popular culture's conventions (174). Eco describes the result of this balancing act as an "aesthetics of seriality" (179) that is characterized by "a dialectic between order and novelty, [. . .] between scheme and innovation" (173). Eco further clarifies that this dialectic affects not just the "contents of the message," but also "the way in which the message transmits those contents" (174). Even if the stories and contents of popular entertainments appear to echo earlier works, changes might thus occur on the levels of plot, presentation, form, and medium – and the appreciation of such differences, in turn, provides part of the pleasure that consumers derive from the reception of popular entertainments. Successful commercial commodities, so the argument goes, are bound to be copied and imitated. At the same time, shifting cultural tastes and increasingly sophisticated audiences encourage innovation and the variation of established patterns. From this perspective, production trends within Hollywood and the enduring popularity of certain genres – such as superhero narratives, for instance – can be understood as serial phenomena, too. Likewise, the cross-medial proliferation of superheroes across comic books, films, digital games, T-shirts, and coffee mugs can also be viewed as the result of ongoing processes of serial iteration that presuppose consumers' familiarity with the respective figures.

A similar understanding of seriality – albeit one that emphasizes repetition over innovation and largely disregards the expertise of consumers – is a key theme of Max Horkheimer and Theodor W. Adorno's theory of the culture industry. In the *Dialectic of Enlightenment*'s famous chapter on the topic, the authors identify the persistence of narrative schemata, stock scenarios, and character types as a defining feature of capitalist mass culture.[1] Horkheimer and Adorno connect the prevalence of established formulae and styles to the profit orientation of an entertainment industry dominated by a few large companies, noting that producers would "reject anything untried as a risk" when faced with the possibility of commercial failure (106; see 94–97). For Horkheimer and Adorno, this situation results in an "exclusion of the new" and an oppressive homogeneity of entertainments that, in the long run, deprives mass culture of the emancipatory potentials that earlier forms of "light art" still possessed (106, 107). In this situation, distinctions between commodities of the same type – "like those between A and B films, or between short stories published in magazines in different price segments" – are superficial and do "not so much reflect real differences as assist in the classification, organization, and identification of consumers" (97). The culture industry thus provides "something [. . .] for everyone so that no one can escape" (97), feeding audiences with an "unending sameness" of products that, in its totality, contributes to the reproduction of a general social and cultural conformity (106). The products of the culture industry, as they suggest, ultimately offer easily digestible experiences and direct consumers' attention away from activities that could challenge the existing social order. In contrast to Eco, the two Frankfurt School scholars thus frame the repetition and variation of well-known patterns and motifs as a problem with serious political implications.

Horkheimer and Adorno's arguments provide an interesting parallel to Eco's 1962 essay on the "The Myth of Superman."[2] In this early piece, Eco notes the thematically redundant "iterative scheme" of Superman comics, which tend to tell essentially similar stories about confrontations between the hero and various villains that invariably end with the return to a pre-existing status quo ("The Myth" 19). Eco argues that the appeals of such repetitive narratives lie in their "indulgent invitation to repose," to enjoy the recurrence of familiar elements and to escape the stresses of "contemporary industrial society" (21; see also "Innovation and Repetition" 164). For both Eco and the Frankfurt School critics, cultural commodities such as feature films, comic books, and popular songs thus take on a stabilizing and integrating function for the societies in which they circulate and, therefore, contribute to the perpetuation of a social order built around capitalist exploitation. But where Eco understands the play of repetition and variation as an opportunity for distracted appreciation, Horkheimer and Adorno view the sameness of mass-cultural commodities not only as boring, but also as actively preempting attempts at imagining a world that is substantially different from the world inhabited by the consumer – a constellation that benefits existing systems of political oppression.

Since its initial formulation, the theory of the culture industry has drawn its share of critiques by younger generations of scholars who have charged Horkheimer and Adorno with painting a picture that may be overly bleak, too totalitarian, and inadequate for the analysis of a pluralistic, postmodern popular culture.[3] Due to the high number of such critiques, offhand dismissals of Horkheimer and Adorno's arguments have become a recurring motif in recent Anglophone cultural and media studies literature, where the chapter on the culture industry is frequently referenced, but just as often labeled as an argumentative dead end not worth pursuing.[4] Horkheimer and Adorno's arguments nonetheless contain a kernel of useful insights about the social function of popular entertainment under capitalism. But to appreciate these insights, one needs to account both for the shortcomings of their theory and for its conceptual basis in Karl Marx's critique of political economy. Doing so also requires an acknowledgement of the "fragmentary" character of the chapter on the culture industry, an aspect that the authors themselves stress in the preface to the *Dialectic of Enlightenment* (xix). Rather than as a final and definite assessment of its subject-matter, the chapter on the culture industry is better understood as an incomplete work-in-progress that charts central tendencies of capitalist mass culture, but disregards or backgrounds important aspects. Two central blind spots of Horkheimer and Adorno's conception of the culture industry lie in its failure to address mass culture's serial aesthetics and the role of informed and self-reflexive consumers (two crucial dimensions stressed by Eco). To compensate for these problems, I will now take a closer look at the evolution and cross-medial spread of the DC Comics character Superman, which demonstrates the co-occurrence of repetition and innovation (rather than just repetition) within commercial entertainment. I then return to Horkheimer and Adorno's thoughts about the "sameness" of cultural commodities and their role for the reproduction of capitalism, contrasting them with Adorno's later writings on the culture industry.

For Horkheimer and Adorno as well as for Eco, the prominence of established formulae and styles is not an exception to the normal operations of the market, but endemic to mass culture. Since practices of imitation and copying reduce risk, producers are bound to emulate already popular products, a constellation that privileges the production of various types of knock-offs, homages, pastiches, or parodies of entertainments that have proven their mass appeal. Jerry Siegel and Joe Shuster's Superman is the product of precisely such borrowings. When Superman made his debut in the June 1938 issue of *Action Comics*, the premise of a crime-fighting protagonist with a secret identity was already known from pulp magazines such as *The Shadow* and movies such as *The Mark of Zorro* (1920) (Daniels 13, 19; Meier 35). Likewise, Superman's name was informed by popularizations of Nietzsche's "*Übermensch*" as they appeared in science-fiction novels such as Philip Wylie's *Gladiator* (1930) (Jones; Hatfield, Heer, and Worcester 4), while the conceit of a strongman-hero with more-than-human powers had long been a central motif of comic strips such as *Popeye* and *Hugo Hercules* (Coogan 7–9). Similarly, Superman's stature and costume evoked the looks of comic strip heroes such as Flash Gordon or Buck Rogers, while the principal setting of most *Superman* stories was named after Fritz Lang's *Metropolis* (1929) (see Daniels 11–31). Instead of appearing as radical innovation, Siegel and Shuster's Superman thus constituted an amalgam of well-established ideas.[5]

Crucially, however, Superman soon proved to be interesting enough to generate a demand for additional stories. DC Comics responded by creating a variety of Supermen for different formats and media. By 1943, Siegel and Shuster's hero starred in three separate ongoing comic book series (*Action Comics*, *Superman*, and *World's Finest Comics*) and in a newspaper strip that was syndicated nationwide. By the end of the same year, the figure also headlined a *Superman* radio serial that would continue to air for several years, had appeared as the protagonist of the novel *The Adventures of Superman* (George Lowther, 1942), and made the jump onto the silver screen as the protagonist of a series of animated short films produced by Fleischer Studios (Daniels 34–58; Gaines 179; Meier 46). Instead of simply repeating a ready-made formula for each new iteration, these additional Supermen often played subtle (and not always intended) variations on the character's backstory and added small innovations to the original concept. As Les Daniels points out in his *Complete History of Superman*, some of the now-canonical features of the figure – his ability to fly (rather than merely leap tall buildings in a single bound), his origin on the planet of Krypton, and the names of his parents – were introduced in media other than the comics (Daniels 35–71). Each new medium furthermore added experiential dimensions to the Superman figure: the radio serial endowed the protagonist with voice and sound, the Fleischer shorts added movement to a hero once confined to static images, the 1948 Columbia film serial introduced actor Kirk Alyn as living personification of the character, and so on. These various versions of Superman were only loosely connected and related to each other extra-narratively, through the recurrence of shared features that were repeated and reconfigured for each new format and medial context (such as Superman's costume, his secret identity as Clark Kent, his status as a defender of truth, justice, and the American way, and so on). Every new incarnation of Superman thus proved to be somewhat different from the preceding ones yet remained easily recognizable as an instance of the same thing.

The success of DC's Superman narratives soon inspired the production of numerous similar titles starring other heroes, thereby laying the foundations for the emergence of superhero comics as a distinct genre. As part of this trend, the three years after 1938 saw the debut of Batman, Wonder Woman, Captain Marvel (later known as Shazam), the Flash, Captain America, and many more.[6] Richard Reynolds associates this rapid growth with the dramatic productivity of the storytelling "model" pioneered by Siegel and Shuster, which already featured elements that continue to be staples of superhero narratives today. These elements include the "lost parents" of the protagonist (Superman is an orphan from an alien planet), thinly-veiled religious undertones (the infant Superman arrives in a comet-like spaceship that looks like the Star of Bethlehem), a concern with justice and the hero's "devotion to those in need," the juxtaposition of a hero with super-powers and people with regular powers, Superman's cover identity as a regular citizen, his status as a figure that operates above the law, and the depiction of science as "a special form of magic" (104–6). What Reynolds describes as a model with "endless story possibilities" is perhaps better understood as a narrative formula that can produce countless similar stories. Writing about Arthur Conan Doyle's Sherlock Holmes stories, novelist Michael Chabon has described such formulae as "storytelling engines" that can generate ever-new output through a repeated recombination of established motifs and plot logics (Chabon 47; see also Mayer, *Fu Manchu* 11). Once Superman had gained sufficient medial exposure, the elements of Siegel and Shuster's narrative machine became available to DC's competitors, who quickly started to imitate, vary, and translate them into new contexts. The history of the superhero genre since the late 1930s can thus be understood as the result of a continuous reinvention, retooling, and re-appropriation of the Superman formula.

The above examples demonstrate that Horkheimer and Adorno's claims about the sameness of commercial cultural production require some qualification. Already during the late 1930s and early 1940s, the cross-medial proliferation of superheroes yielded considerable innovation and diversification, even though changes to the formula occurred within storytelling frameworks that remained recognizably similar. However, reducing Horkheimer and Adorno's claims about the "sameness" and "identity" of mass culture to an argument about the features of cultural commodities means subscribing to a fairly literal interpretation of their theory and ignoring a more fundamental philosophical argument made by the authors. As Heinz Steinert points out, "Adorno is not just saying that 'everything is all the same anyway' and that there is no variation at all. What he is really getting at [in emphasizing repetition and sameness] is that the process of abstraction [. . .] has resulted in culture becoming bound up with domination" (73). Instead of simply arguing for a literal identity of all products of the culture industry, Horkheimer and Adorno suggest that said products share an abstract identity as cultural artifacts that are implicated in the reproduction of capitalist orders.

For the critical theorists, the repetition and variation of success formulae turn out to be complexly related to the specific social context and power relations of capitalist societies, which assign a concrete utility (or use-value) to commercial entertainments. In a 1969 essay on the topic of "Free Time," Adorno elaborates on this social dimension of cultural commodities and leisurely recreational activity. "Free time," so Adorno argues, is "shackled to its opposite," to time that is not free but "heteronomous" and dictated by external needs such as the necessity to work and earn a living (187). The social function of recreational activities is therefore defined by their relation to work and the routines of the working day. In making this claim, Adorno implicitly classifies the products of the culture industry as part of what Marx terms "means of subsistence" – that is, those goods and services that wage-dependent workers consume daily to reconstitute their ability to work (Marx, *Capital* 274–75; Adorno, "Thesen" and "Culture Industry Reconsidered"). Activities such as reading a novel, listening to the radio, or going to the movies thus need to prove their usefulness for consumers and contribute to the reproduction of their labor-power, or otherwise further the productive integration of the individual into society (see Horkheimer and Adorno 109; Adorno, "Free Time" 187–90). The producers of cultural commodities, by contrast, depend on the audience's capacity and willingness to purchase and consume their goods (otherwise, producers would not be able to realize profits and sustain their businesses over time). This interdependency finds its paradigmatic expression in "the 'Fordist' model of capitalism," under which a limitation of working hours, rising levels of individual and social wages, and a clear separation of work and leisure made the mass consumption of consumer goods possible in the first place (Steinert 75; see also Dyer-Witheford 55–56, 74–75).

What interests me about Adorno's thoughts on the relationship between work and leisure time here is that they allow us to conceptualize the production and consumption of cultural commodities as interconnected realms of social practice which are both informed by a serial logic: On the one hand, cultural commodities are the products of an industrial repetition and variation of known formulae. On the other hand, the reception of these commodities is part of a recurring everyday practice that reiterates itself on a regular basis, within slightly varying situations and against a backdrop of preceding media consumption. Cultural commodities – such as feature films, radio and television programming, novels, or comic books – are thus doubly implicated in the reproduction of capitalist orders. As products of a profit-oriented industry, they realize their surplus value by being sold on the market and contribute directly to processes of capital accumulation. As objects of recreational media consumption practices, the products of the culture industry balance familiar and unfamiliar appeals to offer a temporary escape from the routines and (a)rhythms of work, school, or unemployment, but simultaneously prepare consumers to face these realities again. It is this constellation which allows popular media texts to become socially productive. They do so not as isolated works or through singular acts of reception, but as part of what Jason Edwards calls "everyday practices of production and consumption" that (because of their recurring character) reconstitute capitalist orders on a small scale (Edwards 283).

Adorno's essay "Free Time" also calls attention to the fact that cultural commodities participate in the material and practical organization of leisure time and recreational activities.[7] This is especially true of radio, television, and print – the mass media of the Fordist period – whose inflexible publication, broadcasting, and exhibition schedules have historically encouraged reception practices that echoed and complemented the rhythms and routines of the workday (such as being at home during the airing of one's favorite programming, reading the newspaper during breakfast, or visiting the cinema on Sunday afternoons to catch matinée screenings, for example). In such cases, the seriality of media consumption and reliable rhythms of publication offered themselves as occasions around which leisure time could be structured. As result, the routines of Fordist mass culture took on a political significance that echoed the implications of the introduction of Taylorist methods into modern industrial production. Within factory settings, Taylorism increased productivity and "decompos[ed] working-class power" through the segmentation of complex activities according to "the chronometer and clipboard of [. . .] scientific management" and an overall reduction of workers' control over the production process (Dyer-Witheford 73). Similarly, the schedules of analogue mass media participated in a regime of time management that allocated various leisure activities to the scarce resource of consumers' free time, thereby discouraging other kinds of activity (such as political organizing, for example). The repetitive character of practices such as reading the morning newspaper, listening to news broadcasts on the radio, or following a television program week after week furthermore established a virtual connection between larger groups of consumers. In this fashion, media consumption could provide the basis for the processes of "collective serialization" that (explicitly or implicitly) addressed the members of the audience as parts of a larger group or collective (Denson and Sudmann 272–80; see also Mayer, *Fu Manchu* 17–18; Kelleter, *Serial Agencies* 62). Such groups could be defined differently (along cultural or national lines, for example, but also as apolitical communities of enthusiasts, connoisseurs, or fans), but in each case they provided collective identifications that could act as alternatives to more explicitly antagonistic identifiers such as class, for example.

The sketch of the culture industry developed so far – which frames modern mass media and their contents as actively involved in the shaping of recreational practices – inevitably raises questions about the status and agency of consumers. In Adorno's chapter on the culture industry and much of his later writings on the topic, consumers are depicted as defenseless victims of a profit-driven machinery that "integrates from above" (Adorno, "Culture Industry Reconsidered" 98). For Adorno, the entertainment industries produce commodities that cater to individuals' need to reproduce their laboring power and participate in social life. The sale and consumption of these commodities ensure the continued accumulation of surplus value by capitalist corporations, contribute to the continued exploitation of labor, and organize the leisure time of those who man the factory lines, offices, and cashier's desks of the Fordist period. Simultaneously, the industry's products spread ideological messages that "duplicate, reinforce, and strengthen" conformist mindsets and worldviews (Adorno, "Culture Industry Reconsidered" 99). Together, the material and ideological dimensions of the culture industry give rise to "a cycle of manipulation and retroactive need" in which the needs of consumers are already shaped by the formulae, routines, and messages of the culture industry (Horkheimer and Adorno 95).[8] The culture-industrial constellation thus participates in the production of consumers' demands; corporations then meet these demands with products that promote the status quo as the best of all possible worlds. For Horkheimer and Adorno, the closed or unbroken character of this supply-and-demand cycle is at the root of the culture industry's awesome power. Arguably, the authors' insistence on this power is a central reason why the concept has been criticized and dismissed by younger generations of scholars.

Interestingly, however, Adorno himself would later re-address this issue and come to slightly different conclusions. Towards the end of his essay on "Free Time," Adorno problematizes the idea that "the culture industry totally and utterly dominates and controls both the conscious and unconscious of those people at whom it is directed" (195).[9] Reviewing the results of unpublished empirical research on the public reception of a 1966 royal wedding, Adorno points out that the enjoyment of popular entertainments neither precludes the possibility of a critical perspective, nor stunts the audiences' capacity for self-reflection. When interviewed about their perceptions of the wedding and its coverage by the news media, participants of the study first expressed enthusiasm and an appreciative attitude. However, when asked about the "political significance" of the wedding, many interviewees "suddenly showed themselves to be thoroughly realistic and proceeded to evaluate critically the political and social importance of the same event" (196). For Adorno, these responses suggest that "the culture industry and consumer-consciousness cannot simply be equated with one another" (195). In drawing this conclusion, Adorno offers a modification of the culture industry thesis that, by retaining the possibility of critical distance, redistributes some agency back to media audiences. The essay on "Free Time" furthermore suggests that a critical engagement with cultural commodities is not necessarily opposed to their continued enjoyment, and that self-reflexive consumers can both revel in the pleasures of the culture industry and contemplate the political dimensions of the entertainments they consume at the same time.

Adorno's revisions have interesting implications for the theoretical framework developed in the chapter on the culture industry. While "Free Time" grants consumers the capacity of critical reflection, it also continues to insist on the culture industry's tendency to shape and pattern recreational activity. While it introduces the idea of critical or otherwise unruly audiences, Adorno's revised view thus still positions consumers as the "object" (rather than the subject) of the culture industry ("Culture Industry Reconsidered" 99). At the same time, this revision shifts the emphasis from questions of ideological indoctrination to more practical dimensions of commercial cultural production and consumption, a fine-tuning that allows us to ask for the precise means and methods by which cultural commodities are integrated into recreational practice and involved in the organization of free time. "Free Time" also sensitizes us to moments in which the cultural industrial constellation might fail or cease to work. Since recipients are potentially critical, the culture industry's organization of free time re-emerges as an open-ended process that might generate conflicts of interest between producers and consumers. Nonetheless, the relationship between these two parties is not inherently antagonistic, as Adorno does not present consumers and producers as opposite sides in a binary struggle over dominance, but rather as different parts of an interlocking system that revolves around the continued production and consumption of popular entertainments. While consumers might find themselves dissatisfied with some of the culture industry's products, they will still be faced with the need to purchase (and enjoy) cultural commodities of all kinds. Media audiences are not passive and easily duped appendages to an industrial system that feeds them with unending sameness, but their capacity for critical reflection and their ability to choose from a catalogue of products also do not override the need to consume popular entertainments as part of a larger set of recreational practices. Likewise, the ability to reflect on one's consumption practices does not negate the culture industry's tendency to pre-structure the free time of consumers according to the schedules and protocols of medial infrastructures and technologies. The culture industry, in other words, still presents itself as a constellation of economic, cultural, and technological forces that are actively involved in the shaping of consumers' demands and recreational activities, but the outcome of this process is far from guaranteed.

Adorno's acknowledgement of self-reflexivity and critical distance gains additional significance once the seriality of culture-industrial production and consumption is considered. I have noted above that the products of the culture industry are not as uniform as Horkheimer and Adorno suggest. More than just distinctions between price segments, even minor differences in the medium, form, style, and content of cultural commodities offer potentially critical consumers an opportunity to choose – a choice that is made according to taste preferences and expertise, and in response to an evolving product landscape. The seriality of culture-industrial production and consumption allows consumers to adopt the posture of informed experts who base purchasing decisions on past experiences. Producers, however, continue to be interested in media audiences only as customers – but, since market success cannot be taken for granted, producers cannot do business without in some way "adapting to the masses," as Adorno puts it in "Culture Industry Reconsidered" (99; see Horkheimer and Adorno 118). In fact, the serial character of mass cultural production ensures the industry's continued attention to shifting consumer tastes and demands, even though the primary use-value of cultural commodities – that of entertainment – remains unchanged.

However, even in this revised form, the theory of the culture industry does not adequately address the interactions and feedback loops that exist between the spheres of production and consumption. For the Frankfurt School critics, mass media such as film, radio, or television know "[n]o mechanism of reply" through which audiences could exert influence on the products of the culture industry or circulate their own programming on a significant scale (Horkheimer and Adorno 96). For Horkheimer and Adorno, the cultural and textual production of consumers remains confined within an "apocryphal sphere of 'amateurs'" (96). While the chapter on the culture industry already concedes that such amateur production is occasionally absorbed by the industry, the late Adorno still characterizes recreational activities as generally passive, unproductive, and marked by the boredom of laborers who need to make use of the time not spent at work (Adorno, "Free Time" 188–89; 191–93). As a result, the authors of the culture industry thesis conceive of production and consumption as mutually interdependent, but essentially separate spheres. Such a view usefully foregrounds the power asymmetries between the entertainment industry and media audiences but does not account for the manifold interactions and reciprocal flows of information that exist between both sides.

In the preceding chapter I noted that serial narratives unfold in a constant dialogue with sales figures, recipients, and the medial discourses that surround them. Since culture-industrial production is inherently serial, a similar adaptability and responsiveness to fluctuations in demand and profitability characterizes the production of other (not explicitly serialized) cultural commodities as well. In addition, the sphere of amateur production is not always as apocryphal as Horkheimer and Adorno suggest. Abigail De Kosnik has pointed out that participation in the activities of fan communities can foster the audiences' sense of attachment to commercial media objects and inspire the consumption of related commodities. Accordingly, De Kosnik argues that fan activity can be understood as a form of unpaid labor that serves as "unauthorized marketing" for select cultural commodities (99). De Kosnik makes her argument about digital-era popular culture, but corporate actors within the entertainment industries capitalized on the labors of fan audiences in pre-digital times as well. Already during the 1940s and 1950s, the publishers of American comic books used officially sanctioned fan clubs to cultivate their relationships to particularly loyal readers.[10] Over the following decades, the activities of comic book fandom gave rise to fan-oriented conventions, organizations, and publications that continue to accompany, comment on, and interact with the commercial comics production today.[11] The theory of the cultural industry is indifferent to such audience practices because it frames them as external to the operations of the entertainment industries. But this outside status does not automatically render consumers' cultural production insignificant. In fact, the intense attachments of consumers have occasionally become a problem for producers of popular entertainments. During the comic book scare of the mid-1950s, for example, debates about an alleged causal relationship between excessive comics consumption and a rise in juvenile delinquency led to the demise of several comics publishers and the eventual institution of the Comics Code as a voluntary self-censorship guideline (Gardner 68–106; Gabilliet 29–55; Nyberg). While not addressed in the chapter on the culture industry and Adorno's later writings on the subject, such external factors and repercussions are hardly irrelevant to the producers of commercial entertainment. Any serious attempt to update Horkheimer and Adorno's theory thus needs to take into account the productivity of audience practices, their unintended spill-over effects, and potential impact on subsequent cultural production. One way of doing so is to emphasize that culture-industrial production is much more flexible, adaptable, and responsive than Horkheimer and Adorno suggest. This is so not only because commercial entertainment balances repetition with innovation, but also because efforts to monitor and intervene in the activities of media audiences are in the best interest of producers.

The above reading of Horkheimer and Adorno's theory has important implications for the study of commercial popular culture. The first of these involves the meaning of the term culture industry, which, contrary to its widespread usage, does not actually refer to an economic power-bloc in control of mass-cultural production. Instead, the concept denotes a larger social constellation that involves both producers and consumers, as well as products and media-technological infrastructures, in continuing cycles of cultural production, consumption, and re-production. Put differently, "culture industry" refers to a social system that designates free time as a realm for the recreational consumption of cultural commodities (and little else) and which thereby props up existing social orders. The producers that operate within this system, in turn, do not constitute a uniform faction, but compete for the time, money, and attention of consumers; they seek to outdo each other by producing entertainments that offer novel variations on established success formulae.[12] In addition to being informed by the principle of seriality, the products made in this context are shaped by shifts in demand and more general changes in the cultural environment. Ultimately, however, production remains committed to the profit-motive and privileges commercial success above all else. Consumers, conversely, are dependent on the products and routines of the culture industry, which offer distractions and entertainment, structure free time, and provide the fabric of a common popular culture that is shared within larger social collectives. Most consumers furthermore lack direct control over the production process of cultural commodities; as a result, the culture-industrial constellation limits their agency to the capacity to appropriate, criticize, or reject the entertainments they are meant to enjoy. Feedback loops between production and consumption exist nonetheless, as the industry closely monitors both fluctuations in demand and audience responses. Importantly, the people who fulfill the role of producers also are consumers of other culture-industrial contents in their private lives; in fact, some occupations within the entertainment industries require an in-depth familiarity with specific types of cultural commodity.[13] Amateur producers might rise through the ranks of the entertainment industries as well, just as audiences' own cultural production and fan activity might occasionally be coopted by professional producers. More often, however, audiences' own cultural production runs in parallel to the practices of the entertainment industry and provides synergistic effects for the commercial entertainments that inspire it. Finally, the principle of serial repetition and variation is at work on all levels of this system, from the practices of industrial producers and creators to media-technological infrastructures (which are reconfigured by technological innovations and evolving protocols of media use), to the aesthetics of the media content and the recreational activities of audiences. Rather than as a "machine [. . .] rotating on the spot" (Horkheimer and Adorno 106), the culture industry thus presents itself as a highly dynamic and rapidly evolving arrangement of social relations, technological media, and cultural forms that entangles individual reproduction with the industrial production of commercial entertainment.

This understanding of the culture industry as an evolving social system re-focuses the study of commercial popular culture in interesting ways. Firstly, it sensitizes us to the fact that the political significance of cultural commodities does not exclusively manifest itself on the level of content. Instead, it is tied up with their multiple contributions to the reproduction of capitalist orders. Accordingly, it makes little sense to reduce the politics of superhero blockbusters to the dimension of ideology, even though a certain set of political themes and ideological preoccupations cannot be divorced from the basic narrative parameters of the genre. An analysis of the genre's ideological contents, in other words, does not sufficiently capture its specific role within the culture-industrial constellation, nor does it completely illuminate superhero blockbusters' multi-layered contribution to the reproduction of capitalist orders. The reading developed here thus calls for a more thorough inquiry that accounts for the evolving ways in which genre organizes the recreational activities of consumers on a practical level.

My discussion of superhero blockbuster cinema's politics of engagement in Chapters 3 through 5 attempts to offer such an inquiry, but before I can turn to a concrete analysis of the genre, the medial, cultural, and socio-economic changes that have transformed commercial entertainment since Adorno's times need to be accounted for. Towards the beginning of his 1969 essay, Adorno notes that the study of free time and recreational activity should not remain on the level of "abstract generalisation[s]" but acknowledge the specific social and material conditions that shape the realities of work and leisure at any given point in time ("Free Time" 187). These conditions, in turn, develop in lockstep with an incessantly self-modernizing capitalism. Because the theoretical framework outlined so far is rooted in a critical engagement with the mass culture of the Fordist period, its insights cannot be transferred directly to the contemporary situation, especially since prominent voices in recent media and cultural studies have discussed the rise of digital and networked media as a catalyst for a fundamental re-orientation of commercial popular culture. One of the most visible commentators on this shift is Henry Jenkins, whose books on participatory culture (*Textual Poachers*, 1992; *Fans, Bloggers, and Gamers*, 2006; *Convergence Culture*, 2006; and, with Sam Ford and Joshua Green, *Spreadable Media*, 2013) have been widely received by both media scholars and industry professionals. If Jenkins is to be believed, the digitization of our media environment, the rise of the Internet, and the technological convergence of formerly separate media in the supra-medium of digital code have resulted in an increased agency of media audiences, a stronger orientation of producers towards the customers' demands, and a new economic importance of audience-produced content. In summary, Jenkins presents twenty-first century popular culture as driven by the participation of culturally productive, autonomous, and independent media audiences. This view seems irreconcilable with a perspective that frames consumers as potentially critical, but subordinate actors within a culture-industrial constellation that contributes to the reproduction of exploitative social orders. To come to terms with the specificity of digital-era popular culture and the agency of digitally empowered consumers, the next section examines Jenkins's arguments in detail.

DIGITAL-ERA POPULAR CULTURE AND THE SPIRIT OF CAPITALISM

Much of Jenkins's work of the last two decades engages with the impact of digitization and sets out to describe the "cultural logic" of twenty-first-century commercial entertainment (*Convergence* 17; 4–24). Jenkins's *Convergence Culture*, for example, argues that "new media technologies have lowered production and distribution costs, expanded the range of available delivery channels" and changed the ways in which "consumers [. . .] archive, annotate, appropriate, and recirculate media content" (18). The overall result of these changes, as Jenkins suggests, is an increased agency of consumers and a corresponding responsiveness to audience demands on the part of the industry. The accessibility and broad scope of Jenkins's output and his remarkable productivity as an author – his monographs are accompanied by numerous edited volumes, countless shorter academic publications, public appearances, a podcast, and a frequently updated blog – have contributed considerably to the popularization of terms such as "transmedia storytelling," "convergence culture," or "spreadability," which have since been taken up by other scholars and inspired a variety of practice-oriented texts aimed at media professionals.[14] Jenkins's work has been closely connected to industrial practices in other ways as well, as some of his past research has been funded by corporate actors such as "Turner Broadcasting, MTV Networks [. . .], Yahoo!, Internet Group do Brasil, Nagravision" and others (Jenkins, Ford, and Green ix). Very much drawing on trade journals and management literature and generally presenting itself as sympathetic to corporate interests, Jenkins's research ultimately locates itself at the intersection of academic scholarship and practice-oriented industry discourses.

In what follows, I suggest that Jenkins's proximity to corporate interests is not accidental – and that his work on digital-era popular culture participates in a larger ideological discourse that seeks to legitimize the practices of the contemporary entertainment industries. More precisely, I want to argue that Jenkins's work presents itself as an articulation of what sociologists Luc Boltanski and Ève Chiapello call the "spirit of capitalism" – that is, an *"ideology that justifies engagement in capitalism"* and guides the activities of corporate actors on a practical level (8, emphasis in the original). Building on Boltanski and Chiapello's concept, this section discusses Jenkins's work as part of a larger ideological discourse that justifies a particular configuration of capitalism along with a corresponding regime of digital-era popular culture. Understood in this manner, Jenkins's work sheds an interesting light on the guiding principles and imperatives that orient commercial cultural production today. In addition, it can help us understand how the imperatives of larger social formations and modes of production come to inform the practices of actors within the entertainment industry.

In *Convergence Culture*, Jenkins identifies an increased availability, flexibility, and interactivity of media content as crucial aspects of digital-era popular culture. Thanks to a proliferation of distribution channels, wide-spread Internet access, and digital technologies for recreational media consumption, popular entertainments now become more easily accessible, increasingly emancipated from fixed broadcasting and publication schedules, and subject to new practices of appropriation on the part of the consumer (Jenkins, *Convergence Culture* 15–18; see also 65–68). In *Spreadable Media*, Jenkins, Sam Ford, and Joshua Green argue that this new situation is characterized by "an emerging hybrid model of circulation" in which "a mix of top-down and bottom-up forces determine[s] how material is shared across and among cultures" (Jenkins, Ford, and Green 1; see also Jenkins *Convergence* 18). Whereas mass media such as film, television, or print journalism have traditionally operated according to a centralized model of distribution in which "the movement of media content is largely – or totally – controlled by the commercial interests producing and selling it," today "networked communities" of consumers increasingly determine how "media [content] circulates" (Jenkins, Ford, and Green 1, 2; see *Convergence* 3–4). For Jenkins, Ford, and Green, this results in "a movement toward a more participatory model of culture," in which "people [. . .] are shaping, sharing, reframing, and remixing media content in ways which might not have been previously imagined" (2). As the industry now depends on customers' willingness to not only consume, but also share and re-circulate content, producers need to orient themselves more strongly towards the audience's demands (Jenkins, Ford, and Green, 177). Rather than trying to control the flows of commercially produced content, the entertainment industries should thus "value [. . .] the activities of audience members" that "help generate interest in particular brands and franchises" (Jenkins, Ford, and Green 7). This new situation elevates the role of vocal and highly engaged media fans who already engage in the kind of socially communicative reception practices that the industry now seeks to inspire. But Jenkins and his collaborators also stress that producers should prioritize content that is easily accessible, sharable, and able to offer "diversified experiences" to an equally diverse group of recipients (Jenkins, Ford, and Green 6; see also Scott, "*Textual Poachers*" xviii–xxv). By doing so, producers should ideally be able to turn media audiences into "inspirational consumers" and "brand advocates" who willingly promote their favorite brands, franchises, products, and contents within their respective social networks (Jenkins, *Convergence* 73, see 68–74; see Jenkins, Ford, and Green 7).[15] Jenkins, Ford, and Green furthermore discuss the "immersive story worlds" of recent entertainment franchises as a promising strategy to both "prolong audience engagement" and accommodate the interests of different groups of consumers (133, see 132–42; see also Jenkins, *Convergence* 93–130).[16] Not all the developments discussed by Jenkins and his co-authors are entirely new or specific to digital-era formats. The idea of a newly responsive production side, for example, disregards the fact that audience-producer interactions have long been common within the comics industry. Nonetheless, Jenkins's work usefully foregrounds the consequences of a situation in which consumers' textual production becomes generally "accessible to the media industry," as media scholar Göran Bolin puts it (810).

However, while Jenkins's work is widely cited by other scholars, it is not uncontroversial. A key reason for this is Jenkins's insistence on the unambiguously positive effects of digitization and the rise of networked media. Drawing on Pierre Lévy's concept of "collective intelligence," Jenkins argues that the participation in online discourses can teach consumers to use new media technologies in productive and collaborative ways (Jenkins, *Convergence Culture* 232). In this manner, the labors of media users could ultimately "enable a more engaged citizenry" and "help prepare the way for a more meaningful public culture" in which the practices and skills of collective problem-solving are exercised as part of the democratic process (*Convergence Culture* 228, see also 206–39). Jenkins's arguments predate the recent right turn in American politics and the wide-spread utilization of online media by far-right actors – including the use of image boards by members of the alt-right, the circulation of disinformation and conspiracy theories via social media, and the online radicalization of white nationalists – by several years. While Jenkins perhaps could not have anticipated this turn of events, such activities have demonstrated that digital and networked tools can also be employed for fundamentally anti-democratic and violent ends. The fact that far-right activists have used "participatory" media technologies at least since the early 1990s (see Statzel) casts further doubt on Jenkins's discussion of convergence culture's democratizing potentials. Making a similar point, Christian Fuchs has argued that Jenkins's adoption of terms such as "participatory culture" frame the practices of media audiences in the terms of a political science discourse about participatory democracy (67) – a perspective that makes it difficult to address anti-democratic tendencies and tends to see emancipatory tendencies in places where things might be more complicated. For Fuchs, Jenkins's framing is furthermore problematic because it downplays or disregards the profit-orientation of the entertainment industries and the power asymmetries that exist between media corporations and consumers. Not coincidentally, Jenkins's views are at odds with perspectives that stress the exploitative character of corporate attempts to capitalize on audience practices. Writing in the late 1990s, Tiziana Terranova already discussed the "simultaneously voluntarily given and unwaged" work of Internet users as a form of "free labour" that constitutes "an important, yet unacknowledged, source of value in advanced capitalist societies" (74, 73).[17] For Terranova, this unpaid work includes precisely the kind of activities championed by Jenkins (such as the participation in online fora or the circulation of user-generated content, for example). Cultural studies scholars like Mel Stanfill or Abigail De Kosnik have since extended Terranova's argument to the practices of media fans, which typically do "not register as labor at all," but nonetheless fulfill promotional functions for the franchises and properties to which they relate (Stanfill pos. 2973; for an overview of work with similar concerns, see Stanfill pos. 2324–816; Bolin 807–8).

Jenkins and his co-authors have responded to the critiques voiced by Terranova and others by stressing the reciprocal nature of exchanges between producers and consumers, by lobbying for a greater transparency of producers' practices, and by calling for an increased authenticity in the industry's interactions with audiences (Jenkins, Ford, and Green 56–61, 75–84). Implicit in this defense is the assumption that that "economic systems ideally align the perceived interests of all parties involved in a transaction in ways that are consistent, coherent, and fair" (Jenkins, Ford, and Green 52; see *Convergence Culture* 63–64). Arguably, however, the practices of media audiences are complexly entangled with other aspects of their everyday routines, closely related to the rhythms and heteronomies of work, and inextricably bound to other necessities of social life. Recreational media consumption practices are thus subjected to a variety of forces and agencies outside of the control and influence of any consumer. Likewise, the actions of corporate actors occur under competitive conditions and are carried out with a constant eye on profit margins, which means that considerations about meaningful participation and responsible interaction are hardly a priority. It might thus be categorically impossible to balance the needs of consumers and producers. This is so not only because the orientations of the production and consumption sides are considerably different, but because the notion of a successful "equilibrium" between supply and demand itself is a fiction "unfounded in empirical economy," as Ingerid Straume has argued (38, 39).[18] Despite these shortcomings, the descriptions and concepts offered by Jenkins obviously do capture something crucial about the state of contemporary commercial entertainment – if it were not so, his terms would not have been adopted by other scholars and his work would lack a practical utility for media professionals.

Jenkins's work on digital-era popular culture should thus not simply be dismissed as a "hypocritical cover for relations of force," as Boltanksi and Chiapello put it (x). It is more useful to consider his ideas as ideological in the sense of "a set of shared beliefs" that are "inscribed in institutions, bound up with actions, and [. . .] anchored in reality" (3). Ideology in this sense refers to a system of ideas that is shaped by a particular perspective and interest, that provides orientation, offers justifications for the actions of individuals, and allows for the articulation of rules for good behavior. Capitalism, so Boltanski and Chiapello argue, requires such a system of beliefs, justifications, and codes of conduct because it tends to subordinate the needs of individuals to the operations of markets and processes of capital accumulation, but nonetheless depends on their active and willing participation to sustain itself (7–12). As a set of beliefs meant to mobilize individuals, capitalist ideology thus cannot be reduced to claims about capitalism's supposed tendency to foster "general well-being and progress" or the reference to its "emancipatory power [. . .] and political freedom as the collateral of economic freedom" (13). While such commonplaces are indispensable parts of the spirit of capitalism, Boltanski and Chiapello suggest that its central messages "must be integrated into descriptions that are sufficiently substantial and detailed, [. . .] coincide with people's moral experience of daily life and suggest models of action they can grasp" (14). The best example of such an ideological discourse, they argue, can be found in management literature targeted at business executives, managers, and engineers. Literature of this type offers practical advice for corporate actors along with moral justifications that legitimize specific courses of action.

In its orientation towards media industry professionals, its repeated stress on the positive value of consumers' social connections and its calls for fairness in producer-customer interactions, Jenkins's work on digital-era popular culture constitutes an articulation of the spirit of capitalism in the precise sense described by Boltanski and Chiapello. As such, it assumes that the practices of corporate actors and media audiences are both guided by the attempt to maximize benefits – increased profits, a positive brand image and good public relations for producers; access to quality content, increased occasions for meaningful social interaction and community-building on the part of consumers. Jenkins's more specific arguments also considerably overlap with ideas that the two sociologists identify as central to the spirit of contemporary capitalism.[19] Boltanski and Chiapello note that popular management texts published since the 1970s frequently stress a corporate imperative to develop "a sensitivity to differences, [. . .] and receptiveness to a whole range of experiences" (97), the need to value "interaction [and] authentic human relations" (98), "the importance of careful attention to [customers'] wishes," and a "development of individualized relations" (99), as well as the need to create personalized "products that are attuned to demand" (99). The stated reasons for a reorientation of business practices are the same, too: Just as Jenkins identifies the computer-based convergence of formerly separate media and an increased competition between content providers as central to the transformations in early-twenty-first-century entertainment media (*Convergence* 64–68), the larger management discourse attributes the need to adapt to more competitive markets and the "constant progress in information technology" (Boltanski and Chiapello 73). In more than one way, Jenkins's work on digital-era popular culture thus reads like a belated echo to the management literature discussed by Boltanski and Chiapello.

What, then, are the implications of claiming that Jenkins's arguments are expressions of the spirit of capitalism? Firstly, it means that Jenkins's work can be understood both as an attempt to insert a capitalist ideology into media and cultural studies discourses and as a project that makes scholarly insights about the practices of media audiences available to the entertainment industries.[20] Jenkins's work should thus not be read as a disinterested description of certain trends in contemporary popular culture, but rather as an ideological distillation of concepts, beliefs, norms, and "best practices" (Jenkins, Ford, and Green xii) that orient the operations of commercial entertainment at the beginning of the twenty-first century. Secondly, it means that the business strategies and aesthetic practices discussed by Jenkins are part of a larger regime of digital-era capitalism. If Jenkins is correct, this regime puts a premium on attempts to monitor customer demand; acknowledges the diversity of the audience's interests and tastes; seeks to establish affective bonds between creators, products, and consumers; and, ultimately, attempts to harness the cultural and communicative practices of media audiences for commercial gain. Thirdly, identifying Jenkins's ideas as part of an ideological discourse strips his arguments from the sense of inevitability that the usage of terms such as "cultural logic" might otherwise evoke. Jenkins's work frequently seems to imply that the digital media environment requires a specific way of designing and marketing popular narratives and that alternative practices are simply unable to compete. Recognizing this framework as ideologically inflected allows us to see that the practices discussed by Jenkins et al. are not necessarily the only possible response to the impact of digitization, but simply a set of options that is promoted from a specific vantage point.

As one among many articulations of the spirit of contemporary capitalism, Jenkins's participates in the elaboration of a neoliberal management discourse that, by way of countless translations and attempts to implement new ideas in practice, eventually comes to orient contemporary culture-industrial production. Informed by this ideology, commercial popular culture comes to be governed by a new set of imperatives. During the Fordist period, the culture-industrial organization of free time manifested itself, among other things, in the attempt to align the inflexible broadcasting schedules and publication rhythms of the mass media with the recreational practices and routines of consumers. In this classical configuration of the culture industry, the sale and consumption of cultural commodities took center stage and figured as both the goal of producers and an essential part of consumers' leisure activities. At the same time, consumers' own cultural production accompanied the products of the entertainment industries as a non-commercial (or not immediately profitable) activity (even though producers occasionally encouraged fan activity to secure a baseline of sales). By contrast, the dominant ideology of digital-era popular culture conceptualizes media audiences as culturally and textually productive consumers from the outset. This shift in emphasis reframes consumers as potential cultural workers whose practices can be harnessed for promotional gain – and it privileges media contents that can engage audiences over longer periods of time and inspire attendant cultural activities. Borrowing terminology from Pierre Lévy, Jenkins has described such contents as "cultural attractor[s]" that invite, bundle, and fuel all kinds of related activity (Jenkins, *Convergence* 95). Over the course of the following chapters, I argue that recent superhero films embody this "new spirit" of commercial popular culture par excellence. But, since Jenkins's work is invested in attempts to legitimate the practices of digital-era popular culture, its ability to explain the operations of this configuration of commercial entertainment remains limited. To better understand the implications of the turn to a valorization of audience practices, broader transformations in the capitalist mode of production need to be addressed as well.

DIGITAL CAPITALISM, IMMATERIAL LABOR, AND CULTURAL EXTERNALITIES

In his short volume *24/7,* Jonathan Crary offers an engagement with the "consequences of neoliberal globalization" for life in the affluent West that echoes Adorno's interest in the issues of recreation and leisure activity under capitalism (Crary 8). For Crary, the implementation of neoliberal reforms since the 1970s and subsequent processes of digitization have instituted "a global infrastructure for continuous work and consumption" that articulates increasing demands towards individual productivity (3).[21] As result, a fully digitized and networked media environment now enables flexible and modularized working processes as much as a form of media consumption that is no longer bound to private spaces or a clearly defined free time. This situation increases the pressure on individuals to make productive use of their time, effectively "dissolving most of the borders between private and professional time, between work and consumption" (15). Existing under these conditions, so Crary argues, means to live life according to "a principle of continuous functioning" in which one is expected to be constantly working, consuming, or communicating about one's consumption (8). In contrast to the height of Fordism, during which Adorno could still insist on a clear-cut separation between free time and labor, the new "post-Fordist" constellation exhibits a tendency to eliminate pockets of unused time along with the securities that made their unproductive enjoyment possible.

Crary's sketch provides a useful starting point for understanding the larger medial and economic regime under which recent superhero blockbuster films operate. Viewed against the backdrop of a 24/7 culture, the audience practices described by Jenkins appear as expressions of an economic regime that exploits consumers' communicative practices and turns free time into a potential source of surplus value. But neoliberalism and digitization have not changed other aspects of the culture-industrial constellation discussed earlier in this chapter. While the boundaries between work and free time have become more fluid, most recipients still consume popular entertainments as part of recreational practices that are meant to counterbalance the exhausting routines and pressures of everyday life. Likewise, consumers continue to be potentially critical and self-reflexive. Crary's account, however, presents 24/7 culture as a monolithic regime that leaves little room for the subjective agency to unplug and withdraw, if only for a limited time, from the globally networked flows of media content. In his account, digital media provide the infrastructure for the constant and perpetual exploitation of users who are ceaselessly active and productive, but also helplessly shackled to said infrastructure. This one-sided view makes it difficult to discuss countervailing forces or conflicts within the culture-industrial system.

Focusing more specifically on the practices of media audiences, Dan Hassler-Forest's study *Science Fiction, Fantasy, and Politics* sets Jenkins's work of digital-era popular culture into a dialogue with the critical account of capitalist globalization that Antonio Negri and Michael Hardt develop in their books *Empire* (2000) and *Multitude* (2004). Hassler-Forest proceeds from the observation that media franchises such as *Star Trek*, *Game of Thrones*, or *The Walking Dead* both construct "complex, coherent storyworlds" across media and inspire the activities of fans who engage in an ongoing "creative appropriation" of these texts (*Science Fiction* 3). Hassler-Forest sees an "internal contradiction" at work in these phenomena, which for him are "expression[s] of the two faces of global capitalism" (3): On the one hand, "popular storyworlds are constantly being appropriated by capitalism's incontrovertible logic of accumulation," and "audience's creative work is transformed into immaterial labor at the service of media corporations" (4). On the other hand, the creative practices of media fans also seem to actualize a "radical spirit of collectivity" that harbors "an inherently revolutionary potential" (4, 13). This resistant potential comes to the fore in subversive memes, in audience-produced mash-up videos, or discussions on social media, for example, as well as in consumers' overt critiques of media corporations and their products. Hassler-Forest's account thus highlights the ambiguous relationship between the producers and consumers of popular entertainments, emphasizing that fan cultures might yield both an economic productivity *and* a potential unruliness that complicates attempts to capitalize on their activities (*Science Fiction* 13). In contrast to Crary's view, Hassler-Forest's more nuanced perspective allows us to acknowledge that the interests of producers and consumers are not only not identical, but often fraught with conflict – and that entertainment franchises and fan cultures might become sites on which these conflicts play out.

At the same time, Hassler-Forest's suggestion that the practices of media fandom harbor hidden anti-capitalist potentials seems like an overstatement. Arguably, we can just as plausibly understand the "resistant" audience practices discussed by Hassler-Forest as activities of consumers who are used to engage with a variety of entertainment offerings and who make decisions about what to consume based on individual preferences. From such a perspective, a critical view of specific commodities might simply lead to the consumption of other products and to the articulation of criticism, but not to the adoption of an anti-capitalist outlook or a rejection of the culture-industrial system.

Interestingly, however, Hassler-Forest also gestures towards economist Carlo Vercellone's concept of "cognitive capitalism," which allows for a more comprehensive discussion of digitization's impact (*Science Fiction* 10). For Vercellone, the history of capitalism can be understood in terms of three fundamental shifts in the relationship between capital and labor. The first of these shifts marks the rise of mercantile capitalism "between the beginning of the sixteenth and the end of the eighteenth century," a period which sees the appearance of the "entrepreneur who organises production [. . .] by artisans and independent workers" (Vercellone 15, 15n6). The second shift coincides "with the first industrial revolution" and the rise of large factories "specialized in the production of mass, standardized goods" (Vercellone 16). Characterized by a complex division of labor, work within the industrial factory is carried out by masses of workers who operate an array of specialized machinery on shop floors that are surveilled and serviced by a class of more highly qualified managers and engineers (Daum 26–27, 95–97; Dyer-Witheford 74–76). The sophistication of factory machinery here coincides with a "disqualification" of most factory labor, which no longer requires the skills of trained craftsmen (Vercellone 16; 23–6). Finally, what Vercellone labels as cognitive capitalism refers to a third stage that begins with the "social crisis of Fordism" in the 1970s (Vercellone 16).[22] The emergent post-Fordist situation witnesses the successive abandonment of the factory model as the predominant mode of commodity production and the concurrent appearance of new forms of labor as well as increasingly automated, computerized, and networked working environments (Vercellone 16; see also Daum 29–39). Fueled by neoliberal deregulation, the diffusion of digital technology and the decline of the mass factory, cognitive capitalism ushers in "the formation of a knowledge-based economy" and the rise to prominence of tech giants (such as IBM, Apple, or Microsoft) whose businesses are either based on hi-tech products for computer-mediated communication or on services for the generation, organization, and diffusion of information (Vercellone 14).[23] In the years around the turn of the twenty-first century, this digital capitalism has been further energized by the rise of the Internet and the successes of companies such as Google and Facebook, whose services would eventually become central mediators of online activity. As a result of these developments, "the new centre of gravity of the world economy," as Vercellone's colleague Yann Moulier Boutang puts it, shifts from the heartlands of industrial production to California's Silicon Valley (7).

In his own take on these developments, philosopher Maurizio Lazzarato describes the form of work that has become dominant during the post-industrial period as "immaterial labor." In contrast to factory labor, immaterial labor entails the production of the "informational and cultural content" of commodities rather than the material production of things (Lazzarato 132, 136–37; Vercellone 16). For Lazzarato, immaterial labor becomes widespread in all kinds of sectors, reshaping work processes everywhere, from the (now increasingly automated) industrial factory, over the service industries, to work in educational or cultural fields. Importantly, he emphasizes that immaterial labor encompasses a diverse set of "skills involving cybernetics and computer control, [. . .] horizontal and vertical communication," as well as "the kinds of activities involved in defining and fixing cultural and artistic standards, fashions, tastes, consumer norms, and [. . .] public opinion" (132). "[O]nce the privileged domain of the bourgeoisie and its children," these immaterial skills now "become the domain of [. . .] 'mass intellectuality'" and diffused within modern societies as a generally available set of work-related skills (Lazzarato 133).[24] Building on Lazzarato's work, Vercellone suggests that the emergence of this socially "diffuse intellectuality" constitutes a key element in the larger shift towards an economy that is no longer primarily based on the exploitation of deskilled factory work, but instead on forms of labor that involve technical know-how, social communication and cooperation, and the operation of computerized machines (Vercellone 29).

It is easy to see why Hassler-Forest connects his discussion of digital-era entertainment franchises and fan practices to the concept of cognitive capitalism. When Vercellone brings up socially diffused intellectuality as one of the defining aspects of contemporary capitalism, he implicitly refers to the emergence of the same kind of hybrid subject that also figures prominently in Jenkins's work: the figure of the consumer who is also a small-scale creator and distributor of media content, who can occupy this dual position thanks to digital and networked media technologies, and who shifts between both roles due to the necessities and routines of work, education, and recreation. According to Vercellone, cognitive capitalism generalizes the kind of computer-mediated social communication, cooperation, and problem-solving that Jenkins discusses as central to digital-era participatory culture and (at least potentially) turns these practices into an integral aspect of all kinds of social activity.[25] The practices and skills associated with the notion of immaterial labor, in other words, take the form of a diffuse productive potential that also exists outside of formalized labor relationships.

Other scholars have similarly suggested that contemporary capitalism can be understood as an economic regime that relies on digital and networked media to extract profits from the corporate appropriation of accumulated social knowledge and shared collective experience. Timo Daum, for example, argues that digital-era capitalism thrives on the "valorization of user-generated content and the increasing economic appropriation of the complete range of human activity, even if it falls outside of the labor process itself" (224; my translation). For Daum, the platform model of content distribution – which is best exemplified by social media platforms such as Twitter, YouTube, or Facebook – embodies this mode of appropriation particularly well (Daum 112–16). Social media platforms offer free-to-use environments within which users share their own contributions, navigate those of others, and access content by third-party providers. As a result, "the actual work" of content creation is performed "by the audience, by the customers and users" who link to news sources or contribute short messages, video clips, photos, and status updates (Daum 114; my translation).[26] Importantly, however, digital capitalism also relies on algorithmic mechanisms to capture the informational productivity of involuntarily generated user data that, as Mark Andrejevic has argued, is inadvertently generated within "digital enclosures" such as the Internet (2; see also Bolin 801–6; Stanfill pos. 2450–95). Making a similar case, Shoshanna Zuboff has discussed the extraction and analysis of user-data as a central pillar of a "surveillance capitalism" that "unilaterally claims human experience as free raw material for translation into behavioral data" (8; see 8–12). This project hinges on the "total transparency" of user activity, which is continuously logged and surveilled by companies such as Facebook and Google and subsequently used as a basis for targeted advertising, as feedback information for technological development, or as a commodity that can be sold to data-brokers (Daum 113). In all these examples, the digital economy relies on the unrecognized and unpaid immaterial labor of users who provide and manage the content of commercially run websites, post on blogs and social media, share contents across platforms, or perform similar activities.

In his own study of *Cognitive Capitalism*, Boutang uses the concept of "externalities" to stress the significance of this turn towards a valorization of computer-mediated activity (22; see 23–26). According to Boutang, an externality represents a "non-market effect," "something that falls outside the economic," but is nonetheless "acting on it in a continuous fashion and not simply as an initial given" (22). Externalities in this sense are themselves not part of individual economic transactions, business ventures, or commercial enterprises, but impinge still on their operation, yielding an impact that might be positive or negative. The concept of externalities allows us to understand the orientation towards a valorization of user activity as a shift of capital's attention towards areas that have traditionally been considered as the outside of firms, markets, and economic transactions. The socially diffused knowledges and skillsets that Lazzarato has associated with immaterial forms of labor are externalities in this sense, as are concrete manifestations of immaterial labor on social media platforms or other widely-read websites. Free knowledge and information resources such as Wikipedia – which ultimately are products of immaterial labor as well – are yet another example of an externality that can be factored into capitalist valorization processes.

Corporate attempts to control the outside environments of firms have a long history. As Boltanski and Chiapello point out in *The New Spirit of Capitalism*, ...

> The history of "management" can in fact be conceived as involving constant refinement of methods for controlling what occurs in the firm and its environment. [... W]ith certain subdisciplines of management, the will to control was to be extended beyond machines and workforce. With business strategy, control of markets and competition has developed; with marketing, control of the distribution circuit, customers, and their purchasing habits; with purchase management, control of suppliers; with public relations, control of the press and political authorities. (79–80)

Digital capitalism extends this will to control all fields of human activity that involve the operation of digital and networked media. In the digital era, any kind of interaction carried out via networked media technologies thus becomes a potential positive externality that might be exploited by profit-oriented actors, from the streaming of video content and reading of news content online, over the posting of tweets and status updates, to the participation in fan fora or the usage of mobile fitness apps, for example. This means that some of the spill-over effects of media consumption that Adorno might have dismissed as idle expressions of Fordist boredom – such as the community-building practices and textual production of media fans – now become directly integrated into capitalist valorization processes. No longer an economically insignificant phenomenon, the activities of media audiences take on new functions within the culture-industrial constellation, becoming a form of unpaid, value-generating labor that produces much of online discourse and provides informational raw material that can be fed back into algorithm-based services and valorization processes.

The theories of digital capitalism discussed so far reframe Jenkins's arguments and the notion of an "engagement-based paradigm" (discussed in the preceding chapter) in interesting ways. In *Convergence Culture* and *Spreadable Media*, Jenkins and his co-authors articulate a central imperative of commercial popular culture in the age of digital capitalism: Generating sales is no longer enough; instead, cultural commodities now also need to generate user activity on all levels, engage consumers over longer periods of time, and inspire all kinds of related online activity. Against the background of the economic theories discussed above, we can understand this orientation as a project aimed at the mobilization and capture of externalities that can increase a commodity's chances of commercial success – from discussions on fan-sites and other online fan practices to search queries on Google, over clicks, likes, shares, and comments on social media, to the textual production of professional critics and the responses they inspire. But the practices of media audiences might also become negative externalities: Reviewers might circulate scathing critiques that impact viewership numbers, a poor box-office performance might produce negative publicity, fan audiences might decline to support and promote specific titles, the discussion of recent releases on social media might fail to produce the desired outcome, and so on. Producers of cultural commodities thus have an incentive to intervene in online discourse to shape and direct the reception of their products. Strategies such as transmedia storytelling, an aesthetics attuned to the interests of fan cultures, and efforts to turn consumers into "brand advocates" can thus be understood as expressions of a corporate will to manage and control the cultural environment of popular entertainments.

Like other management efforts, attempts to capture positive externalities are not exactly new. I noted earlier in this chapter that the publishers of American comic books began to actively encourage and support fan activities during the 1940s and 1950s. Likewise, the producers of "cult" TV shows such as *Star Trek* have long sought to cultivate good relationships with the members of fan communities and tried to rally their support in times of dipping ratings (see Reeves, Rodgers, and Epstein 27–32). But in the digital era, efforts to mobilize fan-cultural externalities undergo a systematization and refinement, as well as a shift in importance, that transforms them from occasional practices on the margins of commercial popular culture to mainstream phenomena. Along these lines, marketing scholar Robert Kozinets has argued that "business school literature on consumer behavior, marketing and 'Consumer Culture Theory'" began to frame the figure of the culturally productive, socially networked and emotionally engaged "consumer-as-fan [who] becomes an advertiser, entrepreneur, marketer, and producer" as an ideal type of customer in the early 1990s (169–70; see 162–71).[27] Making a similar case, Stanfill suggests that between "1994 and 2009, the word 'fan' and practices traditionally associated with fans were increasingly integrated into media industry logics" (Pos. 103–4). Stanfill relies on the study of interviews with media industry professionals, news reports, fan-oriented websites, as well as of film and television representations of fans to argue that highly engaged fans eventually came to be recognized as an important "constituency that media companies [. . .] actively seek to incorporate, encourage, monetize and manage" (Pos. 145–52). Ultimately, she suggests, the "intensive and extensive engagement" typical of fan cultures emerged as a new norm and mode of media consumption preferred by the industry (Pos. 100–13).[28]

The increased emphasis on fans and fan activity constitutes a particularly salient manifestation of the entertainment industry's will to capitalize on the unpaid immaterial labor and diffuse intellectuality of networked media audiences. But corporate attempts to encourage fannish consumption practices are only one part of a broader project to exert control over the cultural and medial environment. Under digital capitalism, entire fields of online discourse and computer-mediated practice emerge as unconquered sites and territories from which profits, promotional benefits, and productivity gains can be extracted. From the standpoint of corporate actors, the activities of other profit-oriented companies (such as competitors within the same economic sector or commercial news media, for example) represent potential externalities as well. Moreover, the audience activity inspired by cultural commodities such as superhero movies invariably helps to sustain a whole ecosystem of commercially operated online platforms, services, and publications that mediate audiences' access to popular entertainment, including streaming services such as Netflix, Amazon Video, and Disney+, social media, fan-oriented entertainment news websites, traditional news media, and more. For the corporate actors that operate within this ecosystem, the discursive activities that play out across journalistic responses, commentary pieces, academic criticism, and social media chatter, the debates of online fan cultures and other types of online discussion also present themselves as potential externalities that might be harnessed for commercial gain. Superhero blockbuster films and other contemporary entertainments thus need to position themselves within a crowded and incessantly busy media landscape, and their chances at commercial success turn out to be contingent on a variety of external factors that require constant attention and management. Accordingly, attempts to control the environment of corporations and commodities are not only targeted at the practices of media fans and less involved recipients, but also try to harness the productivity of professional consumers and other corporate actors.

Crucially, however, corporate attempts to mobilize and capitalize on cultural externalities do not proceed in a frictionless manner and do not simply integrate the practices of other actors "from above," as Adorno might have put it. Like the survey participants of Adorno's essay on "Free Time" and the resistant media audiences cited by Hassler-Forest, the actors, institutions, and competing products that make up the environment of today's cultural commodities are potentially unruly, which is to say that their interests, needs, and goals rarely are perfectly aligned with the imperatives of the corporate actors that seek to manage them. Efforts to exert control over the cultural environment of commercial entertainments are thus at least potentially fraught with conflict and always run the risk of failing (or of producing unintended results that require further attention and management). As I will show in Chapters 3 through 5, superhero blockbuster films try to preempt such failures through a politics of engagement that, rather than trying to completely determine and pre-structure the reception practices of their viewers, presents itself as open to a range of different responses, modes of consumption, and levels of engagement. More generally, however, the entertainment industry's attempts to mobilize cultural externalities necessarily constitute an open-ended project that cannot determine the practices of consumers completely.

In summary, digital capitalism's reconfigured culture industry connects the profitability of commercial entertainments not only to sales and audience engagement, but also to their ability to manage their cultural and medial environments. Compared to the mass culture of the Fordist period, digital-era popular culture articulates heightened demands for consumers' ongoing and culturally productive engagement with media content. It seeks to solicit such an engagement through practices of serial storytelling, a close monitoring of consumer activity, a new sensitivity to cultural differences, and an attunement to audience demands. One result of this orientation is that much of contemporary entertainment becomes more stressful, more time-consuming, and more apt at inserting itself into the everyday routines of consumers – a tendency evidenced by, for example, the rise of online streaming platforms and the diffusion of mobile smart devices whose notifications interrupt our everyday lives on a regular basis. While the dominant ideology sells these developments as products of a participatory culture that increases the agency of consumers, the more critical perspective advanced here reframes them as results of a culture-industrial constellation that has extended the corporate will to control to hitherto unconquered areas of social and cultural life. The second part of this book examines in more detail how these imperatives play out in the case of superhero blockbuster cinema. For the moment, however, it is worth emphasizing that the genre's aesthetic practices do not simply constitute an arbitrary assortment of idiosyncratic formal tics. Instead, recent superhero movies embody the spirit of twenty-century popular culture in filmic form, and this orientation manifests itself very concretely in the ways in which they tell their stories, the themes they negotiate, and the kinds of cinematic experiences they provide.

COMIC BOOK SUPERHEROES AS UNFREE SYMBOLIC COMMONS

This chapter set out to explore the mechanisms behind the long history and contemporary omnipresence of comic book superheroes and the various narratives, media, and products in (and on) which they appear. It started with the observation that the most iconic superheroes are many-decade-old serial figures with a remarkable ability to reinvent themselves and nonetheless stay recognizably the same. It then went on to argue that processes of serial repetition and innovation characterize not only the cross-medial history of the superhero genre, but also commercial cultural production in general. Offering a re-reading of Horkheimer and Adorno's theory of the culture industry, the chapter considered seriality as a crucial dimension of a larger social constellation that organizes the free time of consumers around the recurring consumption of cultural commodities. At the cusp of the twenty-first century, this organizing function undergoes a shift from a consumption-centric to an engagement-based model, a development that is part of a more general transformation within the capitalist mode of production. This transformation reframes the practices of media audiences as a source of economic surplus value and brings about a new set of corporate attempts to manage the cultural and medial environment of cultural commodities. Extending this argument, the following chapters will explore in more detail to what extent such attempts inform the aesthetic practices of superhero blockbuster films. But before moving on, I want to return to the question of why superheroes from the pages of American comic books have risen to such a conspicuous position within today's popular culture. The answer, I suggest, is bound up with the long publication histories of these figures, which often date back to the beginnings of the superhero genre.

Unlike other popular figures, many of the superheroes owned by DC Comics or Marvel Comics possess long and multi-faceted histories of serial proliferation. Since their birth in the comic books of the late 1930s and early 1940s, superhero narratives have continued to circulate in a variety of formats and media, fueled countless fan activities, repeatedly become the subject of news media coverage, and inspired a wealth of critical commentary. These past proliferations and the cultural responses engendered by them have bestowed a peculiar familiarity on figures such as Superman, Wonder Woman, Captain America, and the like, thereby creating an important precondition for the superhero culture of the early twenty-first century. Something of the significance of this history is captured by the truism that today's superhero blockbusters are "pre-sold" properties that (because they are based on figures and narratives that have already proven their commercial viability) come with a built-in audience (Balio 25–28; Hassler-Forest, *Capitalist Superheroes* 10; Burke 54–55). This idea quite accurately describes the rationale behind most serialization practices, but it gains an additional significance if histories of serial proliferation are understood not just as a thing of the past, but as externalities that, due to the encyclopedic capacities and vast content libraries of the digital era, continue to matter and exert influence on contemporary cultural production. Elena Esposito has argued that the contents of modern mass media – in particular, print, film, radio and television, but also digital media – "provide a background of knowledge that can be taken for granted and considered as shared by everybody" (255; my translation).[29] Recent superhero blockbusters are pre-sold properties only because they are preceded by earlier iterations that have already diffused (and continue to diffuse) a basic knowledge about the genre, its figures, themes, and storytelling formulae within society. This knowledge can be understood as a pop-cultural analogue to the diffuse intellectuality that Vercellone discusses as a feature of cognitive capitalism. The long-standing presence of superhero narratives in various media, formats, and discourses, in other words, has anchored the genre firmly within social memory. As result, contemporary superhero blockbuster cinema can capitalize on its location within a media environment that makes other superhero narratives, preceding iterations of well-known figures, and all kinds of related information readily available.

Superhero blockbusters based on titles from the voluminous back-catalogs of DC Comics or Marvel Comics can thus be understood as examples of a special class of popular entertainments that I call unfree symbolic commons: they are corporately owned, medially omnipresent, immediately recognizable, and easily legible cultural commodities that can capitalize on the presence of earlier iterations within social memory, building on a pre-existing familiarity on the part of the audience.[30] Superhero blockbusters based on DC and Marvel Comics properties thus present themselves as the latest iterations of widely-shared symbolic resources that are readily available as topics of social communication. It is precisely this status that endows superhero figures with their considerable capacity to radiate out into a variety of different cultural fields. As symbolic commons, many of DC's and Marvel's superheroic protagonists have, in some shape or form, been part of the fabric of American popular culture for more than half a century. Consequently, these figures offer themselves as easily recognizable reference points for all kinds of artistic and cultural activity. Both company's iconic superheroes are "unfree" in the sense that they are owned by large media conglomerates and protected by larger institutional and legal frameworks which ensure the enforcement of intellectual property claims. Accordingly, the commercial use of superhero figures and their narratives is limited to a narrow set of actors and otherwise generally prohibited. As popular entertainments, superhero figures and their narratives nonetheless inspire a wealth of official and unofficial, authorized and unauthorized continuations, offshoots, adaptations, and appropriations, as well as various kinds of paratextual discussion, reporting, and debate. These narratives and materials, in turn, add to the medial omnipresence of superhero figures and fuel a self-reinforcing dynamic of proliferation that ensures the continued existence of the genre.

Recent superhero blockbuster cinema's ability to capitalize on often many-decade-long histories of culturally resonant serial unfolding also sets entries of the gerne apart from other types of film. Not coincidentally, recent films about heroes such as Batman, Spider-Man, or Captain America tend to reference the serial prehistories of these figures in relatively obvious ways. After all, the pre-existing media exposure of these figures constitutes a competitive advantage that increases the films' chances of commercial success. But the ability to benefit from a socially diffused knowledge of superhero narratives is not limited to films about the genre's best-known protagonists. Since most superhero movies play variations on well-established storytelling formulae, films based on lesser-known properties can rely on the audiences' basic familiarity with the tropes of the genre as well. To succeed with audiences, however, these films need to do more than merely coast on a pre-established popularity or reiterate already proven ideas. Superhero movies also need to present themselves as state-of-the-art cinematic attractions, find ways to engage culturally productive media consumption practices, and be able to resonate with a broader set of current concerns, topics, and anxieties. The following chapters examine how these operations play out in practice.

NOTES

1. My discussion of the chapter on the culture industry and of Adorno's essay on "Free Time" (below) here expands on ideas first developed in Brinker, "On the Political Economy."
2. Eco's essay on Superman first appeared in English translation in 1972.
3. Naremore and Brantlinger, for example, suggest that the theory of the culture industry cannot account for the coexistence of different artistic traditions (such as avant-garde art, folk-art, popular culture) within a broader field of mass culture. Likewise, Huyssen argues that it represents an elitist defense of modernist art that lacks the vocabulary to conceptualize more popular forms (ix–x, 16–44). Similarly, Kellner claims that Adorno's "undialectical" opposition of mass culture and authentic art cannot account for aesthetics that blur the lines between "high" and "low" cultural forms ("Theodor W. Adorno"). Horkheimer and Adorno's theory furthermore downplays the potential of markets to encourage product differentiation (Steinert 80–81) and performs a problematic gendering of mass culture that associates "lower" cultural forms with feminine qualities, which are then dismissed (see, for example, Horkheimer and Adorno 123). For defenses of Horkheimer and Adorno's theory, see Behrens *Krise* and *Verstummen*; Steinert.
4. On the tendency to dismiss Adorno's work, see Hills, *Fan Cultures* 6–11.
5. The superman example is typical of early American comic books, which often recycled ideas from other genres and media (Mayer, *Fu Manchu* 119–20). Interestingly, the creation of the Superman figure itself constituted a serial chain rather than a singular moment of artistic innovation: While the Superman of *Action Comics* #1 was an instant success, Siegel and Shuster had pitched various versions of the figure to publishers since 1933 (Daniels 10–34).
6. On the proliferation of superhero figures after 1938, see Jewett and Lawrence; Daniels 37; Reynolds 100.
7. To illustrate this point, Adorno notes that the industrial production and mass-marketing of "tents and dormobiles, plus huge quantities of extra equipment" changed the practice of camping from an activity once understood as "a protest against the tedium and

convention of bourgeois life" into an outdoor extension of middle-class comfort (190). Arguably, however, the mass media's time schedules and ability to group consumers into a larger collective play a much more important role for the culture industry's ability to organize free time.
8. As Adorno notes elsewhere, the entertainment industries cater to "needs that are mediated and then fixed into form by the market" ("Thesen" 395; my translation).
9. First presented as a radio lecture in May 1969 and later published as part of the volume *Stichworte*, Adorno's essay "Free Time" counts among his last published works on the culture industry (Adorno died in August of the same year).
10. Matt Yockey notes that Marvel's corporate predecessor Timely Comics promoted the company's own Captain America fan club as early as 1941; Marvel continued such efforts with a series of official fan clubs during the 1960s and 1970s ("Introduction" 8; 26). DC Comics sponsored official fan clubs during the same period as well.
11. On EC comics fandom during the 1950s, see Pustz, *Comic Book Culture* 26–65; Gardner 68–106; on superhero comics fandom of the 1960s and 1970s, see Kelleter and Stein 271–8; on Marvel's courting of fan practices during the 1970s, see Brinker, "Reader Mobilization."
12. The understanding of the culture industry articulated here resonates with Kelleter and Stein's ANT-inspired view of popular culture as an "evolutionary system" that brings together a variety of human and non-human actors and operates without an easily identifiable "personal, economic, or medial central agency" (Kelleter and Stein 263; my translation).
13. On the idea that producers of cultural commodities often are experienced consumers, see Stein 134–5; Kelleter, "Five Ways" 19; as well as my discussion of fannish auteurs in Chapters 3 and 4.
14. For examples of such practice-oriented texts, see Phillips; Dowd, Niederman, Fry, and Steiff; Hayes. See Jenkins, "The Reign, 265n5".
15. Jenkins's *Convergence Culture* lifts the terms "inspirational consumers" and "brand advocates" from Kevin Roberts's *Lovemarks* (2004), a popular management text that argues for the importance of affective bonds between brands and their customers. See my discussion below.
16. For similar summaries of Jenkins's central arguments, see Fuchs 66–67; Stanfill pos. 116–23. Stanfill also offers a brief overview of cultural studies work on fan audiences that echoes Jenkins's narrative.
17. Terranova's concept of free labor is based on Maurizio Lazzarato's notion of "immaterial labor"; see my discussion below.
18. Straume notes that the idea of a balance between supply and demand is a key motif of neoclassical economics – a school of thought that tends to ignore the historical, social, and cultural contexts of economic activities; instead, it relies on the notion of the infallible market, abstract mathematical models and metaphors drawn from the field of thermodynamics to generate economic knowledge (Straume 38–39). Stanfill similarly emphasizes that the entertainment industry's attempts to solicit strong audience engagement occur within in a "structurally unequal media system" that is characterized by power asymmetries between producers and consumers (pos. 345).
19. Boltanski and Chiapello identify three historically specific spirits of capitalism with distinct ideological make-ups. The first of these emerges "at the end of the nineteenth century," the second during the height of the Fordist period after the 1930s, and the third with the rise of a "'globalized' capitalism" and the spread of digital information technologies since the 1970s (19; see also 17–19, xviii–xix).

20. Jenkins's work here performs a similar operation as the management texts discussed by Boltanski and Chiapello, who attribute shifts in the spirit of capitalism since the end of the 1960s to an influx of ideas and motifs from sociological and artistic critiques of capitalism (Boltanski and Chiapello 27–30, 345–46; see also McGuigan 25–28).
21. The terms neoliberalism and post-Fordism refer to overlapping phenomena; in what follows, I use the terms "post-Fordism" and "post-Fordist" to refer to configurations of capitalism that follow those of the Fordist period. "Neoliberalism" and "neoliberal," in turn, denote a political agenda and program that clusters around a promotion of economic deregulation, small government, and free market policies. Simon Springer similarly characterizes neoliberalism as a set of policies aimed at a general "roll-back of state capacities," the privatization of state-owned companies, the dismantling of the welfare state, and a liberalization of the labor market that has resulted in a rise of precarious forms of employment (Springer 153; see also Harvey *Neoliberalism* 3–35; Harvey, "From Fordism"; Dyer-Witheford 76–79). More generally, neoliberalism can also be understood as a political project that seeks to introduce free market economics into areas of social and cultural life not yet subjected to them (Foucault 215–37).
22. Vercellone's argument here is based on the Marxian discussion of the "formal subsumption" and "real subsumption" of labor (see Marx, *Capital* 645; 1019–40). In line with a larger tradition of Marxist theory, Vercellone uses the concept of succeeding developmental stages to discuss general tendencies within the history of capitalism. The phases of Vercellone's account show considerable overlap; specific types of work do not disappear with the beginning of a new stage, but cease to be dominant forms.
23. Vercellone mentions "the technological leap of telematic and microelectronic innovation" and the introduction of "Japanese methods of lean production" as contributing factors in the shift towards a knowledge-based digital economy (14). Vercellone furthermore connects cognitive capitalism to newly prominent forms of property (such as intellectual property), new technology-based business models (such as rent-based models in which profits are realized through the sharing or licensing of services, products, and properties), and an intensified "financial globalization" (23; see also 33–34). Similarly, Daum discusses a variety of disruptive IT-based business models – such as the exploitation of big data resources or endeavors in the so-called share economy – as emblematic of digital-era capitalism (Daum 110–56).
24. Lazzarato also locates the beginning of this shift in the 1970s. On the concept of "mass intellectuality" (which informs the work by Lazzarato and Vercellone discussed here), see Virno; Raunig, *A Thousand Machines* 114–16; Terranova 80–88. On the closely related Marxian concept of the "general intellect," see Marx, *Grundrisse* 585–86; see Raunig, "Einige Fragmente"; Daum 220–23.
25. Along similar lines, Boutang discusses cognitive capitalism as an economic regime "characterized by the rise of immaterial labour and by collective intelligence as a primary factor of production and as the real substance of wealth and value" (Boutang 22).
26. Daum emphasizes that a significant part of the content circulating on social media is created professionally on behalf of corporations, as well as by automated bots (see 119–22); from the standpoint of the platform, however, this third-party content is just another type of user-generated content. Daum discusses the interplay of consumer feedback, user data analysis, and version iteration in software development and digitization projects such as *Google Books* as additional examples for the many ways in which social knowledge is appropriated by corporate actors in the digital era (see 224–31).
27. Kozinets mentions Ken Blanchard's *Raving Fans: A Revolutionary Approach to Customer Service* (1993), Michael J. Wolf's *The Entertainment Economy: How Mega-Media Forces*

Are Transforming Our Lives (1999), Douglas Atkin's *The Culting of Brands: When Customers Become True Believers* (2004), and Kevin Roberts' *Lovemarks* (2004) as examples of a literature that promotes such a view of consumers. The inclusion of *Lovemarks* is instructive here, as it points to an overlap between this type of management literature and the work of industry-oriented media studies scholars such as Jenkins (see Kozinets 163–72; Jenkins, *Convergence Culture* 69, 73, 91, 246).

28. For a more optimistic take on the "mainstreaming" of fan culture, see Scott and Jenkins. Kozinet's and Stanfill's work follows in the footsteps of earlier research that similarly emphasizes alignments between the practices of fan audiences and the interests of corporate cultural producers. See Chapter 4.
29. Esposito here paraphrases Niklas Luhmann, who similarly notes that "whatever we know about our society, or indeed about the world in which we live, we know through the mass media" (Luhmann, *The Reality* 1). The concept of social memory promoted by Luhmann and Esposito does not refer to a collective memory shared by all members of a society, but to historically specific forms and media that allow social systems to remember or forget. For a discussion of how the differing logics of mass media and digital media shape social memory, see Esposito 12–43; 183–368. I return to this idea in Chapter 5.
30. Other examples of unfree symbolic commons include the films and TV series of the *Star Wars* and *Star Trek* franchises, the James Bond films, the *Lord of the Rings* films, and, to a lesser degree, the *Transformers* series, as well as the film franchise built around the *Harry Potter* books.

CHAPTER 2

Superhero Narratives between Seriality and Political Meaning

In his classic essay on "The Myth of Superman," Umberto Eco suggests that the narrative appeals and ideological messages of early Superman comics are intricately linked to an "iterative scheme" for the serial production of essentially similar stories (19).[1] A key ingredient of this scheme is the larger-than-life protagonist who is "equipped with powers superior to those of the common man," but nonetheless remains within "the reach of the reader's self-identification" (14). Superman's powers of superhuman strength, incredible speed, near invulnerability, flight, and heat vision, so Eco notes, are balanced by his alter ego Clark Kent, the "fearful, timid, not overly intelligent, awkward, near-sighted, and submissive" journalist (14). This duality renders Superman/Clark Kent an appealing fantasy that can accommodate the readers' "hope that one day, from the slough of [one's] actual personality, a superman can spring forth who is capable of redeeming years of mediocre existence" (15). But the figure of the omnipotent hero also allows for the telling of a potentially endless series of action-packed adventures. Superman, as Eco notes, is akin to a "mythological character" or "archetype" like Hercules (15), a figure whom "nothing can impede" (16) and who is impervious to the passing of time or the dangers that threaten the lives of mere mortals. Accordingly, Superman comics can put their hero through countless dramatic events and suspenseful confrontations with villains that are (more or less) easily overcome by the protagonist. At the end of each adventure, Superman's interventions return the world to an orderly status quo that is virtually identical to the one that existed before. Subsequently, the next installment can start "from a sort of virtual beginning, ignoring where the preceding event left off" (19). As result, Superman stories "develop in a kind of oneiric climate [. . .] where what has happened before and what has happened after appears extremely hazy," where protagonists and supporting characters do not age and where villains like Lex Luthor are bound to return, no matter how often they are defeated ("The Myth" 17). Likewise, Superman's powers – which would in theory allow him to "take over the government, defeat the army, or alter the equilibrium of planetary politics" (22) – are never used to effect lasting political change. Instead, Superman comics relegate their hero to tasks that do not threaten the narrative status quo (such as fighting crime, averting natural disasters, or stopping cosmic dangers, for example). The iterative scheme of early Superman comics, Eco argues, ultimately contains the fantasy of the omnipotent everyman within a circular and structurally conservative storytelling framework that, in effect, renders each adventure a "high redundance message" that "keeps hammering away at the same meaning": villains will be caught, order will be restored, and society will be defended (21).

Since its initial publication, Eco's essay has been cited by numerous scholars and garnered some criticism for its generalizing claims and apparent indifference to superhero comics' evolving modes of serial storytelling.[2] Interestingly, however, one of Eco's central observations – that the appeals and politics of superhero comics are closely intertwined with their serial form – has received less scholarly attention. On the one hand, Eco notes that superhero comics' tendency to tell and re-tell similar stories results in redundant or repetitive political messaging; on the other hand, he frames the figure of the superpowered hero as ideally suited for serial narration because it invites the invention of countless scenarios in which protagonists can prove their mettle. Taken seriously, this view implies that the stories told by superhero comics are not only the work of writers and artists who encode meanings into texts, but also a product of re-iterated storytelling formulae, generic conventions, and a serial drive to continue – all of which write themselves into the politics of the genre as well.

This chapter makes a similar argument about the stories told within the superhero genre and examines the interplay between their modes of serial narration, their latently political themes, and the continued appeal of superpowered figures. Inspired by Eco's arguments, I also suggest that the content of superhero narratives (in film and elsewhere) cannot be divorced from their serial form. But I maintain that the genre's modes of serial storytelling are more diverse – and not always as circular – as the iterative scheme discussed in "The Myth of Superman." More precisely, the next section draws on work by Shane Denson, Frank Kelleter, and others in order to argue that most superhero narratives rely on variations of two distinct, but closely related modes of serial narration: a linear seriality that arranges events and installments in a narratively continuous sequential order, on the one hand, and a non-linear mode that generates alternate and parallel narrative continuities, on the other. Afterwards, the chapter turns to the relationship between the seriality of superhero narratives and their ideological preoccupations, which also are not as uniform as Eco suggests. Most superhero narratives nonetheless remain committed to a shared conceptual framework that prefigures how political subject-matter can be addressed within the genre. This framework, which I discuss as the political imaginary of superhero narratives, encompasses a set of latently political themes and conventions that the entries of the genre repeat, vary, and subject to innovative revisions – such as the contrast between super-powered figures and other people, or the idea that physical violence presents the best tool for the solution of conflicts, for instance. Finally, the chapter examines the enduring appeal of superhero figures and considers why the notion of the omnipotent hero continues to be attractive to contemporary audiences. Returning to arguments from Eco's essay, I here argue that the figure of the superhero presents itself as a flexible foil for the role conflicts, productivity demands, and crises of personal agency that characterize modern society in general. But I also suggest that the significance of such themes should not be overstated, as the political messages articulated within the genre tend to be simplistic and are often complicated by superhero narratives' serial unfolding.

In making this case, my goal is to come to terms with the ways in which serialized superhero narratives weave connections between figures, texts, and media, as well as to consider the worldviews that they construct and the appeal that they offer. But this chapter also seeks to bridge the gap between my discussion of the politico-economic, ideological, and media-infrastructural matters in the preceding chapter and the more detailed examination of superhero blockbuster cinema's politics of engagement in the second part of this book. In the previous chapter, I suggested that commercial popular culture is inherently serial, informed by practices of repetition and innovation and embedded in a culture-industrial constellation that links recreational media consumption to the reproduction of larger social orders. This chapter examines what happens when seriality comes to inform the narrative operations of popular entertainments more directly. Serial narratives, I suggest, latch onto popular culture's inherent seriality, make it explicit, and turn it into an organizing principle that informs the relationships between individual installments and larger narrative frames. To engage audiences over longer periods of time, serial narratives balance repetition and innovation in their telling of ongoing, periodically unfolding stories. In doing so, they embody the culture industry's tendency to structure and organize leisure time, link otherwise disparate instances of media consumption together, and set them into a larger context. As result, serial narratives invite reception practices that are not similarly available to more self-contained texts – such as following the adventures of protagonists and supporting figures across installments, or using the break in between installments to speculate about upcoming plot developments, for instance. The same is true for serialized superhero narratives.

NON-LINEAR AND LINEAR SERIAL NARRATION

Anglophone cultural and media studies offers no shortage of labels to classify forms of retelling and narrative continuation. These include long established and widely accepted distinctions such as the one between the "series" (referring to a succession of self-contained, episodic stories starring the same characters) and the "serial" (an ongoing narrative that continues across the breaks between installments), as well as more specific terms for television (mini-series, limited series, anthology series) and film (sequel, prequel, spin-off, trilogy, franchise, remake, reboot).[3] Writing about Hollywood cinema, Frank Kelleter and Kathleen Loock observe that the meanings of such terms are often less stable than one might expect, as concepts undergo shifts in cultural currency, fall out of use, and change the over time (130). This makes attempts at articulating definite typologies difficult, as new practices and terms continue to proliferate – with the "pre-boot" (Scahill) and the "requel" (Raya Bravo) being recent examples. For Kelleter and Loock, labels such as the above are thus best understood as names for the products of an "evolving cinematic *formatting practice*" that "generates media-specific modes of variation and organizes them in historically variable categories" (130). This means that any attempt to produce a definite and systematic catalogue of such terms is bound to fail because it tries to impose a static conceptual grid on a set of moving targets.

Such definitional problems can be sidestepped if one focuses not on historically distinct formatting practices but on the types of relations and connections that serial narratives establish between installments and iterations of the same story, figure, or intellectual property. In what follows, I draw on work by Shane Denson, Frank Kelleter, and others to suggest that the serial forms listed above can be understood as variations on or combinations of two basic modes of serialization that establish different kinds of connection between iterations of the same property: a linear seriality that foregrounds narrative continuity across series installments and frames them as parts of an ongoing story, and a non-linear mode that generates a multiplicity of alternate takes on the same narrative or character.[4] Both modes are not exclusive to superhero blockbuster cinema, but commonplace ways of iterating and linking media content that are more generally at work in commercial popular culture. Interestingly, however, most superhero blockbuster films combine linear and non-linear types of seriality. In doing so, they articulate demands for serial engagement that are specific (though not entirely unique) to the genre, prompting audiences to not only follow the adventures of heroes such as Spider-Man across several entries of longer film series, but also to acknowledge the existence of previous and parallel incarnations of the character.

Denson links linear seriality to the kind of narrative "progression, continuation, and development" that is commonly associated with the categories of the series and the serial ("Marvel Comics' Frankenstein" 536). At its most basic, this type of seriality involves the successive unfolding of a narrative across installments, as well as forward-moving, future-oriented plots and a focus on recurring characters. Emphasizing similar aspects, Roger Hagedorn has stressed the profit-oriented character of serial texts, which generally embrace "the narrative potential of commercially imposed textual breaks" to retain consumer interest over longer periods of time and often end "each installment at a point of unresolved narrative tension" (Hagedorn 7).[5] But not all linearly unfolding serial narratives avoid narrative closure completely. Episodic forms of serial storytelling – which are at work in sitcoms such as *Seinfeld* (NBC, 1989–98), classic prime-time television drama series such as the original *Star Trek* (NBC, 1966–69), and in DC's Superman comics of the 1940s and early 1950s – also focus on a set of recurring characters, but usually tell series of self-contained stories that conclude at the end of each installment. For linearly unfolding serial narratives, the suggestion of narrative continuity, of a persistent storyworld that contains all characters and events, and of a forward-moving diegetic time is thus more central than the refusal of closure.[6]

Intra-serial continuity is intricately connected to the idea of character development as well. Denson notes that linear serial narratives are populated by "series characters" that "take on an increased psychological depth and/or ever move complex social involvements" over time ("Marvel Comics' Frankenstein" 536; see also Denson and Mayer; on continuity in superhero comics, see Hoppeler and Rippl). This is true even for episodic forms that do not establish an easily legible order of diegetic events. The narratively "hazy" iterative scheme of early Superman comics, for example, still maintains that all events take place within a narrative world with an established past (which includes Superman's origin on planet Krypton, his youth in Smallville, and so on) that can be referenced if needed. In addition, Superman becomes increasingly resourceful and acquainted with more and more secondary characters (as well as supervillains) as the series progresses. Linear seriality can thus be understood as a cumulative mode of storytelling that adds more narrative detail and diegetic complexity over time, even if installments remain self-contained and storytelling formulae simple.[7]

By stressing linear seriality's pre-occupation with continuity, I do not wish to suggest that the stories told by serial narratives are always coherent, non-contradictory, or laid out in advance. Kelleter notes that serial narratives tend to construct stories on the fly because their initial installments are often already being consumed while later parts are still in production or in the planning stages ("Five Ways" 13). This "temporal overlap [. . .] allows serial audiences to become involved in a narrative's progress," as it enables a feedback loop between consumer responses and industrial storytelling practices (13). As noted in the introduction to this book, the temporally expansive unfolding of serial narratives also exposes their production to a variety of contingencies that might produce delays or require adaptive responses on the part of creatives. Ongoing serial narratives are thus often "more untidy than work-bound structures" and tend to accumulate diegetic inconsistencies as they unfold (17). This is especially true if the people involved in their making change, or if breaks between installments last longer than initially planned. The tendency towards accumulating contradictions can, in fact, be understood as an emergent property of long-running series, as the proliferation of diegetic events, characters, and backstories becomes more and more difficult to oversee as the narrative progresses. The "constantly growing excess of things that have already been told" also means that serial narratives have to "engage in constant continuity management" in order to ensure that the occurrences of later installments still line up with those of previous ones – a challenge that, as Kelleter points out, can also be met retrospectively, through practices such as retconning (which invents new, hitherto unknown backstories for already featured events and characters), for example (17).

Such continuity management is prominently on display in Richard Donner's *Superman* (1978) and its sequel *Superman II* (1980). In the Krypton-set scenes that immediately follow the first film's opening titles, the protagonist's father Jor-El (Marlon Brando) banishes three criminals to the "phantom zone," an inter-dimensional prison. After this, the banished characters disappear from the film, but turn up again in the sequel, which reuses parts of the Krypton-set scenes during its opening moments and shows the villains' arrival on Earth in its second act. In opening with recycled footage, *Superman II* establishes its status as a continuation of an ongoing story and simultaneously absolves audiences from the need to revisit the earlier film. Notably, however, *Superman II*'s Krypton sequence omits the appearance of Brando's character and adds new footage of his wife Lara (Susannah York) – changes that were necessitated by Brando's refusal to appear in the sequel. Instead of merely continuing the subplot begun in the first film, *Superman II* thus adjusts its own diegetic past and effectively deletes the presence of Jor-El. The rest of the sequel then tells a largely self-contained story that otherwise makes little reference to preceding events. Crucially, however, *Superman II* nonetheless signals its status as a sequel through a continuity of production values and stylistic choices, by relying on an otherwise identical cast of recurring characters and by reusing sets, props, costumes, and elements of the score from the first film. This example demonstrates that continuity management affects aspects of film style as well, as noticeable changes and deviations between installments might compromise the impression of a continuous storyworld.[8]

Linear serially is all about telling stories in installments, but it is not necessarily limited to the telling of a single story, nor does it always remain confined to one medium. Most of the feature films of the *Star Trek* franchise, for instance, share a narrative continuity with the episodes of the original series from the 1960s and later follow-up shows about other starships and crews.[9] The modes of serialization at work in American superhero comics also complicate the understanding of linear seriality laid out above. Frank Kelleter and Daniel Stein point out that Marvel Comics in the 1970s began to rely on a "multi-linear" mode of serial storytelling, which located the events of nominally separate series within a shared storyworld (274). In doing so, the company combined most of its titles into an overarching narrative framework of loosely connected series, a constellation that had storylines unfolding in parallel and allowed for occasional crossovers between titles (Kelleter and Stein 274–82; see also Hoppeler and Rippl). The idea of shared narrative worlds and intersecting series informs the storytelling practices of contemporary superhero blockbuster cinema as well. Disney's *Marvel Cinematic Universe* (or *MCU*; since 2008), for instance, constructs a transmedial storyworld across close to thirty blockbuster movies, twelve television drama series, several short films, as well as multiple comic books and short-form web-series.[10] Such transmedial expansions make franchises like the *MCU* decidedly less linear than more conventional forms of seriality, as the inclusion of additional narratives and media multiplies the points of entry from which consumers can start to explore the respective storyworlds. I discuss the storytelling logics of such narrative universes in more detail in the next chapter, but I want to emphasize here that efforts to connect narratives across series and media usually involve the construction of a shared storyworld, practices of continuity management, and the suggestion of linear cause-and-effect chains within the diegesis – all of which become increasingly difficult to maintain as franchises expand over time.

Where linear seriality revolves around the construction of a narrative continuity across installments, non-linear seriality entails the re-staging of an already established narrative or property within a new medium or context. Denson associates this type of seriality with the long careers of serial figures such as Dracula or Frankenstein's Monster, which have inspired countless distinct incarnations since their initial appearance. The many iterations of these narratives and figures nonetheless do not add up to a unified serial text whose installments share a narrative continuity. Rather, non-linear seriality is best understood as a mode of "snowballing accumulation" that produces alternate takes on the same story or figure, providing each with a narrative continuity that is separate from those that came before ("Marvel Comics' Frankenstein" 536; Denson and Mayer; Mayer *Fu Manchu*). Non-linear seriality in this sense is at work in cinematic practices of remaking, "rebooting," or adaptation, and it has long been a staple of the cross-media superhero genre as well.[11] Likewise, it informs more recent superhero narratives. Will Brooker notes, for example, that the films of Christopher Nolan's *Dark Knight* trilogy (2005, 2008, 2012) . . .

> . . . co-exist with a range of distinct Batman texts, each of which presents a slightly different interpretation of the main character and its mythos. In the second half of the 2000s alone, these included the televised cartoon *The Batman* (2004–2008) – aimed at younger viewers, with its continuity quite separate from both the previous animated series and mainstream comics – and its spin-off comic, *The Batman Strikes*; the entirely different animated series *Batman: The Brave and the Bold* (2008–present), with its own spin-off video game and monthly comic book (2010–present); the adult-oriented video game *Arkham Asylum* (2009) and its sequel *Arkham City* (2011), in addition, of course, to the mainstream continuity of the comic book. (77)

Making a similar argument, Russell Backman has pointed to the diverse incarnations of Marvel's X-Men in comics, film, and other media, which establish their relationship to each other through the repetition and variation of "key narrative characteristics" (201). The latter include the concept of super-powered mutants, locales such as the X-Mansion, and characters defined by iconic looks, for example (see also 201–10). Richard Berger similarly suggests that the many versions of Superman relate to others within a "dialogical sphere of influence" in which defining characteristics and popular innovations are transmitted from one iteration to the next, while other elements "drop out" of circulation (87). While not framing their arguments as such, Brooker, Backman, and Berger all describe crucial aspects of non-linear seriality: the practice of reassembling well-known and established narrative elements to tell stories that are new and distinct, and yet reassuringly familiar. The various incarnations of superhero figures thus relate to each other by way of family resemblance, with each iteration echoing others while nonetheless remaining notably distinct.[12]

The products of such non-linear proliferations often call attention to their serial character and thereby establish a more direct link to earlier iterations. The entries of the *X-Men* film series, for example, include numerous subtle references and in-jokes that point to the existence of a larger body of Marvel superhero texts. For Backman, the *X-Men* films thus reward a pre-existing familiarity with other X-Men narratives, "rather than asking the audience to bracket this knowledge" during reception (217). Such references are a good example for superhero movies' ability to operate as – to borrow a formulation from Eco – "catalyzers of collective memories" that can capitalize on a socially diffused knowledge about the genre and its most iconic representatives ("Casablanca" 3).[13] I discuss this kind of referentiality in more detail in the following chapter, but I want to emphasize here that non-linear series might still weave connections between their constituent parts, even if these do not add up to a continuous narrative. Instead, the various incarnations of superhero figures are tied together by overt or subtle references, by stylistic similarities and thematic resonances, as well as by other narrative parallels and intertextual links.

The distinction between linear and non-linear seriality is best understood as one between ideal types – in practice, both types often appear together. Most of DC's and Marvel's superheroes, for example, oscillate between lives as series characters that undergo development over the course of a narrative's unfolding and an existence as frequently re-invented serial figures that turn up in different continuities.[14] Likewise, almost all films discussed in this book combine both forms of seriality, as they present themselves both as installments of ongoing film series (or "cinematic universes") and as reinterpretations of comic book source materials.

The concepts of linear and non-linear seriality are useful analytic tools to examine how the relationships between series, installments, and other iterations of the same property are staged within the films themselves; the next chapter will examine in more detail how superhero blockbusters weave such connections and how their modes of serial reference evolve over time. Before discussing the history of superhero blockbuster cinema, however, I now turn to the political ideology of superhero narratives and the enduring appeal of their central figures – aspects which are intricately linked to the genre's inherent seriality.

THE SUPERHEROIC POLITICAL IMAGINARY

Since its beginning in the late 1930s, the proliferation and cross-medial spread of superhero narratives has produced an almost endless variety of stories – all of which relate to each other within a common frame of reference that is delineated by recurring motifs and frequently re-staged narrative elements. Daniel Stein nonetheless argues that superhero narratives . . .

> . . . are more than a collection of texts that share a common set of themes, character types, visual iconographies, and story structures. In fact, they constitute an evolving serial genre. They emerge from specific modes of production, take on particular physical and medial forms, and collectively articulate a continually shifting set of generic conventions. Every new installment of an ongoing series both activates and (however slightly) varies the total sum of genre enunciations – and it makes certain paratextual and extratextual discourses possible while rendering others impossible, or at least implausible. (135)

Stein here calls attention to the close relationship between the serial dynamics that inform the history of the larger superhero genre and the audience discourses that surround it. To be received as success, superhero narratives need to keep pace with changing tastes and cultural trends, offer interesting revisions of established formulae, and add new ideas that can retain the interest of informed consumers. At the same time, any given superhero narrative also needs to reiterate tropes and conventions deemed central to the genre. The result is an evolving proliferation of similar stories whose concerns are never quite identical. A similar dynamic of repetition and innovation also informs the genre's engagement with political subject-matter: on the one hand, the need to reiterate central motifs and conventions pre-structures and limits what can be expressed by any given superhero narrative; on the other hand, the need to change with the times informs an ongoing elaboration of established storytelling formulae and the occasional injection of new topics and ideas.

In this section, I examine a persistent kernel of latently political themes and conventions that, taken together, constitute what I term the superheroic political imaginary. The latter can be understood as a loosely defined, robust, yet flexible conceptual framework that governs how political themes and subject-matter can be addressed, negotiated, and represented within the genre. My use of "political imaginary" here is inspired by Cornelius Castoriadis, who has argued that societies bring forth specific "social imaginary significations." These include the belief in "God" or "modern rationality," but also concepts such as freedom or autonomy that become "embodied" in a society's "system of norms, institutions [. . .], values, orientations, and goals of collective life, as well as of individual life" (Castoriadis 102; compare Straume 33). The sum of social imaginary significations constitutes the political imaginary of a given society, which (because it is inscribed in institutions and practices) orients life within this society. Political imaginaries thus establish common (if not necessarily commonly accepted) frames of reference, as well as a shared sense of a society's governing structures, power relations, and political processes. In an analogous manner, the superheroic political imaginary comprises key concepts, tropes, and themes that allow for the imagination of fictional social and political orders; it comprises conventions and motifs that are repeated and elaborated on by most (though not necessarily all) entries of the genre. Individual superhero narratives might bring the elements of this superheroic political imaginary into new constellations, so that any given example might present a different worldview and a distinct way to express it. At the same time, elements of this imaginary continue to be shared by all narratives that remain invested in the central conventions of the genre. Inscribed in recurring motifs and subject to ongoing revision, the superheroic political imaginary both enables and constrains superhero narratives' ability to negotiate political subject-matter, as it provides a framework within which such topics can be addressed; moreover, it frames these issues in a particular way. The superheroic political imaginary should therefore not be understood as a fixed schema that is repeated without variation; nor does it completely determine the ideological messages of superhero narratives. Instead, it comprises a set of basic narrative options and parameters that condition what can be expressed within the genre.

The antagonistic relationship between super-powered heroes and powerful villains constitutes a central dimension of this imaginary. In an insightful reading of Christopher Nolan's *The Dark Knight Rises* (2012), David Graeber notes that entries of the genre usually frame superheroes as defenders of a status quo, who deal with threats which the regular authorities are not equipped to handle. This constellation, so Graeber suggests, renders superhero narratives an "inherently fascist space, inhabited only by gangsters, would-be dictators, police, and thugs, with endlessly blurring lines between them." Graeber labels this scenario as fascist because it frames violence as the only viable means to maintain, disrupt, or transform political orders. After all, only the forceful interventions of heroes such as Batman and Superman can ensure that the law is being upheld and that people remain safe. Most of these heroes furthermore are "purely reactive," while their villainous counterparts are "full of plans and projects and ideas" to overthrow the existing order. In addition, superhero narratives rarely depict political actors other than heroes, villains, or the representatives of the state; political action by average citizens and political means other than violence simply are no prominent theme of the genre. Superhero narratives thus tend to limit the ability to threaten or defend a just social order to a small set of powerful actors – superheroes, supervillains, and the state apparatus itself – which all operate at a remove from the lives of regular (that is, non-superpowered) people. Because of this, Graeber implies, superhero narratives are a poor vehicle for political commentary, and films such as *The Dark Knight Rises* "stutter into incoherence" once they are read as allegories for real-world conflicts. Graeber further notes that, in superhero narratives, the "lines of force are always shifting," and that various groups might strike up unlikely alliances at a moment's notice: "Sometimes the cops are legalistic, sometimes they're corrupt [. . .]. Sometimes they pursue the superhero, sometimes they look the other way, sometimes they help. Villains and heroes occasionally team up." The conventions of the genre thus leave room for surprising variations and narrative reversals, thereby enabling the telling of different stories about conflicts between scheming villains, reactive superheroes, and ambivalent state apparatuses.

Graeber's essay usefully summarizes the central political concerns of the genre, and many of his observations have also been made by other authors. Richard Reynolds, for example, stresses the power differential between "[t]he normal and the superpowered," the extralegal status of superheroic activity, and the ambivalent relationship between superheroes and the state (105; see also Dittmer 11; Hughes). Charles Hatfield, Jeet Heer, and Kent Worcester, in turn, emphasize the "prosocial" mission of superheroes, who usually devote their lives to the defense of society or the pursuit of a higher kind of justice (3). This mission is often connected to vaguely articulated, but positively connoted values – such as the credo of "Truth, Justice, and the American Way" proclaimed by the hero of Donner's *Superman*, or the slogan "with great power comes great responsibility" that is repeatedly evoked in Raimi's *Spider-Man* films. Elsewhere, Hatfield points out that the mission of the hero is often contrasted with the goals of one or several "super-antagonists" who "boast similar or complementary powers" (Hatfield 140). Hatfield further suggests that a Manichean conflict between good and evil is at the heart of most superhero narratives (137). Writing about the dystopian *V for Vendetta* (2005), Dan Hassler-Forest stresses that superheroes sometimes turn against the state if "intervention is required in order to transform [society] back into the way it is 'supposed to be'" (*Capitalist Superheroes* 110). Making a similar point, Marc DiPaolo distinguishes "establishment" narratives in which "the superhero acts to preserve the social status quo" from "anti-establishment" stories in which the hero fights "an evil governmental, corporate, or aristocratic villain" (DiPaolo 12). Implicit in all these observations is the subordinate role of people who lack the power and agency of superpowered figures, and who are thus relegated to the roles of victims, bystanders, henchmen, or supporters of the heroes.

The superheroic political imaginary can be understood as the virtual sum of all the possible combinations and constellations into which these elements – superheroes and villains, the state, "regular" people, Manichean conflicts, violence as the most important means of solving conflicts – can be brought. Central to this imaginary is the tendency to relegate political agency (in the broadest sense of the term) to a separate sphere disconnected from the realm of the everyday. In superhero narratives, only the powerful and the exceptional can change the existing order of things. While regular characters often make important contributions to the resolution of narrative conflicts, the genre generally frames the actions of the hero and villains as more consequential.[15] In addition, superhero narratives equate the ability to act on and shape the social world to a willingness to use violence. Entries of the genre also have a penchant for happy endings and conclusions in which heroes prevail and threats are averted or otherwise contained. It is thus tempting to understand superhero narratives as narratives of ideological reassurance – as stories in which good and evil can be easily told apart, in which threats to the social order are met with the violent interventions of hyper-capable specialists, and in which a just social order is ultimately always defended or reinstated. But such reassurance is often counterbalanced by the genre's tendency to put their protagonists through series of similar adventures. Even if villains are defeated and catastrophes averted, comparable (or bigger) threats are bound to surface in the next installment, the next film, the next issue, or the next episode. Not coincidentally, the storyworlds of superhero series tend to be exceedingly dangerous places besieged by frequent alien invasions, nefarious conspiracies, and unceasing crime waves. The serial unfolding of superhero narratives adds an important modification to their basic ideological message: the world might be on the brink of chaos, but all that regular people can do is sit and watch as the heroes sort it all out – and then continue watching as the next scenario unfolds. In its most common configurations, the superheroic political imaginary thus articulates a depoliticizing, immobilizing worldview that frames regular people as subjects without meaningful agency to act on the world around them.[16] Likewise, any sense of reassurance must remain temporary, as the next threat is usually just around the corner.

However, since superhero narratives are an evolving serial genre, not all of them iterate the constituent parts of the superheroic political imaginary in a similar fashion – in fact, many titles and films background political themes in favor of a focus on dramatic origin stories, suspenseful plotting, and high-stakes confrontations between heroes and villains. Other superhero narratives purposefully subvert central conventions of the genre: Zack Snyder's 2008 film adaptation of Alan Moore and Dave Gibbons' *Watchmen*, for instance, features a former superhero as a villain who kills thousands of innocent civilians to further world peace; similarly, *Suicide Squad* (2016) focuses on a group of supervillains who are recruited into government service against their will. Likewise, the *X-Men* franchise's two *Deadpool* films (2016; 2018) star an irreverent protagonist who explicitly rejects prosocial missions and heroic values, while the Amazon Prime television series *The Boys* (since 2019, based on the comic by Garth Ennis and Darick Robertson) tells the story of non-powered vigilantes who take on a group of morally corrupt, corporate-sponsored superheroes. Writing about superhero comics, Geoff Klock discusses similar entries of the genre as "revisionary superhero narratives" that deliberately thematize, question, and work against established conventions. But even such revisionist narratives usually remain committed to elements of the superheroic political imaginary. Not coincidentally, the use of violence as an effective means to solve conflicts or the distinction between heroes and regular people are important themes in all titles listed in this paragraph. The notion of a common political imaginary is thus best understood as a tool for ideological analysis and not as a set of ready-made conclusions that can be applied to any given superhero narrative.

The assertion that entries of the genre share a common political imaginary should not be misunderstood as a statement about their efficacy as tools of ideological indoctrination. As suggested in the preceding chapter, one's enjoyment of cultural commodities does not necessarily imply an uncritical acceptance of their messages, especially if said entertainments offer other, less obviously political appeals (such as spectacular action and special effects) as well. I argue later in this book, however, that the genre's common political imaginary nonetheless plays a significant role for the public reception of superhero blockbuster films, since it encourages allegorical readings that map the genre's categories onto real-world situations and conflicts. Articulated by film critics, reviewers, and other professional consumers, such readings reframe complex political issues as conceptually simple good-versus-evil conflicts. Many superhero movies openly invite such allegorical interpretations and, in doing so, insert elements of the superheroic political imaginary into larger discourses about politics and popular culture. I will return to these issues in Chapter 5. But in order to account for latent ideological messages of the genre more fully, I now turn to the figure of the superhero and the traits that make it appealing to the audiences of a capitalist popular culture.

SUPERHEROIC PERSEVERANCE

In his essay "The Myth of Superman," Eco connects Superman's status as a power fantasy to the figure's historical origins in the era of industrial capitalism. This context, so Eco suggests, renders the eponymous hero a quintessentially modern figure:

> In an industrial society [. . .] where man becomes a number in the realm of the organization which has usurped his decision-making role, he has no means of production [. . .]. Individual strength, if not exerted in sports activities, is left abased when confronted with the strength of machines which determine man's very movements. In such a society the positive hero must embody to an unthinkable degree the power demands that the average citizen nurtures but cannot satisfy. ("The Myth" 14)

The aspects that align Superman with a mythological tradition – such as his immutable, archetypical, and larger-than-life character – thus turn out be intricately connected to the pressures of everyday life under capitalism and "the crisis of agency associated with industrialization and modernity," as Hassler-Forest puts it in his discussion of Eco's essay (*Capitalist Superheroes* 42). Dietmar Dath similarly suggests that superheroes function as projection screens for deeply personal feelings, conflicts, and anxieties. Superheroes, as Dath suggests, can do so because they "supercharge and distort affects, emotions and fantasies" and present themselves as alluring stand-ins for what readers "imagine themselves to be: sometimes one might feel as if one could fly or read the thoughts of others, [. . .] as if one were made of ice, set aflame, invisible, or heavy as a ton" (Dath 9, translation mine; see also Yockey, "Introduction" 12–19). A central appeal of superheroes thus resides in their more-than-human capacity to rise above the humdrum routines of modern life, to perform amazing feats, and to succeed in the face of incredible adversity, as well as in their ability to embody experiences of stress, despair, or exhaustion.

Not coincidentally, personal crises of agency are a prominent motif of the genre, and many superhero narratives confront their protagonists with personal hardships that seem difficult to overcome. A classic storyline in Marvel's *The Invincible Iron Man* comics, for example, chronicles Tony Stark's struggles with alcoholism, repeatedly presents the protagonist as unfit to perform his duties, and culminates in his (temporary) abandonment of the Iron Man identity (and a passing of the torch to supporting character James Rhodes, who uses Iron Man-armor while Stark is out of the picture).[17] Similarly, stress and the inability to perform are recurring concerns in the films of Sam Raimi's *Spider-Man* trilogy (2002, 2004, 2007; Sony/Columbia), which repeatedly thematize the attempts of Peter Parker (Tobey Maguire) to balance his life as a web-slinging crime fighter with his work as a part-time photojournalist, his duties as a college student, and his roles as a romantic partner for Mary-Jane Watson (Kirsten Dunst) and adopted son of Aunt May (Rosemary Harris). Likewise, James Mangold's *Logan* (2017) presents the mutant Wolverine (Hugh Jackman) as an aging hero whose powers have ceased to work reliably, who takes care of an elderly Professor X (Patrick Stewart) and makes ends meet by working as a limousine driver.[18] In presenting such scenarios, these and other superhero narratives negotiate "the much bemoaned role conflicts and corresponding split of the modern individual" that, as Elena Esposito notes, result from the functional differentiation of modern societies into a variety of sub-systems that govern the behavior of individuals (212, my translation).[19] Superhero narratives thus speak to the difficulty of having to perform several roles at the same time – and their ability to do so is a central reason why they have been read as "profound allegories on the subjective experience of modernity" (Dath 3; my translation).

In more than one way, the serial unfolding of most superhero narratives contributes to these allegorical qualities. In most entries of the genre, the protagonists' attempts to master personal challenges parallel the development of more central conflicts between heroes and villains. As result, work/life balance problems and related issues are usually framed as additional obstacles that must be navigated while protagonists are busy pursuing more pressing goals. At first glance, the storylines and installments that thematize such struggles often appear to advance a simple ideological message about individual perseverance in the face of adversity: personal struggles and hardships are to be overcome, not surrendered to; if times get rough, pull through and everything is going to be fine in the end. At first glance, superhero narratives thus appear to offer reassuring and comforting messages for a neoliberal present shaped by the rise of atypical and flexible forms of work, a roll-back of social wages, and the emergence of a media environment that allows us to work everywhere and at every time. However, since most superhero narratives are serial narratives, entries of the genre tend put their heroes through seemingly unceasing series of dramatic situations and follow-up complications as well. As result, even the most tenacious, resilient, and well-adjusted superheroes often cannot master their adventures without incurring considerable personal costs. It is thus tempting to read superheroes as ambivalent figures who embody the pressures and contradictions of life under capitalism. But the serial unfolding of most superhero narratives also complicates this reading: After all, most superheroes possess a more-than-human ability to bounce back from personal crises and adapt to new situations. Even the most devasting traumata thus often turn out to be strangely inconsequential, as the hero is bound to return and perform additional amazing feats in the future. Superheroes' more-than-human perseverance and tenacity is a direct product of the serial drive to continue and tell ever-new and yet fundamentally familiar stories – a drive that takes precedence over matters such as psychological plausibility, logical consistency, or unambiguous political messaging.

In other words, as protagonists of ongoing serial narratives, superheroes have to return for more, even if doing so might strain credulity or undercut the import of earlier narrative developments. The fictional career of the Marvel Comics character Jessica Jones offers an illustrative example of the convoluted narrative trajectories that might result from this constellation: Jones is introduced as a cynical and hard-drinking private investigator and former superhero in the series *Alias* (2001–3); later, she abandons this line of work for a new occupation as reporter (in *The Pulse*, 2004–6); in the years that follow, she becomes a part-time Avenger and second-tier superhero who appears in different Marvel titles; eventually, she turns private detective again in the comic series *Jessica Jones* (since 2016; not to be confused with the Netflix TV series of the same name, which stars a different version of the character). In the process, Jones investigates countless cases, finds herself in numerous life-threatening situations, punches out many villains, gives birth to a daughter, gets married to Luke Cage, has several of her apartments destroyed, joins and quits multiple super-teams, makes abrupt life-changing decisions that appear to contradict established character traits, and ultimately returns to the occupation she had held when she first entered the Marvel Universe. Such turbulent and circular narrative arcs are far from unusual in the world of superhero comics, where the threats posed by the next antagonist, the next cosmic event, or the next sinister plot are always more important than questions of realism or credibility. Consequently, the allegorical qualities of many superhero narratives often turn out to be fleeting, superficial, and contradicted by the events of later installments. But this shallowness should be understood as a strength and not as a flaw of the genre. For recipients interested in political messages, real-world resonances, and deeper levels of meaning, superhero narratives provide just enough to invite allegorical readings; for everyone else, they offer fast-paced plots, spectacular action, and the pleasures of serialized adventure stories whose final resolution can be endlessly deferred.

In Chapter 5, I argue that recent superhero blockbusters frequently offer a similar mix of shallow political meaning and thrilling adventure, and that such films are apt to invite allegorical readings by reviewers and critics who are inclined to find parallels to real-world events. The ability to accommodate such politicizing readings is one example of a remarkable adaptability to new circumstances that characterizes superhero narratives more generally. Informed by a serial drive to continue and multiply, superhero series often cycle through series of vastly different plots, scenarios, and situations. The same is true of the genre as a whole, whose entries tend to bring the elements of the genre's storytelling engine into ever new constellations. In combination with their serial unfolding, this variability allows superhero narratives to quickly respond to ongoing political debates and culturally shared anxieties, and to then filter these concerns through the figure of the superhero and the categories of the superheroic political imaginary. Along these lines, Hassler-Forest discusses films such as *Iron Man* (2008) and *The Dark Knight* (2008) as products of a US-led, neoliberal world-order that reframes the figure of the superhero "as a benevolent peacekeeper who stands for supposedly universal interests" and is ready to intervene in the domestic affairs of other countries (*Capitalist Superheroes* 13). Making a similar case, Liam Burke argues that the good-versus-evil conflicts and globe-trotting adventures at the center of many superhero movies echo a post-9/11 worldview that pits Americans against an international "Axis of Evil" (36–38). These readings accurately describe the political resonance of some entries of the genre, but they can hardly be generalized: after all, not all superhero narratives tell their stories on an international scale, and some superheroes (such as the Punisher and Deadpool, for example) pay little regard to the laws and imperatives of the nation-state. Moreover, as I will show in Chapter 5, even films that focus on the themes described by Hassler-Forest and Burke often invite a range of different interpretations. Overall, the entries of the superhero genre thus present themselves as surprisingly flexible and diverse yet remain committed to a shared narrative framework.

The thematic flexibility discussed above is expressive of a more general ability to adapt to changing social, cultural, and medial environments that superhero narratives share with other popular serial narratives. I suggest in the following chapters that the series and franchises of superhero blockbuster cinema possess a similar capacity for ongoing self-transformation. I also argue that recent entries of the gerne turn the practices and conventions discussed in this chapter into powerful tools for audience mobilization. To begin making that case, the next chapter takes a closer look at blockbuster cinema's evolution across the decades.

NOTES

1. While Eco's essay does not explicitly mention seriality, his later article on "Innovation and Repetition" reframes Superman as an example of commercial popular culture's "aesthetics of seriality." See my discussion in the preceding chapter.
2. On prominent criticisms of Eco's essay, see Singer. Singer notes that Eco's claims hold true for Superman comics of the 1940s and early 1950s, but not for other periods (357–8). Likewise, Hatfield argues that DC Comics titles starring the character began to include references to preceding issues and emphasize narrative continuity in the late 1950s (137–39). On the evolution of superhero comics' serialization practices since the early days of the genre, see Kelleter and Stein.
3. On the series/serial distinction, see Williams 56–58; for a similar list of serial forms, see Kelleter, "Five Ways" 12; on cinematic serialization practices, see Kelleter and Loock.
4. On this distinction, see Denson, "Marvel Comics' Frankenstein" and Kelleter "Five Ways" 18–22.
5. For a similar view, see Hayward 3. Serialized narratives in this sense of the term have been a mainstay of mass print media since the nineteenth century (see Hagedorn 5).
6. I use the term storyworld in Marie-Laure Ryan's sense of the term, which refers to a fictional world (or setting) that encompasses a set of specific and recognizable "existents," such as characters, objects, events, locations, physical laws, and social rules (see Ryan, "Story/Worlds/Media"). Storyworlds can be elaborated by single texts, but multiple texts can be set within the same storyworld.
7. On "cumulative" serial storytelling, see Mittell, *Complex TV* 12–29. In Mittell's usage, the notions of cumulative storytelling and narrative complexity are associated with ongoing, many-episode-spanning storylines and the refusal of narrative closure on the level of installments. Arguably, however, the fictional worlds of linearly unfolding serial narratives always become more complex (that is, multilayered and denser with information) over time – even if plots remain episodic and self-contained.
8. Burke similarly notes that the idea of a shared cinematic universe "necessitate[s] a shared style" (117).
9. The many changes within the *Star Trek* franchise provide another salient example of practices of continuity management. The make-up design of the Klingons, for instance, has not only evolved considerably since the 1960s, but also informed diegetic explanations for the alien race's apparent changes in appearance – *Star Trek: Enterprise* (UPN, 2001–5), for instance, explained the Klingons' changing looks through their infection with a DNA-altering virus. In offering such diegetic justifications for extra-diegetic changes, serial narratives try to gloss over potential ruptures in narrative continuity. Later installments of the franchise, however, have not explicitly addressed similar changes in style, thus relegating the task of bridging such inconsistencies to the viewers.
10. On the overarching storyworlds and intersecting narratives of superhero comics and their function as models for blockbuster cinema, see also Burke 63; Jenkins, "The Reign" 253; Rauscher, "Avengers." My discussion here is informed by Henry Jenkins's understanding of transmedia storytelling, which frames it as a form serial narration that distributes "chunks of meaningful and engaging story information [. . .] not simply across multiple segments within the same medium, but rather across multiple media systems" (Jenkins, "Revenge").
11. In associating the terms remaking, rebooting, and adaptation with the concept of non-linear seriality, I do not wish to erase the differences between them; these terms obviously denote distinct kinds of cinematic re-telling. Kelleter and Loock, however, suggest that all

these practices are similarly "concerned with translating repetition into variation" (125). For a similar understanding of remaking, see Verevis; Loock and Verevis. Recent work on film adaptation also frames it as a practice of narrative repetition and variation; see Burke 84–85; Parody; Loock.
12. A similar dynamic is at work in the broader history of the superhero genre discussed in the preceding chapter – but non-linear seriality gains its distinct character from the recurrence of immediately recognizable and pre-established characters, iconographies, and motifs.
13. Kelleter and Loock similarly note that cinematic remakes generally "address a double audience consisting of those who are familiar with an earlier version and those who are not" and often include "an array of references for viewers in the know" (136). Eco's notion of "catalyzers of collective memories" refers to a mode of intertextuality in which archetypical situations, established character types, or clichés are restaged in popular texts – which thereby evoke the viewers' recollections of other narratives in which these elements appear.
14. This is the case for most serial figures; see Denson and Mayer 186–91.
15. In this regard, superhero narratives are indebted to the dominant political imaginary of Western modernity, which, as Castoriadis notes, also conceptualizes "politics" as the occupation of professional politicians who operate at a remove from the rest of society (109).
16. Eco similarly suggests that the "pedagogic message" of most superhero comics is "immobilistic" and promotes inactivity instead of political action ("The Myth" 21). Advancing a similar reading, Hassler-Forest discusses superhero narratives as "depoliticizing, dehistoricizing" Barthesian myths that spread the dominant ideology of neoliberal capitalism (*Capitalist Superheroes* 44).
17. Stark's alcoholism figures prominently in the "Demon in a Bottle!" storyline that begins with *Iron Man* #120 and ends with issue #128 (running from March through November of 1978; issues by David Michelinie and John Romita Jr.). The theme is picked up again in *Iron Man* #170 (May 1983; Denny O'Neil and Luke McDonnell), in which a relapsing Tony Stark abandons his heroic activities for a significant period; Stark re-assumes the Iron Man identity in issues #199 and #200 (October and November 1985; Denny O'Neil, Herb Trimpe, and Mark Bright).
18. I will return to the example of *Logan* in Chapter 4.
19. Esposito here draws on Luhmann's theory of social systems; on the topic of functional differentiation, see Luhmann, *Die Gesellschaft* 743–76; Esposito 195–212. For Esposito, the functional differentiation of society encompasses subsystems "oriented towards [. . .] specific function[s]," including "politics, the economy, science, the legal system, the educational system, the family, art, religion, and the mass media" (195; my translation). Functional differentiation also involves lower-level organizations that more directly intervene in individual behavior. As Esposito notes: "Everyone can act however one wants, [. . .] but one cannot do so as a member of an organization (like a firm, a school, a political party, a religious congregation, and so on)" (210–11; my translation).

Part II
Politics of Audience Engagement

CHAPTER 3

The Hyper-Referential Style of Storytelling

In just under two minutes and thirty seconds, the title sequence of Louis Leterrier's *The Incredible Hulk* (2008) weaves a dense web of references to other superhero narratives and media. Beginning directly after the studio logos, the sequence opens with a fast-paced montage that combines medical imagery – shots of lab equipment, CT scans, whirring tape machines, pulsating blood vessels viewed through a microscope – with the image of a flashing "Danger" sign and of shots mild-mannered scientist Bruce Banner (Edward Norton) participating in the ill-fated experiment that will transform him into a rage-filled green monster (Figure 3.1). In these moments, Leterrier's film carefully restages key moments from the opening credits of the classic CBS television series *The Incredible Hulk* (1977–82), which featured a similar montage – and thereby locates itself within a longer history of Marvel Comics adaptations.[1] Unlike the show's credits, however, the film's opening also depicts the Hulk destroying the laboratory and hurting Elizabeth Ross (Liv Tyler) and her father General Ross (John Hurt) in the process. The sequence continues with a remorseful Banner sneaking away from a recuperating Elizabeth and the depiction of a many-year-long manhunt for the protagonist, which is relayed through a montage of newspaper headlines, excerpts from electronic communications, shots of armed soldiers and military equipment in the field, and the recurring image of an angry-looking General Ross in front of busy computer screens. Leterrier's *Hulk* here effectively narrates a condensed version of the protagonist's origin story for viewers unfamiliar with it, a choice that further underscores that the film's central characters have appeared in other narratives and media before.[2] Picking up speed, the opening titles eventually culminate in a series of rapid cuts that juxtapose images from the manhunt with shots of the experiment. Before the end of the sequence, the names of prominent

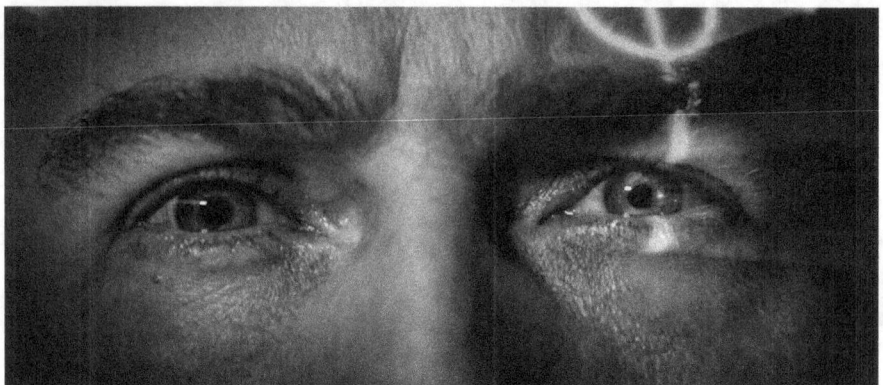

Figure 3.1 The title sequence of 2008's *The Incredible Hulk* reimagines the opening credits of the eponymous 1978 television show for a twenty-first-century audience. Screengrab from Amazon Prime Video.

characters and organizations from the world of Marvel Comics – such as Tony Stark's company Stark Industries, the spy agency S.H.I.E.L.D. and its director Nick Fury, the Hulk's erstwhile sidekick Rick Jones, and the superhero Doc Samson – briefly appear onscreen. In including these references, the opening titles add another layer of intertextual reference and imply the existence of a larger narrative world populated by other Marvel characters – an impression that is confirmed in the film's post-credits sequence, which has Tony Stark (Robert Downey Jr., reprising his role from 2008's *Iron Man*) meeting up with General Ross.

The opening titles of Leterrier's film exemplify the *hyper-referential style* of superhero blockbusters: a mode of storytelling that revolves around a constant indexing of closely related narratives, figures, and media. On the one hand, this style is characterized by a type of intertextuality specific to movies based on DC or Marvel comics properties. This intertextuality comes to the fore in frequent nods, references, and allusions to source materials and preceding as well as upcoming installments of ongoing film series and larger media franchises.[3] On the other hand, the hyper-referential style encompasses stylistic devices that approximate the aesthetics of superhero comics by filmic means. Such devices include the special effects technologies used to realize displays of extraordinary ability, as well as elements of cinematography and mise-en-scène (and, to a lesser degree, editing) that are used to mimic the visual language of the comics medium.[4] This combination of prominent intertextual references and a comics-inspired visual aesthetics is closely tied to superhero blockbusters' status as films that both draw inspiration from comic book sources and operate as installments of ongoing serial narratives. A confluence of linear and non-linear types of serialization is thus at the heart of the hyper-referential style – although not all films based on DC or Marvel superhero comics properties foreground their referentiality to a similar degree.[5] Combining a shared approach to serial storytelling with a similar visual aesthetics, superhero blockbusters' hyper-referential mode of storytelling can be understood as a group style in the sense of a "distinctive, patterned, developed, [and] meaningful use of techniques of the film medium" that is at work in a variety of different, yet formally similar films (Kuhn and Westwell, "Film Style"; on the concept of "group style," see Bordwell, *Narration* 149–55). The hyper-referential style constitutes the centerpiece of superhero blockbusters' politics of audience engagement, as its devices point viewers from one film to the next, delineate pathways from the cinema to other superhero media, and invite a range of culturally productive practices on the part of the audience. As result, films that rely on this style often diverge significantly from the norms of narrative closure and transparent causality that have traditionally been associated with Hollywood cinema.[6] Where other, more classically self-contained films introduce their characters, put them through series of (more or less) unique dramatic events, and end after the most important issues have been resolved, superhero blockbusters focus on already known and well-defined figures; they tell stories inspired by classic comic books and often set up conflicts that are elaborated on in sequels, spin-offs, and other forms of continuation.

This chapter examines the operations of the hyper-referential style, tracks its evolution across the decades, and considers the reception practices it seeks to encourage. Paying particular attention to moments of intertextual and intermedial reference, it thus explores how the genre's common "textual cues and structures [. . .] solicit particular viewing activities," as David Bordwell puts it (*Narration* 150). But this chapter also suggests that the hyper-referential style does not manifest itself in a stable and uniform manner across the decades. Superhero movies released since the year 2000 embrace linear seriality much more strongly than earlier films and, with their practices of world-building and transmedia storytelling, often combine the suggestion of narrative continuity across series installments. Compared to earlier entries of the genre, these more recent films also feature a much higher density of references to superhero comics and other source materials. At the extreme end of the spectrum, movies such as *Justice League* (2017) or *Avengers: Endgame* (2019) present themselves as narratively fragmented films that demand more than a passing familiarity with comic book source materials and the plots of preceding films to be understood. Other recent superhero movies similarly presuppose both detailed background knowledge about the genre and a readiness to follow characters and storylines over longer periods of time. Twenty-first-century superhero blockbusters, as Aaron Taylor argues, thus "interpellate the ordinary viewer as a fan" ("Avengers" 186). In doing so, these films participate in a mainstreaming of fan culture that, in the long run, turns fannish modes of engagement – that is, time-consuming, socially communicative, and emotionally and cognitively involved practices of media consumption – into a new norm.[7]

The following discussion suggests that the above developments are products of a successive intensification of the hyper-referential style that plays out across four overlapping cycles (or waves) of releases.[8] The first of these cycles begins with Richard Donner's *Superman* (1978) and establishes the superhero blockbuster as a profitable format. The second cycle spans the period between 1998 and late 2007 and sees a rapid increase of releases in the genre, as well as an embrace of more complex serialization practices. The third wave (2008–14) then witnesses the genre's rise to the apex of blockbuster cinema, the emergence of the "cinematic universe" as a new model of serialization, and an even higher number of releases in the genre per year. These trends continue during the fourth wave (2014–20), which ushers in an internal diversification of the genre and the appearance of films based on more obscure source materials. The fourth wave ends with the beginning of the COVID-19 pandemic in early 2020, an event that has delayed the production and theatrical release of several superhero films, but also marked a transition to a new era in which video streaming services become increasingly important.

In tracking the evolution of the hyper-referential style across these four waves, I follow Murray Smith, who understands film history as a succession of "smaller-scale changes and shifts" that occur "at both the institutional and aesthetic levels [. . .] within a more broadly continuous system of American commercial filmmaking" (Smith 14). Within this system, Hollywood filmmaking practices undergo "a constant process of adjustment and adaptation to new circumstances," but nonetheless remain committed to the goal of "maximizing of profit through the production of [. . .] narrative films" (Smith 14; for a similar view, see Maltby 34–35). Adopting a similar perspective, the following pages consider changes within the genre as responses to shifts within the Hollywood industry and more general transformations within an increasingly digitized media environment. Relevant changes within Hollywood include the renewed prominence of cinematic serialization at the turn of the millennium, a trend that also informed other commercially successful media franchises from the period – such as those built around the films of the Wachowski siblings' *Matrix* trilogy (1999–2003) or George Lucas' *Star Wars* prequel trilogy (1999–2005), for example.[9] Large-scale developments within the industry – such as company mergers, the trend towards conglomeration, and the rise of companies whose most important capital assets exist in the form of intellectual properties (for instance, Marvel Entertainment) – played an important role here, as did advances in digital filmmaking technology. But the evolution of the hyper-referential style was also informed by corporate attempts to capitalize on newly available cultural externalities that promised to increase the visibility of the genre, helped to endow its entries with additional meaning, and made larger constellations of closely related materials accessible to consumers. These externalities included superhero narratives' often many-decade-long histories of previous serial unfolding, which, as discussed at the end of Chapter 1, became more readily available to digital-era consumers. More importantly, however, twenty-first-century superhero blockbusters also came to benefit from the discourses, platforms, and publications of an increasingly professionalized online fan culture that emerged in the late 1990s and grew considerably over the following decades. Circulating all kinds of paratextual information, this fan-oriented online public eventually became closely entangled with the narrative operations of the genre and increasingly central to viewers' ability to navigate larger clusters of superhero content. The appearance of these externalities can be understood as an epiphenomenon of the more general shift in the capitalist mode of production discussed in Chapter 1. This shift equally included the emergence of a new spirit of capitalism, the rise of immaterial labor as a socially diffuse productivity, and the wide-spread availability of digital consumer electronics and Internet access. The intensification of the hyper-referential style was informed by all these factors and developments; it occurred not as a sudden transformation, but in a series of incremental changes.

THE FIRST WAVE: NON-LINEAR SERIALITY AND MEDIA FRANCHISING, 1978–97

The first wave of superhero blockbuster cinema encompasses two series of films that translate DC Comics properties to the big screen. The first of these two includes *Superman* and its sequels *Superman II* (1980), *Superman III* (1983), and *Superman IV: The Quest for Peace* (1987), as well as the 1984 spin-off *Supergirl*. The second is comprised of Tim Burton's *Batman* (1989) and the subsequent *Batman Returns* (1992), *Batman Forever* (1995), and *Batman & Robin* (1997). Produced squarely within the "blockbuster paradigm" of the New Hollywood era (Burke 59), the films of this first wave operated as part of larger entertainment franchises and occasionally called attention to their pre-histories in comics and other media. More generally, however, these films told self-contained stories that could be consumed in isolation from other narratives. Overall, the entries of the first cycle thus emphasized aspects of non-linear seriality over practices of linear serial storytelling.

Donner's *Superman* is in many ways exemplary of this configuration of the hyper-referential style. While the film includes several nods to earlier Superman stories, it also keeps these references vague and uses them as shorthand for the long cross-medial career of its protagonist. After its opening titles, the film chronicles the events that lead to the destruction of the planet Krypton and the hero's exile on Earth. In doing so, Donner's film narrates a chain of events that was first chronicled in the 1939 *Superman* newspaper comic strip. It then presents several scenes set during Superman's youth in Smallville (the primary setting of the *Superboy* comics), subsequently shows the construction of the hero's Fortress of Solitude (a concept introduced in Superman comics of the 1950s), and eventually cuts to his adult life as a Metropolis-based newspaper reporter (which has been part of the Superman canon since 1938's *Action Comics* #1). Stefan Meier, however, notes that, while *Superman* combines narrative "puzzle pieces of different origin" to tell its story, the film also avoids "explicit linkages to other media" (119, 121, my translation; see also Brasch and Brinker 25–26). As result, Donner's film effectively stages itself as a new beginning of the Superman saga – and simultaneously offers its viewers multiple opportunities to recognize familiar elements from earlier iterations of the property. This channeling of the protagonist's serial prehistory registered prominently with critics of the time. In a glowing review published on the day of the film's release, Roger Ebert, for example, noted "the tremendous advantage that almost everyone in the audience knows the Superman saga from youth" and that the film features "all the old-fashioned things we never really get tired of." Other commentators were less enthusiastic. *The New York Times*' Vincent Canby, for instance, complained: "To enjoy this movie as much as one has the right to expect, one has either to be a Superman nut, the sort of trivia expert who has absorbed all there is about the planet Krypton, or to check one's wits at the door." While differing in their opinions, both critics thus identified the film's appeal as intricately connected to its ability to call up the audience's background knowledge about earlier versions of the Superman figure – even though the film mostly avoided direct references to clearly identifiable source texts.

Other first-wave films similarly construct their narratives out of bits and pieces from various sources. In the process, they often produce interesting revisions of established figures and plots: Burton's *Batman*, for example, presents a new variation on the hero's origin story in which "Bruce Wayne's parents are not killed by the lowlife Joe Chill, but rather by a young Joker" (Burke 100). This innovation enables the film to end with a high "degree of closure," as the eventual defeat of the Joker – who falls to his death during the film's final act – resolves all lingering plot conflicts in one fell swoop (Burke 100). Burke also points out that the protagonist of Burton's film is considerably different from the one featured in DC's Batman comics, which usually present the hero as a level-headed and celibate crusader who relies on non-lethal means of crime-fighting. Burton's Batman, by contrast, "appears to be the model of insanity, [. . .] indulges in a serious, consummated relationship with Vicki Vale" and "kills several adversaries" (Burke 164).[10] *Batman* compensates for these divergences from the source material by retaining iconic settings and locales (such as Gotham City or the Batcave), as well as central supporting characters known from the comics (including Wayne's butler Alfred, police commissioner Gordon, and state attorney Harvey Dent). But like *Superman*, Burton's film does not explicitly reference earlier incarnations of its protagonist and generally keeps allusions to the hero's long cross-medial career to a minimum. Instead, the film evokes the medium of comics through its setting and mise-en-scène; it presents Gotham City as a larger-than-life mix of gothicist skyscrapers, art-deco facades, and narrow alleys, realized by matte paintings, custom-built sets, scale models, and trick photography. The prominent use of matte paintings in particular results in striking vistas that possess a painterly (rather than photo-realistic) quality. *Batman*'s set design and visual style can be understood as example of a "knowingly artificial aesthetic" that, as Burke notes, is frequently found in film adaptations of comic book properties (Burke 104). Visually as well as narratively, *Batman* thus alerts its viewers to its status as a film based on a superhero comic book; yet it also presents itself as a movie that can easily be enjoyed by audiences who are unfamiliar with (or uninterested in) its source materials.

The other entries of the *Superman* and *Batman* series also downplay matters of narrative continuity between installments. Matt Yockey points out that *Superman* films not only rely on self-contained plots, but more generally avoid changes to the diegetic status quo that would need to be addressed in later installments. If Lois Lane dies in the final act of *Superman*, for example, she is resurrected via time travel a few minutes later; similarly, the second film eventually undoes Clark Kent's decision to begin a romantic relationship with Lois through the conceit of a memory-erasing kiss (Yockey, "Somewhere" 29). A similar logic is at work in the *Batman* films of the first wave, which start out as a series of loosely connected, self-contained films but eventually abandon narrative continuity altogether. Burton's *Batman Returns*, for example, references the events of *Batman* in brief dialogues and aligns itself with the earlier film through a continuity in production design and casting. Subsequently, however, any sense of continuity is undone by the Joel Schumacher-directed *Batman Forever*, which performs an abrupt tonal shift to a more openly comedic register, features a visibly different, now partly computer-generated Gotham City, replaces Batman actor Michael Keaton with Val Kilmer (Figure 3.2), and recasts the role of state attorney Harvey Dent (with Tommy Lee Jones replacing Billy Dee Williams). Two years later, *Batman & Robin* followed the mold of *Batman Forever*, but again recast the central character, replacing Val Kilmer with George Clooney. As a result of these changes, the latter two films present themselves as alternate takes on the Batman property with little connection to the preceding entries of the series.

The disinterest in narrative continuity and the evocation of unspecified serial pasts are closely tied to a strategy of media franchising that informs the

Figure 3.2 Michael Keaton stars in 1992's *Batman Returns* (top image); 1995's *Batman Forever* recasts Val Kilmer (bottom) in the title role and thereby produces a rupture in series continuity. Screengrabs from Amazon Prime Video.

films of the first wave on a fundamental level. Understood as, according to Derek Johnson, "the multiplied replication of culture from intellectual property resources," franchising entails the serial production of ever-new cultural commodities from a reservoir of corporately owned popular characters, narratives, and brands (*Media Franchising* 6).[11] DC Comics has engaged in media franchising practices since the early 1940s, when the company began to license the production of radio and film serials based on its superhero comics properties, a project that was paralleled by the mass-marketing of all kinds of superhero-themed toys, trinkets, and other merchandise. DC continued to rely on such practices during the 1970s, when it became part of the Warner

Communications conglomerate (WCI).¹² For WCI, the production of superhero blockbuster films constituted an opportunity to revitalize and expand already established media franchises. As a result, films such as Donner's *Superman* or Burton's *Batman* not only had to generate profits at the box-office, but also needed to perform the secondary function of generating audience interest in closely related narratives and products (which might include anything from soundtrack albums over comic books and digital games to animated television series, toys, and T-shirts). This strategy of cross-promotion hinged on the recognizability of products and narratives as iterations of the same franchise or brand. The films of the first wave ensured this recognizability through the prominent use of iconic logos. In the four films of the *Batman* series, for example, the stylized Batman logo is the first thing viewers see, as variations of it serve as backdrops to the respective opening titles. The same logo was then also used to market a variety of other products. The 1989 holiday season, for instance, saw the release of Batman-themed action figures by manufacturers Mattel, Kenner, and Toybiz. Similarly, *Batman Returns* showcases several Bat-vehicles (including a transforming Batmobile, a glider, and a speedboat) that were available as toys manufactured by Kenner. *Batman Forever* and *Batman & Robin* even open with near-identical sequences that have Batman (and, in the younger film, Robin) posing in long shots that seem designed to promote different iterations of Kenner's Batcave playset that were available during the theatrical runs of the respective film.¹³

In summary, the films of the first wave can be understood as nodal points for two different trajectories of audience engagement: one that was directed towards a (vaguely defined) past of preceding serial iterations, and another that was oriented towards the consumption of merchandising products, toys, and related material. Such attempts to create synergy derived their potency from a marketing strategy that turned the theatrical runs of blockbuster films into widely publicized social events. Mario Cucco argues that the marketing of post-classical Hollywood blockbusters has traditionally relied on a "two-pronged saturation strategy" that combined a "wide" release in as many theaters as possible with expensive advertising campaigns that promoted films across a range of media channels (Cucco 219; see also Grainge 46; Schatz 19–21; Meier 107–13; Shone). By the time of *Batman*'s premiere, the first-run theatrical exhibition window had been reduced to the relatively brief timeframe of two or three months, a period during which a whole range of related commodities could be brought to the market as well (Cucco 219–22; Meier 108–11).¹⁴ This short-term orientation helps to explain why the films of the first cycle emphasize their self-sufficient character: Since the primary function of first-wave superhero blockbusters was to drive the sale of movie tickets and related products, questions of narrative continuity across series installments simply were less important than films' promotional function.

With their unspecific or unmarked reference to a prehistory of preceding incarnations, their status as outsized advertisements for all kinds of related products and their disregard for narrative continuity, the films of the first wave solicited a mode of serial engagement that was non-linear rather than linear. First-wave superhero blockbusters, in other words, were not embedded in tightly structured or hierarchically ordered serial arrangements that demanded a reception in linear sequence. This foregrounding of non-linear seriality corresponded to the pre-digital mass media environment of the period. This environment made films accessible through limited theatrical runs, infrequent television broadcasts, or as relatively pricey home video releases on physical storage media such as VHS, Betamax, or Laser-Disc, a situation that made it difficult to follow the plots of ongoing film series over longer periods of time. The same media landscape also confined the public discussion and circulation of information about popular culture to the relatively exclusive and narrow channels of comics magazines, fanzines, entertainment news magazines, and trade journals, official promotional and marketing materials, the culture sections of the mainstream press, as well as television and radio programs with a focus on popular culture. In this discursive environment, a commenter such as Roger Ebert – who could both write about the history of a character like Superman from the perspective of a fan *and* address a large segment of the US-American public – was the exception rather than the rule. To operate successfully within this environment, first-wave films foregrounded their narrative self-sufficiency and simultaneously delineated a trajectory for serial engagement that pointed to other products and media outside of the cinema.

The first cycle eventually ended in the late 1990s, when the commercial underperformance and poor critical reception of *Batman & Robin* was followed by the release of a string of Marvel-based films whose take on the superhero blockbuster was decidedly different from the DC/Warner model discussed so far.[15] Produced and released by several different studios, these Marvel-based productions discarded the knowingly artificial and stylized look of the Burton/Schumacher *Batman* series in favor of more naturalistic settings, a prominent use of computer-generated imagery for the visualization of superhuman powers, and a more kinetic visual style. The Marvel films of the second wave also emphasized narrative continuity between series installments more strongly than their predecessors, included more explicit references to source materials, and more openly invited the interpretive practices of fan audiences. The beginning of the second wave thus marked an overall shift in the genre's politics of audience engagement: Second-wave films more clearly rewarded a familiarity with extensive serial histories, courted audience participation in online debates about the genre, and more explicitly directed viewers' attention to future installments.

THE SECOND WAVE: NEWFOUND POPULARITY AND THE RISE OF ONLINE FANDOM, 1998–2007

Compared to the first wave, the second cycle saw an explosion of releases in the genre. Altogether, Hollywood released a total of twenty-two mid- or big-budget films based on DC or Marvel Comics properties between the summers of 1998 and 2007, thereby establishing the superhero blockbuster as a prominent production trend. A key reason for this newly competitive situation can be found in a re-orientation of Marvel Entertainment's core business, which, following a period of bankruptcy in the mid-1990s, restructured itself from a mini-conglomerate with stakes in different sectors of the entertainment industry into a newly lean company whose core business entailed the development, maintenance, and licensing of its own intellectual property resources.[16] While Marvel continued to publish comic books, this restructuring included the sale of film rights that brought the company's superhero properties to the big screen. Beginning with a string of box-office successes – including *Blade* (New Line Cinema, 1998), *X-Men* (Fox, 2000), and *Spider-Man* (Columbia/Sony, 2002), all of which spawned sequels soon thereafter – these efforts ushered in a boom period during which several studios released Marvel-based films in quick succession (see Burke 57–58). During the same period, Warner Bros. produced several films based on less prominent DC Comics properties – including *Catwoman* (2002), *Constantine* (2005), and *V for Vendetta* (2005) – eventually rebooting the series of the first cycle with the releases of Christopher Nolan's *Batman Begins* (2005) and Bryan Singer's *Superman Returns* (2006). Overall, the films of the second wave constitute a more heterogenous group than those of the first, with the spectrum ranging from graphically violent, R-rated films such as *The Punisher* (Lionsgate, 2004) over the PG-13-rated, but formally experimental *Hulk* (Universal, 2003) to the openly comedic, family-oriented *Fantastic Four* (20th Century Fox, 2005). The boom of the second wave followed and, to an extent, overlapped with the rise of digital home video, corresponding changes in reception practices, and the emergence of online spaces for discussion of popular culture. These developments contributed to a redefinition of the role of the consumer, who was now re-imagined as part of a newly active, vocal, and socially connected audience whose cultural productivity could be harnessed for promotional gain. Concurrently, the films of the second wave began to embrace practices of linear serial narration and to feature more explicit references to classic comic book source material – a re-orientation that aimed at increasing viewers' engagement with film franchises, home video releases, and fan discourses online.

An increased emphasis on narrative continuity between series installments constituted one of the most notable changes of this period. The entries of Fox's initial *X-Men* trilogy, for example, each seed subplots that are subsequently elaborated on in following films.[17] In the final minutes of the first *X-Men* film, for instance, an amnesiac Wolverine (Hugh Jackman) embarks on a journey to explore his mysterious past. The first act of the sequel *X2* then takes up this story and develops it into one of the film's central plotlines. In the process, the second film also addresses several other dangling threads from the first installment – such as the implied cliffhanger ending, which had the shape-shifting villain Mystique impersonating a high-ranking politician (which is resolved in *X2*'s second act), or the lingering romantic tension between Wolverine and Jean Grey (Famke Janssen), for example. Narrative continuity and ongoing subplots are equally important in Sam Raimi's *Spider-Man* trilogy. Here, the series' ongoing plots center on the shifting interpersonal relationships and tensions between Peter Parker/Spider-Man (Tobey Maguire), his foster parent Aunt May (Rosemary Harris), his on-and-off girlfriend Mary Jane Watson (Kirsten Dunst), and his friend Harry Osborn (James Franco). Over the course of the trilogy, the relationships between these characters are brought into ever new constellations as the dramatic events of each film complicate their private lives considerably. As result, watching these films in sequential order makes a significant difference and allows viewers to infer motivations for actions that might otherwise remain unexplained.

Ongoing subplots are, however, not the only means by which second-wave series establish a sense of narrative continuity. In another marked contrast to the titles of the first wave, superhero movies released after 1998 often evoke the sense of a continuous diegesis that exists beyond the boundaries of individual films. Mark J. P. Wolf describes this storytelling strategy as "world-building," arguing that it requires the establishment of a continuous "space in which things can exist and events can occur; a duration or span of time in which events can occur," as well as an elaboration of characters and details that mark the setting as unique and different from other fictional worlds and the world inhabited by the audience (154). For Wolf, world-building of this kind hinges on the recurrence of known characters and locations, as well as on the presentation of rich detail through "data, exposition and digressions that provide information about a world" (29; for a similar view, see Jenkins, *Convergence Culture* 97–98). Since world-building frames storyworlds as persistent locales that exist somewhat independently from unfolding subplots and the details of character backstories, it can help to establish a sense of continuity and filial relation between narratives whose central plots do not connect directly. World-building is thus particularly productive for film series whose installments are released years apart from each other. Not coincidentally, later entries of Fox's *X-Men* series repeatedly return to important locations that were established in the first film – such as Professor Xavier's School for Gifted Youngsters (which appears in almost all *X-Men* films released between 2000 and 2019), the Weapon X facility at Alkali Lake in the Canadian Rocky Mountains (seen in *X-Men* and *X2*, as well as in *X-Men Origins: Wolverine* [2009] and *X-Men: Apocalypse* [2016]), or the plastic prison that holds the villain Magneto (seen in *X-Men* and *X2*), for example. By contrast, each installment of the *Blade* series takes the eponymous protagonist (Wesley Snipes) to different locales. Here, world-building occurs through the expansion of a shared series mythology, as the second and third films elaborate on the history and culture of the vampires pursued by the hero and his allies.

Despite this genre's embrace of linear seriality, virtually all entries of the second wave can still be consumed as self-contained action and adventure films. This is so because second-wave films generally combine their ongoing storylines and world-building practices with A-plots that offer a high degree of episodic closure.[18] The entries of the *Blade*, *Spider-Man*, and *X-Men* trilogies, for example, all subordinate questions of narrative continuity to central conflicts between heroes and villains, which are resolved in dramatic showdowns at the end of each film. In addition, many second-wave films rely on expository dialogue and flashback sequences to recapitulate relevant past events for the benefit of viewers who have missed preceding installments. Like other blockbusters, most titles released during the second wave also foreground the attractions of spectacular action scenes and state-of-the-art special effects as appeals that operate somewhat independently from the minutiae of serial narration.

In fact, second-wave films generally foreground their spectacular qualities by relying on a more dynamic film style, an overall accelerated pacing, a new generation of special effects, and prominent visual nods to the comics medium. Many of these developments were informed by the advent of "digital cinema" (as Lev Manovich terms it) during the 1990s, which offered new possibilities for the seamless integration of live-action and computer-generated footage. Making a similar point, Burke suggests that the "more malleable digital film image" allowed for a newly accurate "translation of medium specific devices" from comics to the big screen (Burke 170; 171; see also Rauscher, "Marvel Universe on Screen" 23; Vignold 45–46). In particular, many second-wave movies capitalize on the affordances of digital cinema to showcase the more-than-human abilities of super-powered characters. For instance, the *X-Men* films use digital animation to depict Wolverine's healing factor and metal claws, as well as Cyclops' optic force blasts (see Burke 216–20). Similarly, the *Blade* and *Spider-Man* films employ digital doubles as stand-ins for the bodies of actors and stuntmen in scenes that are impractical, dangerous, or impossible to shoot otherwise. Likewise, many second-wave films rely on digitally augmented freeze-frames and "bullet-time" sequences to slow down cinematic discourse time and to allow viewers to scrutinize individual moments in greater detail – devices which, as Burke notes, can be understood as filmic equivalents of comics' ability to diagram movement through sequences of panels

(Burke 190–98, 242–48). To further echo the look of superhero comics, many second-wave films also rely on frequent alternations between close-ups and wider angles, a conspicuous use of Dutch angles, and a general emphasis on "exaggerated depths of field" (Burke 233). Most films of the second cycle furthermore subscribe to an "intensified continuity" style that uses frequent cuts, moving cameras, the juxtaposition of tight framings and wide angles, and a focus on in-frame movement to emphasize narrative momentum (on this style, see Bordwell, *The Way* 121–38). As result, second-wave films generally exhibit a kinetic visual style that favors visceral impact over a transparency of spatial and temporal relations.

The opening minutes of *X2* offer a good example of the intensified comics aesthetic of the second wave. Here, the mutant Nightcrawler (Alan Cumming) infiltrates the White House in an apparent attempt to assassinate the American president (*X2* 0:01:45–05:02). After attracting the attention of secret service agents, the mutant starts using his short-range teleportation powers to fight his way into the Oval Office, leaving behind a colorful trail of (digitally animated) teleportation dust in the process. The film begins this sequence with a series of shots that establish a clearly defined axis of action (from the left side of the frame to the right) and present the movement of characters through space in an easily legible manner. As Nightcrawler gets closer to his target, however, events escalate along with the frequency of cuts; simultaneously, the number of shots from different angles increases rapidly. Eventually, any sense of spatial coherence temporarily collapses as the camera frames the action from both the "right" and the "wrong" side of the 180° line. The action then reaches the Oval Office, where a twenty-second-long slow-motion sequence (created through motion-controlled tracking shots, wire stunts, and digital effects) shows the mutant fighting another group of agents and subsequently attacking the president with a knife. Finally, Nightcrawler teleports away before his victim is seriously harmed. The sequence ends with a close-up of the mutant's knife stuck in the Resolute Desk and the face of the shocked president clearly visible in the background (Figure 3.3). *X2*'s opening scene includes all the signature elements of the second wave's shared visual style: rapid cuts, free-roaming cameras, extremely variable camera angles and focal lengths, digital effects that augment sophisticated action set pieces, bullet-time effects that slow down discourse time, panel-like framings, and – last, but not least – moments in which classical continuity principles are "subordinated to [. . .] immediate shocks, thrills, and spectacular effects" (as Steven Shaviro puts it in his essay on "Post-Continuity" aesthetics).

Viewed from a media-theoretical perspective, such attempts to translate comics-specific devices to the big screen produce paradoxical results. In evoking the looks of superhero comics, the films of the second wave approximate a medium that Marshall McLuhan has famously characterized as "cool"

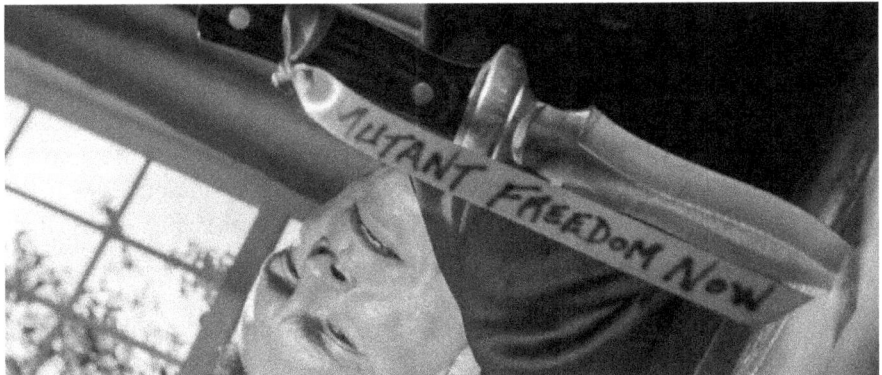

Figure 3.3 The opening scene of *X2* (2002) ends with a shot the composition of which echoes the aesthetics of superhero comics. Screengrab from Amazon Prime Video.

or "low-intensity" (McLuhan 24–27; 178–79). In McLuhan's terminology, "cool media are high in participation and completion by the audience," which is to say that their use involves a non-trivial effort on the part of consumers (McLuhan 25). Comics, for example, demand an active reader who navigates the various codes, formal elements, and material dimensions that constitute and define it as a distinct medium. In the classical case of comics printed on paper, this navigation occurs at a pace determined by the individual reader, who is free to ignore some panels, merely glance at others, and study yet others in greater detail. Film, however, is a "hot" medium that makes strong demands on viewers' focused attention. Where comics allow the reader's eye to wander, the cinematic apparatus presents sequences of images and sounds as an ongoing multi-modal flow that is not as easily subjected to the recipient's control.[19] This experiential intensity is amplified by the accelerated spectacle of second-wave superhero movies, which combine fast-paced plots with frequent bursts of spectacular action and special effects, and which tend to move from one highpoint of dramatic tension to the next. The experiences offered by the two media thus are quite different: Where comic books invite an attitude of readerly contemplation, superhero movies often jerk unexpecting viewers to attention and oscillate between spectacular action and less intense moments.

As noted earlier, second-wave superhero blockbusters also foreground their status as parts of non-linear proliferations more prominently than the films of the first cycle. Films released after 1997 not only continue to borrow characters, motifs, and storylines from a large back-catalogue of earlier superhero narratives, but they also reference specific source materials much more explicitly and often quote clearly identifiable moments from classic superhero comic books. Raimi's first *Spider-Man* film, for example, stages a scene in which a frustrated Peter refuses to stop an escaping criminal in a series of shots that echo a sequence featured in the very first Spider-Man comic (*Spider-Man* 0:42:27–3:05; compare Lee and Ditko). Similarly, *Daredevil* recreates iconic images from different moments in the hero's serial prehistory. One of the very first shots in the film, for example, lifts the image of a bleeding Daredevil atop a Manhattan church from Kevin Smith, Joe Quesada, and Jimmy Palmiotti's 1998/99 "Guardian Devil" story-arc; likewise, a later confrontation between the heroine Elektra and the villain Bullseye is patterned after a sequence of panels from Frank Miller's *Daredevil* #181 (April 1982) (0:03:35–46; 1:38:32–46). Many second-wave films also include multiple nods and homages to celebrated comics creators. In *Daredevil*, the price boxers in the film's fictional New York boxing league carry the names of artists and writers John Romita, Sr., Frank Miller, David Mack, and Brian Michael Bendis (0:15:07–25); later in the film, Kevin Smith cameos as a forensic assistant named after legendary comics artist Jack Kirby (1:29:58).[20] Most of these references require more than a passing familiarity with the history of US-American superhero comics to be understood – in fact, often they are legible only to well-informed and attentive fans who apply time-consuming strategies of computer-assisted close reading. In other instances, references to a canon of classic superhero comics overlap with the strategies of world-building discussed above. In such cases, films include nods to characters, events, and places that are well-established within the story-worlds of superhero comics. In *X2*, for instance, a brief shot of a computer screen reveals the contents of a secret government database about the world's mutant population. Among other things, the display lists the names of Franklin Richards (the son of the *Fantastic Four*'s Mr. Fantastic and the Invisible Woman), the mutant Remy "Gambit" LeBeau, and the Canadian superhero team Alpha Flight (0:23:03–24:09). Similarly, a shot in *Spider-Man* offers a seemingly inconsequential glimpse at a newspaper read by the villain Norman Osborn. However, for viewers of the digital home video version of the film, a freeze frame reveals that the article contains additional information about Osborn's private life, his company, and its contract to create a "super soldier" program for the government (0:33:55–57). In including these bits of otherwise superfluous (and barely visible) narrative information, *X2* and *Spider-Man* point to a history of diegetic events that precedes the plot of the respective film; they simultaneously establish a connection to a larger universe of Marvel stories that viewers might know from other media.

Burke identifies "fanboy" consumers – that is, typically male and affluent comics fans "aged twenty-one or older" who value a perceived fidelity to comic book source material and dedicate considerable amounts of time to debates in online fan forums – as the intended addressees of such references (132; see 136–41). Making a similar case, Aaron Taylor argues that Marvel-based superhero movies "encourage" informed fans "to identify obscure references, teases, in-jokes, graphic semblances, knowing revisions and disseminate their knowledge across various information ecosystems" ("Avengers" 186). Burke's and Taylor's observations are instructive; yet the foregrounded appeal to fan audiences also raises questions about the commercial viability and mass appeal of second-wave films. Jared Gardner notes that even popular comic books rarely sold "more than a hundred thousand an issue" during the first decade of the twenty-first century (183). Accordingly, "comics sales provide[d] nowhere near the number of readers needed to guarantee a successful return on even a small-budget motion picture."[21] But if fanboy consumers were just a small subgroup of a much larger audience, why did second-wave superhero movies go to such lengths to cater to their interests?

Attempting to provide an explanation, scholars such as Burke, Taylor, and Suzanne Scott have pointed to a more general cultural shift that began with the rise of online fandom during the 1990s. Burke, for instance, discusses media fans as "digitally bolstered consumer[s]" with a disproportionate influence on the public reception of Hollywood films (Burke 18; cf. 133–41). Burke points to the scathingly negative pre-release coverage of *Batman & Robin* on fan-oriented websites such as *Ain't It Cool News* (*AICN*, since 1996) and notes that the responses of online fandom can make or break the box-office success of comic book films. Similarly, Taylor suggests that the members of "opinionated and outspoken fan cultures" act as "subcultural gatekeepers" who shape the debates of "a more dispersed film-going community" ("Avengers" 191). Within this scenario, dedicated and knowledgeable comic book fans are a small, but vocal niche audience that – thanks to the bullhorn of online media – has managed to make its demands heard by Hollywood studios. Burke and Taylor both emphasize that fannish expertise eventually comes to inform work behind the camera as well. Burke, for instance, notes that the rise of online fandom was paralleled by a "changing of the guard" within the industry that elevated fannish filmmakers, producers, and executives to influential positions (74; cf. 74–77). Likewise, Taylor points to the careers of filmmaker Joss Whedon and Marvel Studios executive Kevin Feige, who have worked in both the comics and film industries ("Avengers" 187). Making a similar case, Scott discusses directors such as Whedon or Zack Snyder as embodiments of the "fanboy auteur" archetype ("Undead Author" 440). Fanboy auteurs, so Scott suggests, combine a public "self-identification as fans" with the "perceived ability to speak the promotional language of both visionary auteur and faithful fanboy" in order to present themselves as informed and passionate pop culture enthusiasts who have managed to "convert their subcultural capital into economic capital" (440, 442).

While the above arguments describe the new prominence of fannish critics and auteurs quite well, the role of online fan media deserves further scrutiny. Burke, Taylor, and Scott all present the fan-orientation of recent comic book movies as the result of an overlap between the demands of a small elite of expert fans and the interests of like-minded allies within the entertainment industry, a perspective that echoes Henry Jenkins's claims about the responsiveness of digital-era popular culture. This view runs the risk of misrepresenting the power relations between fan culture and entertainment industry, as it reiterates the problematic idea that Hollywood's offerings merely respond to the demands of consumers – an assumption that obfuscates how larger social constellations (such as the separation between work and free time, and the need to sell and reproduce one's ability to work) participate in the shaping of consumers' needs and desires. In addition, Burke's and Taylor's arguments disregard the internal hierarchies and differences in opinion that characterize online fandom at the beginning of the twenty-first century. A close inspection of the user commentary and film reviews on a site like *AICN*, for example, quickly reveals a diversity of opinions and many (at times heated) disagreements among users. Jonathan Gray notes that the category of the "fan" does not sufficiently capture the heterogenous character of such discourses and points out that popular media franchises are just as often consumed and discussed by anti-fans ("who strongly dislike a particular text or genre") and non-fans (who adopt a neutral stance towards particular titles but might nonetheless participate in fan discourses) ("New Audiences" 70). Finally, the focus on fanboys and other fannish consumers makes it difficult to understand the role played by fan-oriented websites. Burke and Taylor frame online fan forums as neutral communication channels in a quasi-democratic process that articulates fandom's demands towards the industry. Arguably, however, fan-sites are not just channels for the articulation of consumer demand. Instead, they are better understood as important discursive nodes within a lively online fan public that is shaped by a variety of different actors and encompasses a variety of forums, publications, and platforms. During the years of the second wave, fanboys are a visible part of this constellation, but the Hollywood industry responds to the larger discourses that unfold within this online public – and not to the opinions of an elite group of fannish consumers.

To illustrate this argument, a closer look at a website such as *AICN* should be helpful. *AICN* was started as private homepage by its founder Harry Knowles, but eventually evolved into a professionally managed and commercially run online publication with a staff of regular contributors.[22] By the beginning of the second wave, *AICN* still presented itself as a site for fans run by fans but published content in the manner of a traditional entertainment news outlet: It offered reviews of recently released films and daily updates on upcoming genre productions in a variety of media. In doing so, *AICN* competed with other websites that offered similar contents – such as *Comic Book Resources* (since 1995), *Dark Horizons* (since 1997), *PopMatters* (since 1999), *Superhero Hype* (since 2002), or *Comic Book Movie* (since 2003), for example. As businesses in the era of cognitive capitalism, these websites were subjected to the same imperatives as the films, television shows, comic series, and media franchises on which they reported – which is to say that they needed to find ways to generate user activity and secure readers' continued engagement. Sites such as *AICN* achieved this goal by covering otherwise un(der)reported niche topics, by presenting scoops about new film releases, by cultivating their image as fan-oriented publications, and by presenting their commentary sections as spaces for open-ended debate. Together with online databases such as *IMDb.com*, user-operated discussion boards, fan-blogs, wikis, and the social media platforms that emerged towards the end of the second wave, fan-oriented news websites eventually came to form the backbone of a fan-oriented online public that provided a constant feed of reviews, news items, and "hot takes," along with forums for communal conversation. In other words, sites such as *AICN* indeed were (and continue to be) spaces in which the options of fans are articulated – but they also operated as commercial news media that generated public attention for superhero movies and other cultural commodities.

The emergence and subsequent entrenchment of the fan-oriented online public marks an important change in the transition from the first wave to the second. More precisely, it marks the point at which the practices of media fans become subjected to the valorization mechanisms of cognitive capitalism. Compared to the primarily print-based fan media of earlier decades, the new online fan public was much easier to access and open to a larger, geographically more dispersed audience. It also invited the participation of users who did not explicitly identify as fans, as well as interventions by marketers and promoters who sought to situate their products within fan-cultural discourses. Within the politico-economic framework developed in the first chapter, the discourses that unfolded within this fan public can be understood as the collective product of the (paid and unpaid) immaterial labor of anyone who participated in them – as the sum total of the work done by fannish film critics and other professional consumers, by users browsing fan-sites and writing in commentary sections, by the authors of posts on blogs and social media, as well as by corporate actors circulating press releases and promotional materials. Since the reach of this fan-oriented public sphere expanded well beyond an elite audience of fanboys, Hollywood could not afford to ignore the "media buzz" it produced – after all, the responses of online fandom now constituted not only potential public relations assets, but also possible public relations crises. In the years around the turn to the twenty-first century, the discourses of online fandom thus emerged as an important cultural externality that needed to be managed by producers. It is against this background that superhero blockbusters began to foreground their appeal to comic book fandom – and entries of the genre did so, not because they needed to win over a small group of fanboy gatekeepers, but because they sought to insert themselves more generally into the discourses and practices of online fandom.

In summary, the films of the second wave presented themselves as products of an entertainment industry that reconceptualized the media fan as an ideal type of consumer, that catered more directly to the perceived interests of fans, and that tried to insert its products into the news coverage, debates, and interpretive practices of online fandom. To this effect, the films of the second cycle delineated possible trajectories of serial engagement much more clearly, pointed more explicitly to a canon of classic stories, and asked viewers to consume films in the order established by release dates. At the same time, second-wave superhero movies went to great lengths to remain appealing to viewers disinterested in ongoing subplots, the intricacies of fictional worlds, or the relationship to source materials. Centering on self-contained conflicts and foregrounding the cinematic attraction of fast-paced action and spectacular special effects, the superhero movies released between 1998 and the end of 2007 thus continued to accommodate a traditional way of watching that occurred primarily at the movie theater and with little to no follow-up interaction online. In other words, the films of the second wave framed fannish engagement not as a necessary requirement, but as a privileged mode of reception.

THE THIRD WAVE: RISE OF THE CINEMATIC UNIVERSE, 2008–14

The third wave began with another re-orientation of Marvel Entertainment's core business, which, during the final years of the second wave, shifted from the licensing of film rights to the in-house production of feature films. While film licensing resulted in considerable profits for Marvel, it also gave the company little control over the production process and left it with returns that were small in comparison to those of its Hollywood partners (see Johnson, "Cinematic" 10–12). To capitalize on the company's intellectual property assets more effectively, Marvel began to expand its operations into film financing and production in 2005.[23] After announcing its plans to create a series of narratively interconnected superhero films at the 2006 San Diego Comic Con, Marvel eventually released *Iron Man* (distributed by Paramount) and *The Incredible Hulk* (distributed by Universal) in 2008. A year later, the company was bought by the Disney conglomerate. Under Disney's auspices, Marvel expanded its series with *Iron Man 2* (2010), *Thor* (2011), *Captain America: The First Avenger* (2011), the cross-over movie *Marvel's The Avengers* (2012), as well as the sequels *Thor: The Dark World* (2013) and *Iron Man 3* (2013). Collectively titled *Marvel Cinematic Universe* (*MCU*), these Marvel-produced films relied on the multi-linear model of serialization discussed in the preceding chapter. Within this model, the adventures of superheroes such as Iron

Man or Captain America unfolded across nominally separate film series – but, at the same time, all films of the *MCU* were set within a shared storyworld that allowed their plots to overlap and intersect (on the concept of storyworld, see Ryan, "Story/World/Media"). Marvel eventually expanded the *MCU* to media and formats, adding a series of short films, numerous tie-in comics, and the ABC television series *Agents of S.H.I.E.L.D.* (2014–20) during subsequent years of the third wave.

The commercial successes of the *MCU* soon inspired other studios to reorganize their own superhero franchises into similarly multi-tiered operations. Retaining the film rights to several Marvel properties, Fox cancelled plans for further entries in its underperforming *Fantastic Four* and *Daredevil/Elektra* series and instead expanded the *X-Men* franchise with spin-offs about Wolverine (*X-Men Origins: Wolverine*, 2009; *The Wolverine*, 2013) and prequels about a younger generation of characters (*X-Men: First Class*, 2011; *X-Men: Days of Future Past*, 2014). Likewise, the Sony-owned Columbia Pictures rebooted its *Spider-Man* franchise with *The Amazing Spider-Man* (2012), which was positioned as the launching pad for a Spider-Man-centric cinematic universe. Sony eventually abandoned these plans after the lackluster box-office performance of *The Amazing Spider-Man 2: Rise of Electro* (2014). Meanwhile, Warner Bros. released a string of films that continued to operate within the narrative parameters of the second wave. These films included Christopher Nolan's Batman films *The Dark Knight* (2008) and *The Dark Knight Rises* (2012), Zack Snyder's *Watchmen* (2008), the superhero Western *Jonah Hex* (2010), and the sci-fi adventure *Green Lantern* (2011). In 2013, Warner eventually positioned the Superman-reboot *Man of Steel* as the first installment of a shared DC cinematic universe. In total, the third wave saw a further increase in the number and frequency of releases in the genre, which added twenty-three films over a period of six and a half years. By the end of the cycle in the summer of 2014, the field had nonetheless been narrowed down to three remaining franchises that all followed the "universe" model: Warner Bros. DC-based films, Fox's *X-Men* films, and Disney's *MCU*.[24]

The gradual adoption of the universe model by the remaining franchises resulted in another intensification of the hyper-referential style that manifested itself most obviously in less self-contained films and stronger demands for ongoing serial engagement. These developments were prominently on display in the films of the *MCU*, which foregrounded linkages between each other and embraced innovative practices of transmedia storytelling. Apart from this, third-wave films continued to combine state-of-the-art cinematic spectacles with ongoing storylines and frequent references to a variety of (now increasingly obscure) comic book source materials. The third wave furthermore coincided with significant growth of online fandom. In the years after 2008, an increasing number of commercially operated fan-oriented entertainment news websites, blogs, user-operated wikis, and social media platforms provided a new abundance of paratextual information about the superhero genre. This expanded fan public continued to function as a space in which the immaterial labor of consumers added to (or detracted from) the visibility and status of superhero movies. But online fandom now took on crucial expository functions as well, as its sites and discourses increasingly began to operate as (to borrow a concept from Jason Mittell) "orienting paratexts" that provided meta-information about the third wave's sprawling storyworlds (*Complex TV* 263; see also 261–63; on the production of fan paratexts as a form of labor, see Stanfill pos. 2640–96). Covering everything from production news over reviews of new releases to explanations of film's intertextual references, think-pieces on the status of the genre, and ceaseless user commentary, online fandom eventually became closely entangled with the narrative operations of the genre.

The complex modes of serial narration at work in the *MCU* were central to the developments described above.[25] Collectively, the entries of the *MCU* constitute what Ruth Mayer calls a "serial cluster" – that is, a narrative unit or set with "a fictional logic and continuity of its own," within which chains of cause-and-effect radiate out from one installment to the next (*Fu Manchu*, 9, cf. 25). At the cinema, the *MCU*'s serial unfolding proceeded in a relatively linear fashion. The diegetic events of *Iron Man*, for example, were followed by those of *The Incredible Hulk* and impacted the plot of *Iron Man 2*, which, in turn, foreshadowed events from *Thor*. Soon afterwards, *Captain America: The First Avenger* introduced its star-spangled protagonist to the franchise; eventually, the Hulk, Iron Man, Thor, and Captain America joined forces in *The Avengers* (Figure 3.4) and later returned for separate adventures in *Iron Man 3*, *Thor: The Dark World*, *Captain America: The Winter Soldier*, and so on.[26] Within this framework, minor characters and plot-relevant objects routinely crossed over from one sub-series into the next: Agent Phil Coulson, for example, was introduced in *Iron Man* as a supporting character, reappeared in *Iron Man 2* and *Thor*, died in *The Avengers*, and was ultimately resurrected in *Agents of S.H.I.E.L.D.* a year later. The films of the *MCU* furthermore advanced an overarching story-arc about the villain Thanos's quest to collect a set of mystical, power-granting artifacts called Infinity Stones. Beginning with the appearance of one of the stones in *Captain America: The First Avenger*, Thanos and the objects of his desire eventually turned up in several films. Beyond this, the various parts of the *MCU* featured ongoing B-storylines that revolved around the shifting relationships between recurring characters.

Notably, however, the franchise's expansion into television and short films complicated this linearity by introducing additional, media-specific models of serialization.[27] While the *MCU*'s films premiered several months apart from each other, *Agents of S.H.I.E.L.D.* followed the schedule of the American television season and released its installments in far quicker succession.

Figure 3.4 *Marvel's The Avengers* (2012) assembles the heroes of the *Marvel Cinematic Universe* for a shared adventure. Screengrab from Disney+.

An example of what Mittell has called "narratively complex television" (*Complex TV*), *Agents of S.H.I.E.L.D.* balanced episodically contained plots with developing character relationships and longer arcs that unfolded through startling plot twists and unexpected revelations. Simultaneously, the show repeatedly foregrounded its connection to the films of the franchise: The alien invasions, government conspiracies and character deaths that occurred in the movies, for example, produced lasting consequences for the titular group of agents, whose adventures often dealt with the fallout of such events. *Agents of S.H.I.E.L.D.*'s pilot episode, for instance, takes up a central plot element from *Iron Man 3* – the experimental "Extremis" bio-technology that villain Aldrich Killian (Guy Pearce) uses to exact his revenge against Tony Stark – and turns it into an element of the first season's story-arc, which eventually comes to center on the schemes of the nefarious terrorist organization HYDRA. Starting with the episode "T.A.H.I.T.I." the show develops this storyline into an extended crossover event with *Captain America: The Winter Soldier*, which was released to theaters a few days after the airing of the episode. In the film, a HYDRA plot results in the dissolution of S.H.I.E.L.D. and the disavowal of its agents by the US government; accordingly, the next eight episodes of *Agents of S.H.I.E.L.D.* focus on the consequences of this dramatic revelation.[28] In this manner, *Agents of S.H.I.E.L.D.*'s first season presented itself as both prologue and narrative extension to the events of the second Captain America film.

By contrast, the *MCU*'s short films – dubbed *Marvel One-Shots* – connected only tangentially to the plots of the feature films. Originally included on the *MCU*'s home video releases, as well as circulating via online video portals, the

One-Shots offer brief vignettes set in the aftermath of the blockbuster films.[29] Telling small-scale stories about the fate of minor characters, the *One-Shots* presented themselves as an anthology of loosely connected stories rather than one continuous serial narrative. But within the larger narrative architecture of the *MCU*, the shorts nonetheless provided some of the connective tissue that interlinked the various parts of the franchise. The 2013 short *Agent Carter* (which was included as bonus content on the *Iron Man 3* home video release), for example, elaborates on the post-World War II career of Agent Peggy Carter (a supporting character introduced in the first *Captain America*-film; portrayed by Hayley Atwell) and teases future appearances of the operative, who eventually received her own television series in 2015 and subsequently turned up in other films of the franchise.

The above examples illustrate the asymmetrical relationship between the blockbuster movies and the rest of the *MCU*: While the television shows and short films responded to the dramatic events depicted in the blockbusters, the events that occurred in the *One-Shots* or on *Agents of S.H.I.E.L.D.* – which told their stories on a much smaller scale and with much smaller budgets – did not reverberate through the rest of franchise in quite the same way. But while the show and the *One-Shots* remained subordinated to the narratively more significant feature films, the former nonetheless presented themselves as entryways into the larger storyworld that can also be enjoyed on their own terms.

Like the films of the second wave, the various entries of the *MCU* include frequent and explicit references to canonical source materials to position themselves within the discourses of the fan public. In some cases, this occurs through a self-reflexive thematization of the franchise's prehistory in other media – as in *The Incredible Hulk*'s opening titles discussed at the beginning of this chapter, for example. In other cases, the *MCU*'s nods to classic Marvel titles foreshadow future releases. Some of the company's iconic superheroes, for instance, are referenced in films that precede their official entry into the *MCU*: Captain America's iconic shield turns up in Tony Stark's basement in *Iron Man* and then again in *Iron Man 2* (each time visible only for a few seconds), while dialogue in *The Winter Soldier* mentions Marvel's house-magician Dr. Strange, who joined the franchise during the fourth wave. The *MCU*'s frequent use of brief mid- and post-credits sequences follows a similar logic. Starting with the first entry of the series, the closing credits of all the *MCU*'s films include brief scenes that often function as teasers for upcoming attractions. *Iron Man*'s credits, for example, foreshadow the first *Avengers*-film through an appearance of Nick Fury; likewise, *Iron Man 2* ends with the discovery of Thor's Hammer Mjölnir by Agent Coulson, while *The Winter Soldier* introduces the characters Baron von Strucker, Quicksilver, and Scarlet Witch, who later reappear in *Avengers: Age of Ultron* (2015). References of this kind seek to secure the engagement of fan audiences on two interlocking levels: on the one hand, they reward familiarity with the canon of Marvel comics; on the other hand, they invite speculation about upcoming plot developments. In such moments, fannish expertise thus becomes a prerequisite for the ability to anticipate possible futures of the franchise.

In summary, the *MCU* can be understood as a multi-linear, multi-format, multi-platform serial narrative, that – thanks to its combination of movies, broadcast TV, and home video – can engage its audience more frequently, more regularly, and with shorter breaks in between releases than other series or franchises. The various parts of the *MCU* furthermore allow it to target different audiences: The PG-13-rated blockbuster films, for instance, are made to appeal to a broad audience of "avid filmgoers aged ten to twenty-four" and the group of so-called "Boomers with Kids" that includes "children, parents and grandparents in the eight-to-eighty demographic" (Balio 26). By contrast, *Agents of S.H.I.E.L.D.* targets a smaller audience of television viewers, while the *One-Shots* promote home video releases and tie-in comics address the smaller group of consumers who read superhero comic books. Likewise, the *MCU*'s structure of loosely connected, but thematically distinct sub-series allows the franchise to branch out into different genres and release a superhero origin story like *Iron Man* alongside a fantasy vehicle like *Thor: The Dark World*, a conspiracy thriller like *The Winter Soldier*, or a sci-fi/espionage procedural like *Agents of S.H.I.E.L.D.* By the end of the third wave, the *MCU* not only presented itself as a fast-growing franchise that offered several dozen hours of entertainment content to consumers, but also integrated different types of material into a constantly expanding narrative framework. At this point in time, the ideal consumer of the *MCU* viewed all the franchise's feature films in the cinema or at home, watched every episode of *Agents of S.H.I.E.L.D.*, purchased DVDs and Blu-Rays to access *One-Shots* and other bonus content, and actively participated in the debates and interpretive practices of online fandom. Taken together, the entries of Disney's *MCU* thus rewarded strong audience engagement much more so than films released during the preceding two cycles.

Like the more explicit fan orientation of second-wave films, the *MCU*'s storytelling practices raise questions about the franchise's appeal to a mass audience and the average viewer's ability to navigate such sprawling narrative architectures. The concept of hypertext – which denotes a non-linear network of self-contained texts held together by intertextual "connections and relations," as George Landow puts it in his definition of the term (174) – constitutes a useful starting point to explore these questions. Viewed in its entirety, the *MCU* presents itself as a quasi-hypertextual network that encompasses a core of feature films and a secondary body of television, short film, and comics narratives. As a hypertext-like structure, the *MCU* does not necessarily demand an engagement that proceeds linearly along the order of releases. This is so because most films of the franchise offer a high degree of episodic closure and subordinate ongoing subplots to central conflicts that are resolved at the end of their respective run-time. Accordingly, each film can function as an entry-point into the larger hypertextual network. But each entry of the *MCU* also constitutes a node that indexes various other parts of a larger, constantly expanding body of old and new superhero content that can be traversed in different ways. The result is a modular structure that, like other forms of hypertext, can be navigated "nonsequentially" (Landow 174) and that can accommodate casual engagements which explore only part of the larger textual network.[30] The accessibility of the *MCU* is furthermore predicated on its embeddedness in actual hypertextual structures. During the years of the third wave, these included commercial video-on-demand services and streaming platforms such as Amazon Video, Netflix, or Apple's iTunes, which started their operations towards the end of the second cycle and rose to prominence in the following years.[31] All of these services employed hypertextual user interfaces to guide users through large catalogs of audiovisual content. Netflix and Amazon also relied on sophisticated recommendation algorithms to point viewers to thematically related films. In doing so, these streaming services enabled an easy navigation of the superhero genre's complicated intertextual references and narrative architectures.

For a significant part of the audience, the engagement with superhero blockbuster films was also mediated by the paratextual discourses of the fan-oriented online public. This public significantly increased in size after the end of the second wave and eventually came to include content on social media such as Facebook and Twitter, as well as video platforms such as YouTube, along with an increasing number of fan-oriented blogs and websites that provided a ceaseless barrage of news, reviews, and commentary about superhero blockbusters and other genres. In doing so, these sites and platforms effectively pre-mediated various aspects of upcoming releases – from casting choices over possible plot points to connections to other series installments – before films ever made it to theaters. In this respect, community-run wikis about the superhero genre – such as the *Marvel Database* (since 2005), the *DC Comics Database* (since 2009), or the *Marvel Cinematic Universe Wiki* (since 2010) – also constituted a relevant resource. Paul Booth discusses such sites as "portals of information" that collect and disseminate specialized fan knowledge, thereby rendering the narrative operations of popular series and franchises transparent to a broader audience (372). During the height of the third wave, the *Marvel Cinematic Universe Wiki*, for example, encompassed several thousand articles on the many entries, characters, and events of the franchise, as well as a great deal of background information about the production of individual installments. Together with the other paratextual materials circulating within online fandom and the interfaces of video-on-demand platforms, wikis and fan-sites helped to make the operations of multi-linear franchises such as the *MCU* accessible to consumers. As result, the genre's increasingly complex modes of serial storytelling and intertextual reference met an audience that was (at least potentially) well-equipped to parse them.

As the most rapidly expanding and commercially successful series of the third wave, Disney's *MCU* eventually became a model for other studios. Interestingly, however, some time would pass until the *MCU*'s architecture was successfully replicated by competing franchises. Before the summer of 2014, only Fox's *X-Men* franchise had added enough installments to become a multi-linear series that could rival Disney's Marvel films. The remaining cinematic universes did not really take off before the beginning of the next cycle. By then, the *MCU* had already familiarized audiences with basic outlines of this model of serial storytelling. Together with the fan-cultural discourses that surrounded it, the *MCU* contributed to a further mainstreaming of consumption practices that were once primarily associated with media fandom – such as eagerly anticipating upcoming feature films and reading about them before visiting the cinema, sharing one's opinions about popular entertainments via fan-oriented publications, and teasing out intertextual connections. In doing so, the *MCU* helped prepare the ground for the next wave of superhero blockbuster cinema, which would establish this mode of consumption as the new norm.

THE FOURTH WAVE: NEW DIVERSITY AND NARRATIVE FRAGMENTATION, 2014–20

Despite a smaller number of ongoing series in the genre, the fourth cycle witnessed another increase in the frequency and number of releases. During this phase, Disney alone expanded its *MCU* with twenty-one additional movies, eleven television series, and additional tie-ins in comics and other media. Almost all other films released after the spring of 2014 similarly positioned themselves as entries of larger cinematic universes. Fox, for example, released a commercially under-performing *Fantastic Four* reboot in 2015, but afterwards refocused its efforts on the expansion of the *X-Men* franchise, to which it added the feature films *Deadpool* (2016), *X-Men: Apocalypse* (2016), *Logan* (2017), *Deadpool 2* (2018), *Dark Phoenix* (2019), and *New Mutants* (2020), as well as the television series *Legion* (FX, 2017–19) and *The Gifted* (Fox, 2017–19). Warner Bros. expanded the multi-linear series begun by *Man of Steel* – now called *DC Extended Universe* (*DCEU*) – with 2016's *Batman V. Superman: Dawn of Justice* and *Suicide Squad*, 2017's *Wonder Woman* and *Justice League*, 2018's *Aquaman*, 2019's *Shazam!*, as well as 2020's *Birds of Prey: The Emancipation of Harley Quinn* and *Wonder Woman 1984*.[32] In addition, Warner released the critically acclaimed *Joker* (2019), which did not share a narrative continuity with the films of the *DCEU*. Together, Disney, Warner, Fox, and Sony (which re-entered the field with 2018's *Venom*) released a total of thirty-one films during the fourth wave. The fourth cycle thus represents a period of rapid growth, but the genre's expansion almost ground to a complete halt during the COVID-19 pandemic in 2020; the pandemic's beginning marked the end of the fourth wave. Due to the public health risks associated with the theatrical exhibition of feature films, dwindling numbers of cinema-goers and subsequent lockdowns, only three superhero movies based on DC or Marvel comics were released theatrically during all of 2020 – three less than during each of the preceding four years.[33] In response, Warner took the unprecedented step of releasing *Wonder Woman 1984* simultaneously to US-American theaters and via its streaming service HBO Max. Eventually, Warner announced that its entire 2021 slate would be released in a similar fashion (Barnes and Sperling). Warner's decision not only signaled Hollywood's difficulties in responding to the pandemic, but also reflected the increasing importance of online video platforms as distribution channels for feature-length films more generally. Disney would eventually follow suit with its July 2021 release of *Black Widow*, which, after having been pushed back from its originally scheduled premiere in May of 2020, was eventually released to both theaters and the conglomerate's own Disney+ streaming platform.

Overall, the entries of the fourth wave offered a greater thematic and stylistic diversity than those of the preceding cycles, a development driven by competition within an increasingly crowded genre and the appearance of films based on lesser-known titles. Whereas attempts to adapt more obscure superhero properties before had resulted in the production of commercially underperforming films, releases such as *Guardians of the Galaxy* (whose premiere marks the beginning of the cycle; Disney, 2014), *Ant-Man* (Disney, 2015), or *Deadpool* now became box-office hits that were followed by sequels soon thereafter. Importing motifs and themes from other genres, these and other films broadened superhero blockbuster cinema's already flexible storytelling parameters further – with *Guardians of the Galaxy* presenting itself as a space opera in the tradition of *Star Wars*, *Ant-Man* telling a superhero origin story within the framework of a heist movie, and the self-aware *Deadpool* fashioning itself as an R-rated comedy, for example. During the same period, the Zack Snyder-directed films of the *DCEU* re-introduced a deliberately stylized comic book aesthetic into the genre. The celebrated *Logan* and *Joker* took the opposite path and presented themselves as somber character studies built around the performances of their charismatic lead actors. In different ways, all these films also foregrounded their character as serial narratives and continued to reward a familiarity with (now at times quite obscure) comic book source materials and paratextual fan discourses online. Like the *MCU* of the third wave, most films of the fourth wave furthermore invited viewers to explore larger narrative architectures and hyper-referential networks. In fact, due to the new prominence of the universe-model, superhero blockbusters now encouraged well-informed and time-consuming modes of serial engagement more strongly than ever before.

These increased demands for audience engagement were particularly clearly on display in the many team-up and cross-over movies of the fourth wave. Continuing a trend begun by *The Avengers*, several fourth-wave films signaled such team-ups in their titles – like the *DCEU*'s *Batman V. Superman: Dawn of Justice* and *Justice League* (Figure 3.5), or the *MCU*'s *Avengers* films for instance. But even films named after individual heroes now often featured the protagonists of other sub-series: *Spider-Man: Homecoming* (Disney, 2018), for example, stars the titular hero (Tom Holland) alongside Iron Man; *Thor: Ragnarok* pairs its nominal protagonist (Chris Hemsworth) with the Hulk (Mark Ruffalo); and *Captain America: Civil War* includes appearances by most of the *MCU*'s heroes. Likewise, *Batman V. Superman* also features Wonder Woman (Gal Gadot), as well as cameo appearances by The Flash (Ezra Miller), Aquaman (Jason Momoa), and Cyborg (Ray Fisher). The high frequency of such team-ups during the fourth wave can be understood as result of the competition within an increasingly crowded genre. Writing about twenty-first century "Quality TV" series, Andreas Jahn-Sudmann and Frank Kelleter describe this phenomenon as a tendency towards "serial outbidding" and

Figure 3.5 Batman (Ben Affleck), Superman (Henry Cavill), and Wonder Woman (Gal Gadot) team up in 2018's *Justice League*. Screengrab from Amazon Prime Video.

note that competing serial narratives often attempt to outperform each other through a successive raising of narrative stakes:

> In terms of narrative technique, this might mean that the same story is presented again, but in a heightened (and thereby potentially new) form – with *more* characters, visibly *higher* production values, or *more spectacular* special effects, for example. Thanks to such escalations, the same product can be sold again, but this time as a novelty that is different from others and different from earlier iterations of itself. (Kelleter and Jahn-Sudmann 207; emphasis in the original, translation mine)

The *MCU* films of the fourth wave illustrate this dynamic particularly well, as they not only involve more and more superheroes, but also use these figures to stage ever more elaborate action sequences with the help of increasingly sophisticated special effects.

Many fourth-wave films furthermore presuppose a working background knowledge about comic book source materials and other superhero narratives on the part of the viewer. As a result, their plots often appear to be constructed around conspicuous narrative gaps: In some moments, motivations for characters' actions are implied rather than spelled out; at other times, films hint at or allude to the significance of events and figures that are established and developed in other installments and media. In *Avengers: Age of Ultron* (2015), for example, the allegiance of twin superheroes Quicksilver and Scarlet Witch shifts multiple times, as both characters go from brainwashed HYDRA operatives over allies of the villain Ultron to being members of the Avengers. Since the film devotes little screen-time to these shifts, Quicksilver and Scarlet Witch's actions might appear to be unmotivated or even erratic. But viewers familiar with the turbulent serial pre-history of these characters might already expect that both will eventually ally themselves with the film's heroes. Other fourth-wave films feature similar moments: *Batman V. Superman*, for instance, opens with a sequence that intercuts the murder of Bruce Wayne's parents with their subsequent funeral and young Bruce's discovery of the Batcave. Since the film is neither a re-telling of Batman's origin story nor an exploration of the hero's childhood traumas, the events of the sequence appear to be disconnected from the rest of the plot (especially since they are not explicitly referred to again later). Informed viewers, however, easily recognize that these events have been told many times before: The killing of Wayne's parents, for example, was first featured in 1939's *Detective Comics* #33 and has since not only been restaged several times in the comics, but also appeared in Tim Burton's *Batman*, Joel Schumacher's *Batman Forever*, and Christopher Nolan's *Batman Begins*. The subsequent funeral scene and young Bruce's discovery of the Batcave, however, recreate similar sequences from Frank Miller and Dave Mazzuchelli's *Batman:*

Year One (1987). *Batman V. Superman*'s opening scene thus includes fragments from earlier iterations of the character to signal the film's fidelity to the spirit of canonical versions of the Batman figure – a necessary task, as the film introduces a new version of the caped crusader (portrayed by Ben Affleck) who reappears in other entries of the *DCEU* later. In doing so, *Batman V. Superman* indexes a larger body of earlier narratives in which the hero's motivations are thematized and negotiated in greater detail. Like *Age of Ultron*, *Batman V. Superman* thus expects that audiences are either already familiar with its figures or willing to consult paratextual materials that might fill their narrative gaps.

In both *Age of Ultron* and *Batman V. Superman*, the tendency towards narrative fragmentation coincides with a more explicit focus on ongoing plots and repeated references to the future (rather than the past or serial prehistory) of the respective storyworld. During *Age of Ultron*'s second hour, for instance, Thor meets up with his associate Dr. Selvig to investigate the meaning of a hallucination bestowed on him by Scarlet Witch. Eventually, he receives a prophetic vision of Thanos's quest for the Infinity Stones (*Age of Ultron* 1:12:44–1:14:10). For the rest of the film, the exact meaning of this vision remains unclear, but viewers in the know could easily read the sequence as a teaser for the upcoming *Thor: Ragnarok* and *Avengers: Infinity War*, which were already slated for release (and subject to much fan speculation) when *Age of Ultron* arrived in theaters.[34] Similarly, a dream-sequence in *Batman V. Superman* shows Batman roaming the wastelands of a post-apocalyptic future, where he is confronted by an evil version of Superman. Immediately afterwards, a barely awoken Bruce Wayne is visited by a spectral figure who warns him about disastrous events to come (0:51:38–55:57). *Batman V. Superman* does not thematize the significance of this dream sequence further, but viewers who followed the coverage of the film on fan-sites – where trailer footage had prompted discussion months before the film's theatrical release – could easily surmise that the film here foreshadowed events that might play out in upcoming installments of the *DCEU*. In such moments, the anticipation of yet-unrealized serial futures became a factor that impinged on viewers' enjoyment of films in the present – a shift from the third wave's politics of engagement, which generally relegated references to future events to narratively less significant post-credits sequences.

2018's *Avengers: Infinity War* and its 2019 sequel *Avengers: Endgame* eventually abandoned self-contained central plots altogether and framed themselves as closely interlinked final chapters of the "Infinity Saga" about Thanos and his quest for the Infinity Stones. Released around the tenth anniversary of Disney's *MCU*, *Infinity War* involves almost all the franchise's superheroes and many supporting characters in a protracted showdown against the villain, who, over the course of the film, manages to assemble all six of the sought-after artifacts. *Infinity War* dedicates little time to a recapitulation of past events, the re-introduction of important characters, or the set-up of its central conflict.

Instead, the film opens in medias res with the aftermath of an offscreen battle and proceeds to kill off several recurring characters – a turn of events that presupposes a pre-existing attachment to figures like Loki (Tom Hiddleston) or Heimdall (Idris Elba). *Infinity War* eventually reveals Thanos's plan to use the power of the stones to erase half of all sentient life in the universe. For the rest of the film, the *MCU*'s heroes mount a last-ditch effort to stop the villain, but eventually fail to do so. *Infinity War*'s finale then has the villain murdering half of the storyworld's population with a snap of his fingers. This turn of events diverges significantly from the happy endings that occur in almost all other entries of the genre, especially because it results in the death of several superheroes, including Spider-Man and Black Panther (Chadwick Boseman) – even though further films about these figures were already slated for release by the time *Infinity War* landed in theaters. *Infinity War*'s finale thus directed viewers' attention towards the then-upcoming *Avengers: Endgame*, which promised to resolve, undo, or at least address the events of the preceding film. *Endgame* eventually did so by sending the remaining Avengers on a time-travel adventure that revisited key scenes from earlier installments, exploring hitherto unseen periods of the storyworld's history, and restaging *Infinity War*'s climactic battle scene in a different setting (and with even more superheroes than before).

The plots of *Infinity War* and *Endgame* demand more than a superficial familiarity with the events of preceding installments in order to be understood. But contrary to what one might assume, these demands did not negatively impact the commercial performance of both films, which eventually became the highest-grossing releases of 2018 and 2019. This popularity cannot be properly understood without attention to the cultural activity that clustered around both films – activity which generated publicity for the *MCU*, circulated information about the plots of past and upcoming films, and provided guidance on how to best engage with the franchise. In 2018, for example, *Infinity War*'s unexpected conclusion triggered countless responses within the online fan public and beyond, where it sparked a range of baffled attempts at interpretation, speculations about upcoming installments of the *MCU*, and close readings of previous films.[35] Writing about twenty-first-century television dramas, Mittell discusses twists, turns, and surprising revelations as examples of "narrative special effects" that "call attention to the narration's construction," invite viewers to "revel in the creative mechanics" of serial storytelling, and often trigger significant discussion and debate among members of the audience (*Complex TV* 42–43). A similar dynamic is on display here: As a divergence from the *MCU*'s established storytelling norms, Thanos's surprising triumph yielded a considerable discursive productivity that, in the weeks after its theatrical premiere, kept *Infinity War* within the spotlight of fan-oriented publications and more traditional news media. The online fan public, in turn, added to this publicity by circulating glowing reviews and critical commentary, as well as by offering forums for communal discussion that kept viewers engaged during the temporal break which separated the film and its sequel. The hype around *Infinity War* eventually ebbed in the weeks after the film's premiere – only to be revived by the social media marketing campaign for *Endgame* a year later. The latter included a Twitter post with an open letter by the film's directors Anthony and Joe Russo, who urged viewers not to share details about the plot on social media (@Russo_Brothers). Labeled with the hashtag #Don'tSpoilTheEndgame, the Russos' post generated close to 200,000 likes and countless retweets; it was soon followed by a series of short promotional videos in which the stars of the film repeated the same call. Picked up by fan-oriented websites and more traditional news media soon after, the campaign eventually generated a considerable amount of traffic and managed to rekindle the hype caused by *Infinity War*. The hype around *Infinity War* and *Endgame* demonstrates the increasingly close interlocking of fan-cultural discourses and narrative operations during the years of the fourth wave: First, the twist ending of a serialized superhero movie prompted a wealth of paratextual responses that increased the film's visibility; subsequently, another set of paratextual materials instructed consumers about how to approach the next installment.

Overall, the films of the fourth wave embody a further intensification of the hyper-referential style, albeit one that is incremental when compared to the shifts of the preceding cycles. In many ways, the superhero blockbusters released after the summer of 2014 continue to operate like the *MCU* films of the third wave, which is to say that they encourage time-consuming engagements with larger serial clusters through world-building, ongoing subplots, cross-over appearances, and omnipresent references to comics source materials. Notably, however, not all fourth-wave films foreground their serial character to a similar extent. The *DCEU*'s *Shazam!* and *Birds of Prey*, for instance, tell relatively self-contained stories. But even these movies situate their events within larger storyworlds, make frequent references to preceding films and comic book sources, and prepare the ground for future adventures. Compared to the films of the third cycle, fourth-wave films thus put their doubly serial character – their status as films that are part of larger non-linear serial proliferations as well as installments of ongoing multi-linear series – even more explicitly on display. Delegating some of their narrative operations (such as providing exposition about characters' motivations and backstories) to online paratexts and banking on viewers' familiarity with preceding releases and serial prehistories in other media, these recent films exhibit a considerable readiness to frustrate or irritate viewers unacquainted with the genre. As result, fannish consumption practices – that is, watching series rather than installments, reading narratives against the discourses of online fandom, being on the lookout for intertextual references, and discussing recent releases with like-minded viewers online – became the default way of engaging with fourth-wave superhero blockbusters.

As noted earlier, media other than film and distribution channels other than the cinema became increasingly important during the final years of the fourth wave. In part, this was because a slew of live-action superhero programming on television added to the visibility of superhero blockbusters. Disney's *MCU*, for example, expanded its storyworld with eleven television shows, which included the Netflix series *Daredevil* (2015–18), *Jessica Jones* (2015–19), *Luke Cage* (2016–18), *Iron Fist* (2017–18), *The Defenders* (2017), and *The Punisher* (2017–19). While the Netflix shows were all set in the *MCU*'s version of Manhattan, shared a set of supporting characters, and contributed to a larger narrative arc that culminated in *The Defenders* (which brought the protagonists of the preceding four series together), they also presented themselves only tangentially related to the films of the franchise.[36] Fox's *X-Men* franchise similarly located the short-lived television series *Legion* and *The Gifted* in 2018 within the world of the feature films, but kept their narratives separate from the plots of the movies. The Warner conglomerate followed a different path and premiered multiple television series without diegetic connections to the *DCEU*.[37] Ultimately, most of the superhero shows released during this period presented themselves as relatively independent from the films of the fourth wave, but nonetheless promoted their blockbuster siblings by circulating alternate takes on established characters, properties, and iconographies. Crucially, however, the years after 2014 also witnessed the appearance of conglomerate-owned streaming services that became one-stop-shops for all kinds of televisual and cinematic superhero content. WarnerMedia, for example, launched its DC Universe, a platform dedicated to animated and live-action programming based on DC Comics properties, in 2018. In addition to granting users access to the relevant titles from the conglomerate's extensive film and television back-catalogs, the platform also offered original content in the form of the live-action TV series *Titans* (since 2018), *Doom Patrol* (since 2019), *Swamp Thing* (2019), and *Stargirl* (since 2020; also airing on The CW). The Warner-owned HBO Max eventually absorbed DC Universe in early 2021. This move – together with the simultaneous release of *Wonder Woman 1984* to theaters and HBO Max in December 2020, as well as the subsequent video-on-demand premiere of other blockbuster films – heralded an increasingly central role of streaming services for the future of the genre. This trend was further underscored by Disney's 2019 launch of its own streaming platform Disney+ – which, in turn, was preceded by Disney's acquisition of the 21st Century Fox corporation. The merger enabled Disney to add Fox's Marvel-based films (including the entries of the *X-Men* and *Fantastic Four* franchises) to its new streaming service and brought the rights to produce additional movies based on these properties back home to the (now Disney-owned) Marvel Entertainment. As noted earlier, Disney+ also hosted the online premiere of 2021's *Black Widow*, an event that was prefaced by the release of the newly-produced *MCU* television series *WandaVision*, *The Falcon and the Winter Soldier*, and *Loki* earlier that year.

Ultimately, the operation of their own streaming services put the Warner and Disney conglomerates into a privileged position at the onset of the COVID-19 pandemic. While the new imperatives of social distancing and at-home consumption soon compromised revenues from theatrical exhibition, platforms such as Disney+, HBO Max, Netflix, and Amazon Video continued to make a plethora of new and old superhero content available to viewers, thereby ensuring the enduring popularity of the genre. The history of superhero blockbuster cinema will thus undoubtedly continue after the end of the pandemic – but, by then, it will be closely tied to the profitability and proliferation of such video streaming services, which are bound to play an increasingly central role for the distribution of Hollywood films in the years to come.

CONCLUSION

From 1978's *Superman* to 2020's *Wonder Woman 1984* and 2021's *Black Widow*, the hyper-referential style of storytelling has been about capitalizing on viewers' memory of earlier superhero narratives as much as it has been about encouraging further media consumption. This project proceeded (and continues to proceed) through the employment of intertextual and intermedial references that index bodies of closely related media content. From the first wave's product tie-ins and vague references to unspecified serial prehistories, over the foregrounded referentiality and explicit fan-orientation of the second, to the quasi-hypertextual narrative universes of the third and fourth cycles, the evolution of the hyper-referential style has proceeded through the adoption of ever more demanding modes of serial storytelling, increasingly explicit attempts to encourage fannish reception practices, and, eventually, a close interlocking of films' storytelling strategies and paratextual online discourses. This trajectory is expressive of larger transformations within the capitalist mode of production since the beginning of the post-Fordist period. The four waves of superhero blockbuster cinema parallel the four decades of capitalist development that also witnessed the rise of digital and networked media, an increasing centrality of immaterial forms of labor, a new significance of intangible forms of property (such as trademarks, copyrights, or production licenses), and a reconfigured, increasingly Internet-based economy. I have suggested in the first chapter that these technological and economic changes were closely related to shifts in the ideological discourses and practices of capitalism's managerial class. The latter eventually embraced a new spirit of capitalism that, as Luc Boltanski and Ève Chiapello argue, calls for constant product innovation, attention to the demands of an internally diverse consumer base, a close monitoring of customer activity, and efforts to forge long-lasting relationships between producers and consumers. Superhero blockbuster cinema absorbed these lessons with some delay. But by the 2000s and 2010s, the entries of the genre had been reconfigured into potent cultural attractors that capitalized on the histories of serial unfolding that preceded them, sought to engage audiences over longer periods of time as well as across media, and tried to turn online discourses about the genre into positive externalities.

Thusly reconfigured, superhero blockbuster cinema first framed fannish modes of consumption as an ideal and then presupposed them as a new norm. In the twenty-first century, superhero movies could do so because the media and discourses of the fan-oriented online public made a plethora of information about the genre available to a potentially global audience of interested consumers. As result, anyone could become a fan – but even viewers who did not identify as fans often engaged in practices that have traditionally been associated with media fandom (such as computer-assisted close reading, the browsing of fan-sites, participation in discussions on social media, and so on). Superhero blockbusters released since the beginning of the second wave thus operated within a media environment that more generally eroded the distinction between fannish engagement and other reception practices. These developments were part of an emergent regime of digital-era popular culture that took on a new role in the organization of consumers' free time and recreational activity. Before the rise of the Internet as a generalized communications medium, audiences' cultural and textual production rarely factored into the business models of the big media conglomerates and their subsidiaries. But by the late 1990s, the diffusion of digital and networked media and the entrenchment of neoliberal policies had brought about a significant reconfiguration of the consumption-based model. Recreational media consumption and value-productive work now increasingly took place outside of dedicated localities and clearly delineated chunks of free time; simultaneously, the spread of digital and networked consumer electronics and the rise of transnational online publics turned audience discourses into a new kind of economic resource. Rather than functioning primarily as vehicles for the sale of commodities, superhero films (and other types of popular serial entertainment) now came to operate as potent tools for the mobilization of all kinds of attendant cultural activity – and the digital media environment of the early twenty-first century, in turn, transformed this activity into potentially value-productive forms of immaterial labor.

Cases such as *Infinity War* and *Endgame* notwithstanding, many entries of the genre remained open to less demanding modes of engagement. The genre's cinematic universes, for instance, accommodate occasional sojourns as much as they invite viewers to explore every nook and cranny of their storyworlds; likewise, several fourth-wave films featured a continued focus on self-contained central conflicts that were resolved by the end of the film. If post-Fordist capitalism, as David Harvey famously argues, is a regime of "flexible accumulation" (Harvey, "From Fordism" 147), then recent superhero blockbusters are perhaps best understood as remarkably flexible cultural commodities that can insert themselves into different modes of recreational media consumption, circulate via a variety of medial distribution channels, and prompt responses with diverse public discourses. Ultimately, this versatility and ability to connect were central to the genre's popularity during the first two decades of the twenty-first century – but whether this success story can continue remains to be seen.

NOTES

1. I here repeat some of the observations made in Brinker, "Transmedia" 220–21. For a similar discussion of this scene, see Vignold 81–2.
2. Leterrier's film is nonetheless *not* a direct continuation of an earlier story, as the narrative continuity of the film is separate from that of the TV series and unconnected to Ang Lee's *Hulk* (2003), the then most recent cinematic incarnation of the figure.
3. Gerard Genette defines intertextuality as "a relation of co-presence between two or more texts [. . .] the literal presence of one text within another" (quoted in Macksay XVIII). Understood in this general sense, intertextuality includes diverse modes of reference and connection between works. The intertextuality of the hyper-referential style is of a narrower sort, as it either involves references to superhero narratives which share a narrative continuity with the film that cites them, or references to other, closely related properties in larger non-linear serial proliferations.
4. Morton similarly discusses such approximations to the comics medium as a form of "stylistic remediation" (5). Devices employed to this end might include shot compositions that recreate specific comic book panels, an intentional use of colors, the casting of actors whose physiques approximate the muscle-clad bodies of comic book superheroes, and elements of costume, make-up, and set design that echo the look of iconic characters and locations (see Burke 178–227; 230–60; and my discussion below).
5. On linear and non-linear types of seriality, see Denson "Frankenstein" and my discussion in the preceding chapter.
6. The hyper-referential style can be understood as variant of a more wide-spread post-classical Hollywood style. On Hollywood's norms of narrative unity and coherence, see Bordwell, Thompson and Smith 98–100. Arguing against Bordwell and Thompson, Richard Maltby has suggested that "Hollywood's commercial aesthetic is too opportunistic to prize coherence, organic unity, or even the absence of contradiction" (Maltby 35). While Maltby's case is convincing, the films that employ the hyper-referential style are arguably more fragmented, modular, and intertextual than other Hollywood movies.
7. See Chapter 1. For an understanding of fan activity as highly engaged media consumption, see Pustz, "Comics and Fandom."
8. In this chapter, I use the terms "cycle" and "wave" synonymously, as shorthand for a group of thematically and stylistically closely related films that rely on the repetition and variation of similar scenarios, characters, and narrative schemata (see Kuhn and Westwell, "Cycle," "Superhero film"). For a superficially similar periodization of comic book film adaptations, see Burke 107–21.

9. See my discussion in the Introduction. For a discussion of transmedia storytelling and intertextuality in the *Matrix* franchise, see Jenkins, *Convergence Culture* 98–130.
10. Burton himself justified these differences with the need to appeal to a mass audience, noting that *Batman* was "too big a budget movie to worry about what a fan of a comic would say" (quoted in Uricchio and Pearson, 206; see Burke 131, 162). On Burton's *Batman*, see also Morton 54–61.
11. For a discussion of media franchising as serial cultural production, see also Johnson "Learning to Share" 9–19, and my discussion in the Introduction.
12. DC Comics has been part of the Warner conglomerate since 1972 (see Gabilliet 62). The corporate structure of the Warner conglomerate has been re-organized several times since then; today, DC Comics is a subsidiary of Warner Bros. Entertainment Inc. (the studio formerly known as Warner Bros. Pictures), which itself is a subsidiary of WarnerMedia.
13. On the "toyetic" appeal of the Batman films, see Owczarski 142–47. For a discussion of the various tie-ins to Burton's *Batman* and product placement within the film, see Meehan; for a discussion of comic book tie-ins to Donner's *Superman*, see Meier 120–22. On the significance of superhero logos, see Brooker 80; Uricchio and Pearson 230–31; Hassler-Forest 78–86.
14. Cucco contrasts this focus on short-term revenues with the distribution strategies common during Hollywood's classical period, which "followed a hierarchical structure: first, the film came out in the most important theaters in the main towns, then in the secondary ones (where the tickets were cheaper), moving progressively from the biggest towns to country and suburban areas. This process could last up to a whole year" (221; see also Kelleter and Loock 134–35).
15. On the negative reception of *Batman & Robin*, see Gray 131–32; Owczarski 145–47; Burke 136.
16. For discussions of this period in the history of Marvel Entertainment, see Johnson, "Will" 66–72; Burke 58–59, 72–73; Flanagan, McKenny, and Livingstone 67–71; Vignold 57–60.
17. On serial storytelling in the films of the *X-Men* franchise, see also Vignold 45–55; Rauscher, "Marvel Universe on Screen."
18. On the distinction between A-plots and B-plots, see Newman.
19. For a comparison of the two media along similar lines, see McCloud 7–8; McLuhan 24; 310–23.
20. Like other Marvel films, *Daredevil* also features a brief cameo by long-time Marvel Comics editor Stan Lee. For a discussion of Lee's cameos, see Jeffries.
21. Gardner here refers to a 2011 report on domestic American comics sales; Burke makes a similar case about comic book sales around the turn to the twenty-first century (Burke 132).
22. At the time of writing, *AICN* is one of the oldest fan-oriented websites still in operation. Knowles ran the site until 2017, when he resigned following allegations of sexual assault; the site is now run by his sister Dannie Knowles.
23. For overviews on the company's licensing and film production practices during the 2000s and 2010s, see Flanagan, McKenny, and Livingstone; Johnson, "Cinematic"; Vignold 56–73.
24. After abandoning plans for additional sequels to *The Amazing Spider-Man*, Sony – which had also produced *Ghost Rider* (2007) and *Ghost Rider: Spirit of Vengeance* (2011) – did not release another superhero film until 2017, when it joined forces with the Disney-owned Marvel to make *Spider-Man: Homecoming*. Lionsgate and Universal abandoned their plans for further Marvel-based films after the relative commercial failures of *Hulk* (2003) and *Punisher: War Zone* (2008), respectively.

25. This discussion of the *MCU*'s serialization strategies (up until the consideration of hypertextual structures) expands on arguments made earlier in Brinker, "Transmedia" and repeats some of the ideas developed there.
26. While most of *Captain America: The First Avenger*'s narrative is set during World War II, the film is not, strictly speaking, an exception to the linear temporality of the *MCU*'s cinematic arm, as its core events are framed as an analepsis by scenes set in the early-twenty-first-century timeframe of the other films.
27. For the sake of brevity, my discussion of the *MCU*'s transmedial spread here disregards the numerous comic-book tie-ins to the franchise, which encompass both new narratives set within the franchise's shared storyworld and reprints of classic stories.
28. On *The Winter Soldier*, see Chapter 5. The relevant episodes of *Agents of S.H.I.E.L.D.* are "T.A.H.I.T.I.," "Yes Men," "End of the Beginning," "Turn, Turn, Turn," "Providence," "The Only Light in the Darkness," "Nothing Personal," "Ragtag," and "Beginning of the End."
29. The *Marvel One-Shots* encompass the shorts *The Consultant* (included on the *Thor* Blu-ray), *A Funny Thing Happened on the Way to Thor's Hammer* (included on the *Captain America: The First Avenger* release), *Item 47* (bonus content for *Marvel's The Avengers*), *Agent Carter* (*Iron Man 3*), and *All Hail the King* (*Thor: The Dark World*). Aside from expanding the storyworld, the *One-Shots* served to test the waters for future installments of the franchise: The positive reception of the *Item 47* and *Agent Carter* shorts, for example, informed Marvel Studios' green-lighting ABC's *Agents of S.H.I.E.L.D.* and *Agent Carter* (see Breznican). For a longer discussion of the *One-Shots*, see Graves.
30. In this respect, the *MCU* is typical of transmedial serial narratives of the digital era, which, as Denson and Sudmann note, frequently invite the "piecemeal exploration of singular, more or less coherent worlds that span the borders of various media [. . .] while simultaneously exhibiting a high degree of formal openness with regards to the narrative order of texts, thus allowing for a variable order of consumption" (Denson and Sudmann 265).
31. The iTunes store added video in the fall of 2005; Amazon and Netflix started their streaming services in 2006 and 2007, respectively.
32. The label *DCEU* is not officially used by Warner and its subsidiaries. Coined by *Entertainment Weekly* writer Keith Staskiewicz in 2015, the name has nonetheless been adopted by fan-cultural discourses and press coverage of the franchise (see Auger; Staskiewicz).
33. Of these three, *Birds of Prey* was released in February, before the pandemic prompted lockdowns in the US and other Western countries. *New Mutants* was released to theaters in August. All three films generated box-office returns that were small in comparison to those of superhero movies released during the preceding years.
34. Marvel Studios announced the production of and release dates for *Thor: Ragnarok* and *Avengers: Infinity War* in October 2014; *Age of Ultron* premiered to domestic US-American theaters in May 2015 (Siegel).
35. For exemplary reaction from *io9*, see Lussier, "Thanks," "After Avengers," "Mark Ruffalo"; Pulliam-Moore, "Why Do You Hurt Us," "Report"; Muncy, "The Russo Brothers".
36. The Netflix shows occasionally reference the events and characters of the feature films in dialogues and through details hidden in the mise-en-scène, but refrain from making more explicit connections. During the years of the fourth wave, the *MCU* also added the ABC television series *Agent Carter* (2015–16) and *Inhumans* (2017), the Hulu shows *Runaways* (2017–19) and *Helstrom* (2020), as well as Freeform's *Cloak & Dagger* (2018–19).

37. These included several additions to the so-called *Arrowverse* – a shared televisual universe of shows based on DC comics characters that began with The CW's *Arrow* (2012–20) and which, starting with *The Flash* (since 2014), added five additional live-action series and two animated web-series until the end of 2020. Other DC-based productions by Warner include the popular *Gotham* (Fox, 2014–19) and the short-lived *Constantine* (NBC, 2014), *Powerless* (NBC, 2017), and *Krypton* (SyFy, 2018–19).

CHAPTER 4

The Superhero Blockbuster as Fan Management

James Mangold's *Logan* (2017), the tenth entry in Fox's *X-Men* series and the final installment of a trilogy about the mutant Wolverine, is a film about exhaustion – of bodies, lives, and the ability to tell an innovative story about a superhero who can overcome virtually every obstacle. Set in a dystopian near future in which most mutants have been killed by a genetically engineered plague, Mangold's film has Wolverine (also known as Logan, played by Hugh Jackman) caring for a senile and frail Professor X (Patrick Stewart). To make ends meet, the protagonist has picked up work as a limousine driver, ferrying unpleasant strangers along and across the Texas/Mexico border. This joyless occupation is made more burdensome by the fact that he is slowly dying from Adamantium poisoning, since his self-healing powers have lost their former potency. As result, the 197-year-old Logan is now a mere shadow of himself, constantly tired and self-medicating with cheap alcohol. Underscoring this depiction of the superhero as a burn-out, Mangold's film repeatedly shows its protagonist getting hurt, struggling to regain his posture despite injury, falling asleep, or drifting in and out of consciousness. The camera repeatedly lingers on close-ups of his face, its deep wrinkles, graying beard, and prominent battle scars. The theme of exhaustion resonates with the struggle against the conventions of superhero blockbuster cinema that more generally informs Mangold's film. Where other superhero movies tell family-friendly stories about hyper-competent protagonists, including action scenes that are violent but rarely graphic and culminate in spectacular displays of world-saving heroism, *Logan* features a liberal use of profane language, numerous displays of graphic violence, and a showdown that is decidedly small-scale. The film also takes aim at the conceit of the super-powered hero itself. One hour into the film, the protagonist discovers two issues of the *X-Men* comic book owned

Figure 4.1 In 2017's *Logan*, Wolverine (Hugh Jackman) finds an *X-Men* comic book – a moment that self-reflexively addresses fans' investment in the conventions of the genre. Screengrab from Amazon Prime Video.

by mutant girl Laura (Dafne Keen) and breaks out into an annoyed rant: "You do know they're all bullshit, right? . . . In the real world, people die and no self-promoting asshole in a fucking leotard can stop it!" (*Logan* 0:56:21–57:03; see Figure 4.1). In a final divergence from generic conventions, the film ends with the hero succumbing to his injuries, dying, and being buried somewhere in the Canadian wilderness. Where preceding *X-Men* films put Wolverine's superhuman ability to recover from injury prominently on display, *Logan* lays him to rest – but not without re-affirming the protagonist's status as a selfless hero. During the film's final act, Wolverine sacrifices his life to defend a group of mutant children against evil pursuers. Letting the character go out with a final heroic act, Mangold's film ultimately presents itself as a solemn swan song for a perennially youthful character whose actor was slowly but surely aging out of the role.

However, the film's break with conventions did not occur in a medial vacuum. By the time of its theatrical release, a several-year-long online marketing campaign had already spread the message about the film's unconventionality through a variety of media channels. Rumors about Jackman's impending departure from the Wolverine role had been circulating since the film's official announcement in late March of 2014 and were eventually confirmed in the spring of 2015 by a message posted to the actors' personal Instagram account (Jackman; see also Schaefer; Gilman; McMillan, "Hugh"; Perry). Prompting a flurry of responses, Jackman's post kicked off an extensive promotional campaign that utilized a variety of social media platforms to generate interest in the upcoming film. As part of this campaign, a 2015 tweet by Jackman's account asked users what they expected from Wolverine's last outing. This request yielded thousands of suggestions, with many users advocating for a more violent and adult take on the character (see "Hugh Jackman"; Bell, "Here's What Fans Want"; Kocharekar). During the following two years, public awareness was maintained by a steady drip-feed of production news and anticipatory media coverage that highlighted the film's status as the final chapter in the actor's seventeen-year-long association with the franchise (for examples, see Pao; Truitt; Opam). Picking up steam after the end of principal photography, the film's marketing campaign released a teaser poster and a series of meticulously staged black-and-white production stills that highlighted the film's "grown-up" aesthetic sensibilities in the fall of 2016 (see Holub "Boyd," "Hugh," "'Logan'"). Over the following months, interviews with *Logan*'s cast, director, and screenwriters continued to emphasize the film's difference from other superhero movies: its serious tone, R-rated violence, and Western-influenced cinematography (see Chitwood, "Wolverine 3"; White; Collura; Gettell; Coggan). Finally, *Logan*'s adult orientation was also on display in a series of promotional trailers that framed the film as a somber and violent affair.[1] When *Logan* premiered in the spring of 2017, 20th Century Fox and its marketing partners had thus already pitched the film as an atypical or unorthodox entry of the genre. This positioning was eventually echoed in reviews of the film as well, many of which stressed its "genuine and special" status within the genre (Hatchett), its "arthouse" ambitions (Lussier, "*Logan*"), and its "brutal, gory violence" (Cerny, "Logan").[2]

The *Logan* example accentuates a dimension of superhero blockbusters' politics of engagement that this chapter discusses as a project of "fan management." Playing out at the intersection of marketing efforts, online discourses, fan activity, and films' narrative and aesthetic practices, fan management entails the purposeful employment of textual and extra-textual means to enroll and secure the support of online fandom. Targeting the participants and institutions of a fan-oriented media public, fan management is at work both within superhero blockbusters and across a variety of paratextual discourses that accompany and promote the respective films before, during, and after their theatrical runs. Informed by producers' and marketers' close attention to the opinions of professional and non-professional consumers, fan management practices seek to insert cultural-industrial products (such as superhero blockbuster films) into the discourses of the online fan public and tries to generate publicity for the respective commodity. On a textual level, this project expresses itself in attempts to signal a fidelity to the spirit and style of comic book source materials. But fan management also encompasses efforts to incorporate topics, motifs, and attitudes from fannish discourses into superhero movies and the marketing campaigns that promote them. Such attempts to "speak the language" of online fandom express themselves, for example, in the form of inside jokes, in self-reflexive commentary on the state of the superhero genre, or in attempts to distance films from other releases. Fan management is also on display in the prominent role that actors and filmmakers take on for films' marketing campaigns. In the case of *Logan*, for instance, Jackman's personal involvement and the use of his social media accounts not only signaled a responsiveness to audience demands, but also effectively constructed an image of the star as an approachable everyman who himself was a fan of the material.[3] In this manner, *Logan*'s marketing team could frame the film as a product for fans made by fans and articulate a concept of fannish community that included consumers alongside stars, directors, and producers. This chapter argues that such a sensitivity to the interests of online fan cultures is expressive of – that is, both symptomatic of and productive for – more widespread corporate attempts to generate a high volume of online discursive activity about superhero blockbuster films. This discursive activity, in turn, not only increases the overall cultural visibility of specific films, but also delineates a trajectory for audience engagement that bridges the gaps between theatrical releases. Yet, at their most basic, fan management practices seek to harness the unpaid immaterial labor of media audiences to generate a positive "buzz" about specific cultural commodities and create a hospitable discursive environment for them. Fan management practices thus exemplify both the engagement-centric paradigm of twenty-first-century popular culture and digital capitalism's attempts at exploiting economically productive cultural externalities.

This chapter argues that practices of fan management have become increasingly central to the commercial success of recent superhero blockbusters. Essentially a strategy to generate visibility within the competitive media landscape of the digital era, fan management seeks to shape public opinion about the blockbuster films in a manner that supports the profit-interest of producers and film studios. But since fan management practices often precede the theatrical release of feature films, they can also be understood as a tool to generate and shape audience demand. In that sense, fan management practices such as the ones discussed above can be understood as strategic interventions in the discourses of online fandom; these begin well before films make it to theaters and help to prepare the ground for their reception by the fan public. The means employed towards this end include strategies of marketing and promotion that are also used to promote other types of films. Niccolò Gallio, for example, points out that Hollywood movies have been advertised with the help of immersive transmedia experiences and web-based marketing campaigns since the late 1990s and that the "standard promotional plan for blockbusters" during the mid-2010s included "digital tie-in platforms" that offered "different entry points to the story" (Gallio 23; 19–24; compare Burke 154). Fan management combines such online marketing practices with the explicit fan-orientation typical of twenty-first-century superhero movies.

To make this case, the main part of this chapter discusses two case-studies from the fourth wave of superhero blockbuster cinema: the Tim Miller-directed

Deadpool (Fox, 2016; like *Logan*, the film is part of the *X-Men* franchise) and David Ayer's *Suicide Squad* (2016; part of Warner's *DC Extended Universe*). Like *Logan*, both films foreground their difference from other titles by playing up the more idiosyncratic elements of their source materials – juvenile humor and self-reflexive tendencies in the case of *Deadpool*, and a perspectival shift that turns supervillains into protagonists in the case of *Suicide Squad*. Interestingly, however, the fan management practices employed for these two films yielded decidedly different outcomes. While the marketing efforts for *Deadpool* managed to enroll the support of fans to rescue an abortive project from development hell and helped turn it into a positively reviewed and highly profitable film, the heavily promoted *Suicide Squad* generated a generally negative critical response and underperformed at the box-office. The main part of this chapter examines how, in both cases, practices of fan management played out across marketing campaigns and the films themselves. It also explores how these practices succeeded or failed to mobilize fan support. Finally, the conclusion considers the entangled cinematic afterlives of the films discussed in this chapter. But before examining these examples, I now turn to the conceptual foundations of my inquiry.

CONCEPTUALIZING FAN MANAGEMENT

As noted in the first chapter, corporate attempts to target and capitalize on fans and their activities are hardly new. The producers of American comic books, for example, began to promote official fan clubs during the 1940s and continued to court fan audiences during the following decades. Starting in the mid-1990s, a convergence of economic, media-technological, and ideological shifts eventually ushered in a general reconceptualization of the figure of the media fan. Such fans were now imagined as an ideal type of consumer who not only spent more money on popular entertainments than other, less engaged consumers, but also engaged in socially communicative practices that producers and marketers could exploit for promotional gain. Fan studies scholarship has since recognized this shift in the corporate valuation of fannish activity as well. Matt Hills's 2002 book *Fan Cultures*, for example, notes that the fans of cult television series such as *Doctor Who* (BBC, since 1963) have long been the target of "niche marketing" practices that strive to "reflect authentic values of fan culture back to the fan" (19). For Hills, such practices include the production and sale of explicitly fan-oriented content such as tie-in novels, audio dramas, and various kinds of merchandise (*Fan Cultures* 12–13). Quoting a 1994 article by Virginia Nightingale, Hills characterizes such targeting of fans as a type of "managerial activity" that accommodates "the quixotic preoccupations" of fan audiences to cultivate a loyal customer base for specialized niche products (Nightingale 124;

quoted in Hills, *Fan Cultures* 19). Mel Stanfill's 2020 study *Exploiting Fandom* similarly suggests that the entertainment industries' courting of fans can be understood as part of a "system of management" that seeks to encourage and normalize specific kinds of highly engaged fan activity (pos. 222). Stanfill, who also uses the terminology of fan management, acknowledges the active role that recent industry discourse assigns to fans – who are no longer just viewed as loyal consumers, but conceptualized as highly engaged media users who actively promote their favorite entertainments. Echoing arguments made by Henry Jenkins and others, Stanfill argues that fan activity on social media functions as "promotional labor" that generates visibility for cultural commodities and that producers generally encourage such activity to generate "buzz, sharing, and free advertising" (pos. 2572). Stanfill also points out that the business models of today's online marketing firms are often built around the concept of "fan distribution" and the production of content that is meant to be recirculated by members of the audience (pos. 2629; compare 2606). Offering a slightly different take on the fan-orientation of recent Hollywood blockbusters, Aaron Taylor has used the term "cultic management" as shorthand for the "strategic co-option of potentially unruly niche audiences" by Hollywood filmmakers who adapt, remake, or otherwise reiterate popular source materials with already established fan bases (Taylor, "Avengers" 181; see also Taylor, "How to See"). In particular, Taylor suggests that Hollywood films often include "symbolic placatory gestures" that are meant to authenticate themselves in the eyes of informed consumers ("Avengers" 181). For Taylor, such gestures include the hiring of directors associated with other cult properties and the casting of lead actors who can plausibly perform a fan identity, as well as the borrowing of storytelling strategies, plot elements, and iconic imagery from well-liked source materials (190–92).

Hills's, Stanfill's, and Taylor's discussions of corporate attempts to capitalize on fan activities provide good starting points to understand the phenomena discussed here. But the strong emphasis on the role of fannish consumers – who, in the work cited above, either serve as the target of niche marketing practices, take on the role of cultural "gatekeepers" (Taylor, "Avengers" 182) whose opinions shape a more general public opinion, or act as unpaid workers who promote and market commercially produced content – downplays the role of other actors who also participate in the media hype that accompanies the theatrical run of blockbuster films. I have argued in the preceding chapters that the practices of fannish consumers account only for part of the cultural activity that clusters around superhero movies. In particular, the influence of fans is dwarfed by that of commercially operated online publications such as *Ain't It Cool News/AICN*, *ComicBookResources*, *comicbookmovie*, *Nerdist*, and others. These act as central nodes for the promotion of new releases in the genre, recirculate official promotional materials, and provide a space for fan discussion and the spreading of rumors about upcoming releases. Importantly, however, the gradual mainstreaming of fan culture since the late 1990s has made the distinction between fan-oriented publications and the mainstream press more and more difficult, as some traditional news media have begun to cover similar subject-matter as well. The responses to the *Logan* marketing campaign cited at the beginning of this chapter, for example, range from reports and reviews by traditional news organizations such as the BBC, *The Daily Mail*, *USA Today*, and the *Los Angeles Times*, over pieces published by entertainment news outlets such as *The Hollywood Reporter* and *Entertainment Weekly*, to posts on more narrowly fan-oriented websites such as *SuperHeroHype*, *The Mary Sue*, and *io9*. What I discuss as fan management is thus not a niche marketing practice exclusively aimed at fannish consumers. Rather, it targets a diffuse fan-oriented media public than includes fans in the traditional sense of the term as well as traditional news media, fan-sites catering to niche audiences, and different groups of professional consumers who write about popular culture for a living (such as reviewers, critics, and, to a lesser extent, academics).

Fan management can also be understood as a set of practices that seeks to turn the theatrical runs of superhero movies into temporally expansive media events that begin before films make it to theaters and come to an end as films move to secondary markets for home video. In making this case, I draw on Hills recent discussion of "unfolding media events," which suggests that paratextual materials play a central role for the generation of "hype [. . .] within media culture" (*Doctor Who* 26). For Hills, unfolding events encompass "an array of textual and paratextual materials that follow an inter-related (and sometimes contingently delayed or rescheduled) release chronology" (*Doctor Who* 25). The theatrical runs of blockbuster movies are unfolding events in this sense, as they not only take place over longer periods of time, but they are also preceded and accompanied by large-scale marketing efforts that render a "lack of knowledge about [the films'] existence virtually impossible" (Stringer 1). Hills furthermore stresses that paratextual promotional materials invariably leave their mark on the reception of the commodities they promote – by establishing a connection to earlier iterations of the same intellectual property, evoking the memory of other texts, or shaping consumers' expectations of things to come, for example (*Doctor Who* 11–25; for a similar argument, see Gray *Show Sold Separately*).

For Hills, media events are generally defined by an "unfolding temporality of anticipation and remembrance" that begins well before the eventual "event" itself and continues after its core elements have already played out (24):

> The unfolding event [. . .] follows a hermeneutic arc [. . .] which exceeds any one text – it is prefigured via audience expectations and producer-audience interactions, configured via an array of (para)textual

materials, and subsequently refigured by audience understandings and further producer-audience exchanges, as well as by forms of cultural recognition (reviews, features, awards). (25)

The fan management practices that interest me here similarly unfold across both time and paratextual materials. They also play out within superhero movies themselves, which have to live up to the hype and promotional narratives that precede them. The serial prehistories of superhero blockbuster films – which often are only the latest iterations of intellectual properties that have been the basis for other narratives in film, comics, and other media before – play an important role here as well.

What I call fan management can thus be understood as a set of interlocking marketing, public relations, and filmmaking practices that seek to turn superhero blockbuster films into highly visible media events. Such events usually germinate within the discourses of online fandom, but ideally radiate out into a wider media public and thereby increase films' chance of commercial success. At its most basic, fan management seeks to generate cultural visibility and positive media attention for the commodities it tries to promote. To do so, it seeks to enroll the support of other (professional and non-professional) actors that can carry forth or amplify its message. This project is thus predicated on the cooperation of fannish consumers, fan-oriented publications, and other actors within the fan-oriented online public. These actors, however, are not ignorant about the commercial interests that operate on the various levels of superhero fan culture. In fact, a realist attitude about the profit-orientation of film studios and an awareness of efforts to enroll the support of fans are well represented within fan discourses.[4] To further complicate things, fan audiences are internally diverse and not at all united in their stance towards specific genres, franchises, series, or films. As result, the professional and non-professional consumers targeted by fan management practices are at least potentially unruly and not always willing to lend their support. Moreover, Frank Kelleter and Daniel Stein point out that superhero comics properties often inspire "authorization conflicts" over the legitimacy of corporate claims to specific stories and characters (Kelleter and Stein, 260–61; my translation). Fueled by a fannish sense of ownership and expertise, such conflicts pit well-informed consumers against profit-oriented producers and often play out within the discourses of the online fan public – and thus across the same media, platforms, and publications that marketers target to promote their products. Corporate efforts to manage fan discourses thus do not take place "behind the back" of easily duped audiences and should not be misunderstood as some sort of hidden manipulation. Rather, fan management occurs in plain view of the audience; it involves the navigation of various lines of conflict within online fandom, attention to the competing demands of professional and non-professional consumers, as well as a balancing of economic imperatives and the practical realities of the filmmaking process. Fan management can thus be understood as a potentially conflictual effort that, like other elements of superhero blockbuster cinema's politics of engagement, does not always achieve its desired outcome.

Since fan management hinges on the ability of producers, filmmakers, and marketers to engage with the discourses of online fandom, it is difficult to conceptualize within a traditional cultural studies framework that remains committed to a binary view of unruly and potentially anti-consumerist media audiences, on the one hand, and a profit-driven culture industry, on the other.[5] Arguing against such a view, Frank Kelleter and Daniel Stein note that "commercial mass communications" have a tendency to cause "a proliferation of, and competition between, competencies and responsibilities, roles and self-identifications" (260, my translation; see also Taylor, "Avengers" 183). In general, this tendency complicates clear-cut distinctions between "producers" and "consumers," "fans" and "creators." As Stein emphasizes elsewhere, long-running serial narratives often "blur such distinctions by variously turning producers into consumers, authors into readers, and vice versa":

> If you want to write, say, an authoritative Batman story at the beginning of the twenty-first century, you have to be knowledgeable about the history of the series, its position within the superhero genre, its transmedial extensions, and so forth. Which means: You essentially have to be a dedicated reader of Batman stories in order to become a competent author. And for many such a reader a personal investment with the series motivates different forms of authorship outside the sphere of professional cultural production, from fan letters and fan fiction to the editing of fanzines, the drawing of amateur comics, the presentation of criticism on Internet blogs, and more – all of which may, in one way or another, feed back into official comic book production. (Stein 134–35)

Stein's observations not only apply to many of the corporate actors involved in the making of superhero movies, but also to journalists and critics who cover news and developments in the genre for fan-oriented and mainstream press publications. Fannish dedication and expertise are, in other words, not an exclusive preserve of the consumption side of popular culture but dispersed across the different fields and levels of practice that produce and sustain the superhero blockbuster as a cultural phenomenon. The remainder of this chapter will nonetheless continue to use terms such as "fans," "fannish consumers," "professional consumers," "corporate actors," and "producers" to discuss practices of fan management. Yet, in doing so, I do not wish to suggest that these terms are mutually exclusive. Instead, they refer to roles that people, at different moments, occupy within a larger culture-industrial system. These roles are not equally accessible to everyone (that is, not every fan can turn their engagement with superhero culture into a job that pays), but some people do, in fact, occupy several of these roles at the same time.

FAN MANAGEMENT AND THE MANY LIVES OF DEADPOOL

After being stuck in development for more than a decade, Fox's *Deadpool* gained a new lease of life on July 27, 2014, when a clip of computer-animated test footage was leaked to the Internet.[6] Originally created by director Tim Miller's animation company Blur as a proof-of-concept and presented to Fox executives sometime between the summer of 2011 and the end of 2012, the clip features a wisecracking Deadpool addressing the camera, jumping from a highway overpass onto a speeding SUV, killing all of its villainous passengers, and causing a crash that propels the vehicle into the air ("Deadpool Leaked Footage"). Barely two minutes long, the footage showcased what Miller, screenwriters Rhett Reese and Paul Wernick, and star Ryan Reynolds (who provided voice work for the clip) envisioned for their film: an emphasis on self-aware yet juvenile humor, fast-paced action, and gratuitous violence. In doing so, the footage also crystallized key reasons for Fox's hesitance to green-light the project, as it pitched a movie whose intended R-rating and association with Reynolds – who had starred in the commercially under-performing *Green Lantern* (2011) and portrayed a significantly different version of Deadpool in the critically panned *X-Men Origins: Wolverine* (2009) before – made it an inherently risky venture (see Kit, "Did Deadpool"). Had it not leaked, the footage would have remained a little-known detail about a long-simmering project that seemed to pick up steam after the first Wolverine film, but never entered an official production phase.[7] Once released online, however, the clip spread quickly through platforms such as YouTube or Dailymotion and soon attracted the attention of websites such as *SuperHeroHype*, *Ain't It Cool News* (*AICN*), *io9*, and *The Daily Dot*, where it generated a significant amount of user commentary. Responding to the emerging media buzz, Fox announced the production of *Deadpool* a week later, fast-tracking the film for a February 2016 release (see Burlingame; Pollard).

At first glance, the *Deadpool* case seems to exemplify the participatory logics of digital-era popular culture discussed by Henry Jenkins and others. Viewed from that perspective, the positive reception of the leaked footage appears as the fundamentally democratic articulation of a fannish volonté générale that, because of fandom's newly gained influence within a wider online public, prompted a response by corporate actors (see Chapter 1). However, while it might be tempting to subscribe to such a reading, it is worth emphasizing that, in the case of *Deadpool*, the participation of non-professional consumers remained restricted to the public articulation of opinions about professionally produced test footage. By early 2014, the development stages for *Deadpool* had largely been completed; accordingly, users who voiced their approval of the clip were hardly in a position to provide meaningful input to a film that merely lacked the final confirmation and budget allocation to enter production.[8] Rather than as prelude to a collective participation in the multi-layered and extensive decision-making processes of studio executives, producers, and filmmakers, the *Deadpool* leak is better understood as a crowd-sourced test screening that allowed the studio to better assess the risks associated with an already developed project. The leak's successful mobilization of online fandom not only generated considerable amount of media attention for an already developed project, but also indicated the existence of a loyal fanbase whose members might be willing to see a *Deadpool* film in theaters. Both factors suddenly turned the making of the film – which, with a production budget of fifty-eight million US-dollars, ended up considerably cheaper than other entries of the genre – into a reasonable proposition.

The leaked *Deadpool* test footage also provides an illustrative example for the kind of "symbolic placatory gestures" discussed by Taylor, as the clip features a version of Deadpool that is closely patterned after the figure's comic book incarnations. Originally created by artist Rob Liefeld and writer Fabian Nicieza for a 1991 issue of the *X-Men* spin-off series *The New Mutants*, Deadpool (also known as Wade Wilson) was initially introduced as a quipping anti-hero whose "sarcastic, abrasive personality" was meant to "counter [. . .] the stoicism and machismo of so many of the other characters in the book" (Nicieza, quoted in Lussier, "The Unlikely Origins"). Deadpool subsequently returned as a series regular in several different Marvel titles, where he evolved into a self-reflexive character who was fond of addressing the reader directly.[9] The leaked test footage establishes a close affinity to this later, medially self-aware version of the character. Not coincidentally, the clip opens with a direct address to the camera and a joke about the protagonists iconic red-and-black costume. It then proceeds to put other defining aspects of the character – such as his martial arts prowess and ability to heal from any kind of physical injury, as well as his penchant for snide remarks and over-the-top violence – prominently on display. Just as significant as these elements, however, is that this version of Deadpool is notably different from the one that Reynolds portrayed in *X-Men Origins: Wolverine*. While the earlier film included a subplot about a wisecracking Wade Wilson and his transformation into a super-powered assassin, it also turned the character into a mute and brainwashed killer, a turn of events that contributed to the generally poor reception of *X-Men Origins* within online fandom.[10] The clip's inclusion of a Deadpool that hewed closer to its comic book counterpart thus constituted a direct response to the negative reception of *X-Men Origins*. Accordingly, informed fans could read the test footage as an attempt to repair the damage caused by the earlier film.

On the fan-oriented websites that recirculated the clip, Miller, Reese, Wernick, and Reynolds's take on the character nonetheless occasioned a range of different responses. Paid contributors to fan-sites, for instance, tended to frame the clip as the well-made leftover from an abortive project that should have merited the support of its studio. Along these lines, *io9*'s Rob Bricken called the clip "heartbreakingly perfect" ("Ryan Reynolds"), while *The Mary Sue*'s Dan Van Winkle suggested that the footage as "will make you wish this were a real movie you could go see" ("Deadpool").[11] Regular users, however, expressed a more diverse set of opinions. On *AICN*, for instance, user commentary included measured praise ("They definitively got it more right [. . .] than they did in the Wolverine movie") and enthusiastic responses ("the Deadpool I've been waiting 10 years to see"; "Hey FOX! My friends and I would all pay money to see a two-hour R rated version of this"), as well as outright rejection ("Deadpool? More like Deadpoop"; "Bad CGI and bad jokes. I can see why the studio passed on this"; "This is C-level Deadpool") and critical takes that suspected a carefully orchestrated "viral marketing" stunt (Oliver). Despite these disagreements, the clip still generated enough traffic and user activity to bring the long-simmering *Deadpool* project back into the public spotlight.

The official marketing campaign for *Deadpool*, which began soon after the film's production had been confirmed by Fox, continued to foreground the self-reflexive humor and fannish expertise that was already on display in the leaked test footage. The campaign was kicked off in March 2015 with a promotional image posted to Reynolds's Twitter account. Showing the actor in costume on a bear-skin rug in front of a fireplace, the image echoed a 1972 *Cosmopolitan* nude spread of Burt Reynolds – and thus used an obscure intertextual reference to a joke about the long production history of the film.[12] Over the course of the following months, the *Deadpool* marketing team continued to dole out other, often similarly irreverent and self-reflexive promotional materials – including several short video clips features Reynolds in costume, as well as poster art and conceptual design sketches, on-set photos and film stills – across a variety of platforms.[13] In July, the marketing campaign continued with a widely publicized *Deadpool*-themed panel and advance premiere of the film's trailer at San Diego Comic Con.[14] The trailer, which was officially released in early August, included several shots that resembled moments from leaked test footage (which itself was based on a scene from the first act of Reese and Wernick's script), thereby linking *Deadpool*'s upcoming theatrical premiere directly to the media buzz that had rescued the project from development hell a year before. Notably, the release of the first trailer was preceded by a short "trailer trailer" that announced the release of a Deadpool feature "from the studio that inexplicably sowed his fucking mouth shut the first time" (for exemplary coverage, see Dornbusch) and succeeded by a second trailer that highlighted the film's one-liners and supporting characters. Designed for viral circulation on video platforms, social media, and fan-oriented websites, these contents were accompanied by more conventional promotional efforts that included movie posters, billboards, TV spots, press releases, and interviews with news media, as well as appearances by the film's stars on late-night talk shows. During the same period, these efforts were further paralleled by activities on Ryan Reynolds's social media accounts, which actively promoted the film among the actors' followers as well.

Covering a wide range of different media and formats, the marketing efforts for *Deadpool* highlight a dimension of audience engagement that precedes the reception of feature films. They also call attention to the symbiotic relationship that exists between superhero blockbuster films and fan-oriented websites. The materials released as part of the *Deadpool* marketing campaign bridged the period between the leak of the test footage and the film's premiere and delineated a path that interested fans could trace from social media across various websites to a movie theater near them. On the one hand, users who followed this trajectory created page-views and traffic for the commercially operated sites and services that recirculated the official marketing materials for the film. On the other hand, the same users also increased the visibility of the marketing materials themselves, as well as of the film that was promoted by them.

By consistently presenting *Deadpool* as beholden to the spirit of (a particular iteration of) its comic book source material, the marketing campaign furthermore shaped the audience expectations that eventually had to be met by the film itself. Accordingly, the movie that premiered on February 12, 2016, went to great lengths to present itself as finely attuned to the discourses of the online fan public. This orientation is already on display in its opening sequence, which superimposes the film's titles over a tracking shot that moves through a frozen-in-time moment from the car crash first seen in the leaked footage (*Deadpool* 0:00:24–02:30). Set to the sounds of Juice Newton's 1981 pop-rock single "Angel of the Morning," the sequence begins within the interior of the car, with the camera capturing a glowing-red cigarette lighter suspended in mid-air. Subsequently, the camera tracks slowly through the rest of the vehicle, across the pain-stricken face of one of its passengers, a coffee cup (labeled as belonging to "Rob L.") spilling its contents, a gun being fired by someone outside the frame, and the cover page of a 2010 issue of *People Magazine* that promotes Ryan Reynolds's status as the "Sexiest Man Alive." Without a cut, the camera then passes through the metal frame of the car to its exterior, circling around a body being catapulted onto the street and capturing a glimpse of a *Green Lantern* trading card (depicting Reynolds in costume as the eponymous hero) that appears to be falling out of the passenger's wallet.

The shot then returns us to the interior of the vehicle, where it reveals that a costumed Deadpool is both assaulting the driver and grabbing the underpants of another man. Finally, the camera moves outside the car again and the sequence ends with a panoramic view of the entire crash (Figure 4.2). The camera's focus on minute details and its slow, spiraling movement through digitally generated space position the spectator as a distanced observer who can marvel at the immaculately staged crash, a perspective that echoes that of an attentive reader of comic books, who can similarly linger on moments that seem frozen in time.[15] With its reference to Deadpool co-creator Rob Liefeld (via the coffee cup) and its nods to significant stages in Reynolds's career, the sequence furthermore signals an in-depth familiarity with the discourses of an online fan culture, summarizing and condensing key talking points about film into a visually appealing tableau. In doing so, *Deadpool*'s very first moments both authenticate the film as a product informed by fannish expertise and evoke the look and feel of the comics medium.

Just as crucially, however, the opening sequence also serves as the backdrop for a self-depreciating joke that is articulated in the sequence's superimposed titles. The titles begin with the names of the studios that made the film, but are soon revealed as a commentary on the conventions of the superhero genre:

> Twentieth Century Fox Presents – In Association with Marvel Entertainment – Some Douchebag's Film – Starring God's Perfect Idiot – A Hot Chick – A British Villain – The Comic Relief – A Moody Teen – A CGI Character – A Gratuitous Cameo – Produced By Asshats – Written By The Real Heroes Here – Directed By An Overpaid Tool. (*Deadpool* 0:00:52–02:30)

Figure 4.2 The title sequence of 2016's *Deadpool* ends on a digitally rendered tableau that evokes the imagery of superhero comics. Screengrab from Amazon Prime Video.

Approximating the colloquial and mocking tone often found in commentary sections of fan-oriented websites, these titles seem to be written from the perspective of a critical, sarcastic, and well-informed fan. They further underscore the self-reflexive, irreverent, and juvenile humor of the film that follows.

The rest of the film finds additional ways to evoke the spirit of its comic book source materials. In Marvel's *Deadpool* comic book series (1997–2002), the protagonist not only often addresses the reader directly, but occasionally takes command of other, ostensibly non-diegetic elements and sections of the magazine (such as letters pages or in-panel narrative boxes) as well. Miller's *Deadpool* approximates such self-reflexive moments by turning its hero into an interventionist narrator who not only comments on the story via voice-over, but actively intervenes in the flow of story information. During the first hour of the film, for example, voice-overs by Deadpool are repeatedly used to signal the transition from the diegetic present of the narrative to the protagonist's origin story (which is told in a series of flashbacks). The first of these moments occurs in the aftermath of Deadpool's first confrontation with the henchmen of villain Ajax (Ed Skrein). Once Deadpool impales the last of his opponents, events suddenly grind to an unexpected halt as time freezes and the camera starts to circle the characters. At this point, Deadpool begins to comment on the events onscreen, stressing the film's difference from other entries in the genre:

> You're probably thinking: "My boyfriend said this was a superhero movie, but that guy in a red suit just turned that other guy into a fucking kebab!" Well, I may be super, but I am no hero. And yeah, technically, this is a murder. But some of the best love stories start with a murder. And that's exactly what this is. A love story. And to tell it right, I gotta take you back to way before I squeezed this ass into red spandex. (*Deadpool* 0:14:02–31)

After the camera comes to rest on a close-up of Deadpool's spandex-clad buttocks, the film cuts to the behind of another man and the caption "Two Years Earlier." The film then presents a number of scenes about Deadpool's earlier life as mercenary Wade Wilson, his romance with the escort Vanessa (Morena Baccarin), and the eventual cancer diagnosis that precedes his transformation into a super-powered antihero before it cuts back to the aftermath of the battle. Similar combinations of voice-over narration and temporal jumps are used several times afterwards, until the last thirty-five minutes of the film again proceed linearly, moving forward in time from the scene of the crash and culminating in an extended showdown between Deadpool and the villains.

Deadpool combines this non-linear plot with a hyperactive referencing of other texts and narratives. In the preceding chapter, I have argued that superhero movies often include nods and allusions to closely related narrative materials. But compared to other entries of the genre, Miller's *Deadpool* casts a much wider net and not only includes several jokes about earlier *X-Men* films, but also references to all kinds of other properties – such as superhero movies by other studios (like Warner's *Green Lantern* and New Line Cinema's *Blade II*), cult texts from other genres and media (like Cartoon Network's *Adventure Time*), and different phases of George Michael's music career during the 1980s. On the one hand, such seemingly random nods to bits and pieces of American popular culture echo a similar tendency present in the *Deadpool* comics of the late 1990s.[16] On the other hand, the film here stages its protagonist as an opinionated media fan, a characterization that resonates with the idea of the fan as an ideal type of consumer.

Deadpool's irreverent tone, fannish expertise, and foregrounded hyper-referentiality eventually supported the film's reception by fan-cultural critics. In a piece written for the science-fiction and pop-culture blog *io9*, site contributor Charlie Jane Anders, for example, praised *Deadpool* as an ultra-violent "meta commentary on superheroes and fan culture' and noted its many "digs at our relationship with pop culture in general" (Anders, "Deadpool"). *Nerdist*'s Luke Thompson similarly commended the film's "new and more accurate Deadpool," the countless "nerd culture references," and the protagonist's tendency to voice his opinion about "random pop-cultural touchstones" (Thompson, "Review"; for a similar review, see Chitwood, "Deadpool"). This assessment of *Deadpool*'s perceived strengths was even shared by reviewers who disliked the film. *The Mary Sue*'s Lesley Coffin, for instance, criticized the film's "cynicism," but noted that it was "true to the comic" and laden with "pop culture references, frat-boy humor, and lots of [. . .] breaking of the fourth wall" (Coffin). The shared tenor of these reviews was hardly coincidental, as *Deadpool* invites precisely the kind of reception practices that fan-cultural reviewers need to exercise as part of their work as professional consumers. Starring a fan as protagonist and foregrounding its status as a pop-cultural intertext, *Deadpool* rewards viewers who can recognize a divergence from genre conventions, who appreciate its self-reflexive play with discourse time, and who can trace its many references back to source materials. *Deadpool* thus seems tailor-made for an audience of attentive and informed fan-cultural critics. By reviewing and analyzing the film along these lines, sites such as *io9*, *Nerdist*, and *The Mary Sue* authenticated Miller's *Deadpool* as an object worthy of the fan culture's attention. At the same time, they generated a considerable amount of online traffic and cultural visibility for a film whose extensive marketing campaign not only targeted media fans specifically, but also addressed a more general movie-going audience. In this way, *Deadpool*'s reception by fan-oriented websites contributed to the overall commercial success of a film that, soon after its premiere, went on to become the world's highest grossing R-rated film (Berman).

In soliciting the approval and support of fannish consumers (professional or otherwise), *Deadpool* and the marketing efforts that accompanied it harnessed the immaterial labors of media audiences for commercial gain – a practice that, as I have suggested in Chapter 1, can be understood as typical of popular entertainment in the era of cognitive capitalism. But the film's courting of fan audiences is problematic in other respects as well. Stanfill notes that, in "industry logics, fans are constructed as white men, and being a fan is framed as normal by linking it to children and family" (pos. 3237). As result, fan-oriented properties often seem to "reinforce the cultural common sense of privilege as a natural property of white, heterosexual masculinity and produce being a fan as white." A similar case can be made for Miller's *Deadpool*, which centers on a white male protagonist who is both a media fan and the romantic partner of a woman that the opening titles introduce as "A Hot Chick." As in many R-rated comedies, much of the humor in *Deadpool* furthermore takes the form of "raunchy" jokes that cater to a heterosexual male audience. While the film's above-average box-office returns suggest a considerable mass appeal, available survey data about *Deadpool*'s US-American theatrical run also indicate that more than half of the movie-goers who saw the film self-identified as male and Caucasian (Groves). While the significance of such statistical data should not be overestimated – not least because the domestic theatrical run only accounts for a fraction of the film's overall audience – these numbers nonetheless indicate that *Deadpool* is, in some respects, a fairly conventional example of the genre. Miller's film thus affirms rather than challenges the normative conception of the media fan as white and heterosexual fanboy consumer. Arguably, *Deadpool* does so because its own attempts to mobilize the fan-oriented online public are informed by the same norm.

Miller's *Deadpool* and the marketing practices that clustered around it provide an instructive example for the fan management practices at work within contemporary superhero blockbuster cinema. They also represent an enormously successful example of such practices, as the film not only managed to solicit the support of key voices within online fandom before its premiere, but eventually also managed to satisfy much of the fan expectations that had mounted in anticipation of its release. However, as my next case study will demonstrate, not all entries of the genre are equally successful in shaping their own reception.

SUICIDE SQUAD AND THE FAILURE OF FAN MANAGEMENT

When director David Ayer's *Suicide Squad* premiered in early August of 2016, the majority of professional reviewers agreed that it was a "completely disappointing disaster" (as the *Los Angeles Times*' Libby Hill put it in her sampling of responses to Ayer's movie).[17] Reviews published on fan-oriented websites generally echoed this reception, even if individual fan-cultural critics often were slightly more charitable in their assessment of the film. *AICN*'s Eric Vespe, for instance, argued that *Suicide Squad* was "beautifully shot, impeccably cast," but "frustratingly incoherent," as it had the feel of "a jumble of scenes thrown into a randomizer program." Fellow *AICN* reviewer Steve Prokopny, in turn, criticized the film for its too large cast of central characters, conventional story, and uneven plotting. A more positive review by *ComingSoon*'s Alan Cerny characterized *Suicide Squad*'s ensemble cast as "entertaining," but noted the film's "ugly and grey" appearance and lack of "logistical sense." Non-professional movie-goers, however, did not always agree. A few days after its release, Ayer's film scored an average user score of 6.7 out of 10 on *Metacritic* (indicating "generally favorable reviews" by users) and a 69-per-cent approval rating on *RottenTomatoes*. These user ratings contrasted with the much more negative reviews by professional critics, which produced an aggregated "metascore" of forty out of a hundred and a "tomatometer" score of 27 per cent, respectively.[18] This contrast between the opinions of professional and non-professional consumers also manifested itself in the commentary sections of sites like *io9*, where some users complained about the critical reception of the film and accused reviewers of bias against Warner's *DC Extended Universe* (*DCEU*). These protests eventually spawned a *change.org* petition that called for an end of the "unfair" treatment of DC-based superhero movies and demanded an immediate shutdown of RottenTomatotes.[19] The critics' negative assessments also did not keep the film from making money at the box-office, where *Suicide Squad* grossed more than *Logan* and only a little less than *Deadpool*. Arguably, however, Ayer's PG-13 rated film might have made even more money had the reviews been more favorable.[20]

It is tempting to explain the relative failure of *Suicide Squad* simply by pronouncing it a bad movie that failed to satisfy critics, but such a claim posits a simplistic relationship between artistic quality and commercial performance. It also disregards the many user ratings that offered a positive assessment of the film. *Suicide Squad*'s lackluster reviews are thus better understood as the result of a partial failure to manage the discourses of an online fan culture. In what follows, I suggest that this failure resulted from a confluence of factors. Most centrally, these factors included the film's relationship to other, also poorly reviewed entries of Warner's *DCEU*, its embrace of formal excess, and a marketing campaign that failed to generate a positive media buzz during the run-up to *Suicide Squad*'s premiere.

Ayer's film was announced as the third entry of the *DCEU* in the fall of 2014; over the following months, it garnered considerable attention by fan-oriented media and entertainment news websites.[21] This coverage received additional fuel in the spring of 2015, when the official marketing campaign for the film began to release a series of set photos posted to Ayer's personal Twitter account.[22] One of the first images posted by Ayer was a portrait of Jared Leto in make-up as the Joker, in which the actor's face was slightly out-of-focus and obscured by a camera aimed at the spectator. Posted on April 10, the image evoked the cover image of Alan Moore and Brian Bolland's classic 1988 comic *Batman: The Killing Joke* and soon prompted a considerable amount of reporting and speculation on fan-oriented websites (for examples, see Tracey; O'Brien; Kendrick; Melrose; Goodman). Releasing additional images over the course of the following days, Ayer's account eventually posted a picture that offered the unobstructed view of a topless and heavily tattooed Joker. The character's new look – which featured a prominent forehead tattoo that spelled out the word "damaged" in cursive font – soon became the object of criticism and mockery on fan sites and social media (see Eddy, "Jared Leto's Joker"). The film's marketing campaign rebounded from this misstep with the release of a favorably reviewed teaser trailer in July 2015, a similarly received longer trailer in January of the following year, and additional promotional materials – all of which were extensively covered by fan-oriented publications. Aside from the negative response to the Joker's new looks, most of the fan public's coverage of *Suicide Squad* thus remained neutral or positive. But this changed in March 2016, when the release of the poorly reviewed *Batman V. Superman: Dawn of Justice* (Dir. Zack Snyder) effected a shift in the reception of Ayer's film.

Slated for release in August 2016, *Suicide Squad* was the third installment in Warner's *DCEU* franchise and preceded by two Zack Snyder-directed films (*Batman V. Superman* and 2013's *Man of Steel*) whose theatrical runs were also overshadowed by failures of fan management. Prefiguring the eventual reception of Ayer's film, *Man of Steel* and *Batman V. Superman* both garnered many negative reviews from professional critics but scored considerably higher in the audience-ratings sections of review aggregators such as *Metacritic* and *RottenTomatoes*. Within the online fan public, the poor critical reception of *Batman V. Superman* also inspired numerous commentary pieces that expressed skepticism and doubt about the future of the *DCEU*. Since this discourse coincided with the pre-release marketing campaign for *Suicide Squad*, it soon began to include Ayer's film as well.[23] For instance, a few days before *Suicide Squad*'s premiere, *The Hollywood Reporter* published a report about the film that detailed rumors about its rushed production, lack of creative direction, and meddling by studio executives – claims that were picked up by fan-oriented sites soon after.[24] Critical coverage of Ayer's movie took on a particularly vocal tone on *io9*, which soon became one of the key sites for the articulation of fannish discontent with Warner's *DCEU*. *io9*'s reporting during this period included a mixed review that discussed *Suicide Squad* as "a strange blend of different tones, stories, and pacing" (Lussier, "Movie Review"), an article on the film's troubled production (Whitbrook), and two longer commentary pieces by site contributor Katharine Trendacosta, which focused on the state of Warner's franchise (Trendacosta, "What Warner Bros. Needs to Do"; "Warner Bros. Needs to Stop").[25] In the first of her articles, Trendacosta argued that "virtually every decision made by Warner Bros. [. . .] has been bad" and that studio executives had diluted the artistic unity of Ayer's film by outsourcing its final edit to an external company ("What Warner Bros. Needs to Do"). In a shorter follow-up article, Trendacosta framed Warner Bros. as unresponsive to criticism and suggested that continued journalistic scrutiny was needed to improve the quality of future superhero movies by the studio ("Warner Bros. Needs to Stop"). *io9*'s coverage of *Suicide Squad* provides a good example for what Kelleter and Stein call authorization conflicts: Here, authors who were both professional journalists and self-described fans articulated a well-informed argument about the perceived failures of a popular text, thereby challenging the authority of the corporate actors and institutions involved in its making. In doing so, *io9*'s paid contributors refused to endorse a film that they perceived as aesthetically muddled as the franchise entries that had preceded it. In doing so, Trendacosta and her colleagues performed exactly the "gatekeeper" function that Taylor attributes to non-professional fannish consumers.

After *Suicide Squad*'s theatrical release, the film's already disadvantageous positioning within fan-cultural discourses was exacerbated by formal aspects that prevented a more positive reception by critics. Like *Deadpool*, *Suicide Squad* tells its story non-linearly, with frequent digressions into earlier timeframes that serve to establish parts of the backstory and provide motivation for characters' actions in the present. But where Miller's film uses a handful of pro- and analepses to relate Deadpool's origin story, *Suicide Squad* uses flashbacks both less consistently and at a higher frequency. The first twenty minutes of Ayer's film, for example, use a dinner conversation between intelligence officer Amanda Waller (Viola Davis) and two Pentagon officials as a framing device for seven short vignettes that establish the backstories of the titular squad's various members. These include the assassin Deadshot (Will Smith), the Joker's girlfriend Harley Quinn (Margot Robbie), the villains Captain Boomerang (Jai Courtney), Diablo (Jay Hernandez), Killer Croc (Adewale Akinnuoye-Agbaje), and Enchantress (Cara Delevingne), as well as squad leader Rick Flag (Joel Kinnaman) (0:05:09–19:07). The next twenty minutes of the film then proceed linearly and depict Waller's attempts to recruit the villains, the Joker making plans to break Harley out of prison, Enchantress freeing her imprisoned brother Incubus (Alain Chanoine), the sibling's attack on Midway City, and the squad's preparations for a mission to rescue an unidentified "high value target" from the metropolis (0:19:07–47:20). The rest of the film then features four additional flashbacks – one brief sequence that teases the backstory for Flag's assistant Katana (Karen Fukuhara) (0:47:20–28), one that elaborates

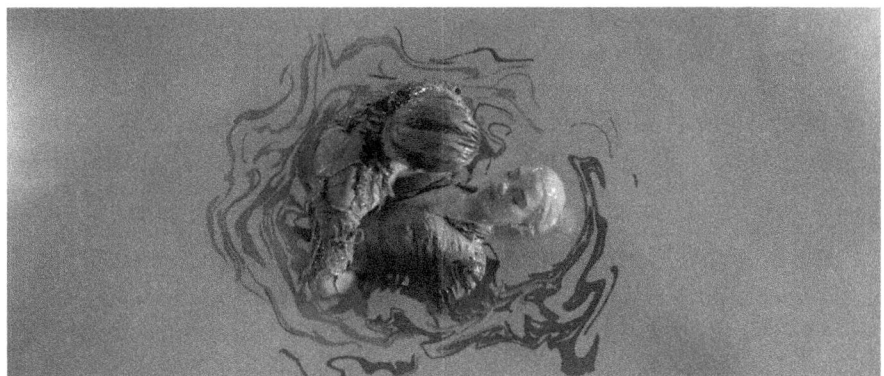

Figure 4.3 In 2016's *Suicide Squad*, a flashback sequence narrates part of the Joker's (Jared Leto) and Harley Quinn's (Margot Robbie) backstory – a scene that directs narrative momentum away from the film's central plotline. Screengrab from Amazon Prime Video.

on the romance between Harley and the Joker (1:05:55–08:02; see Figure 4.3), one that repeats and extends a scene from earlier in the film (1:21:19–57), and a final sequence that reveals more about Diablo's past (1:24:26–25:11). One result of this non-linear narrative structure – in which analepses are sometimes accompanied by voice-over narration and sometimes not, sometimes add to the characters' backstories and sometimes restage scenes from earlier in the film – is that *Suicide Squad* feels shot through with several self-contained but relatively inconsequential micro-narratives that do not always contribute to the central storyline.

The film's frequent use of analepses is an example of what Kristin Thompson has termed "cinematic excess" – that is, a use of storytelling devices that "draw attention to themselves far beyond their importance in the functioning of the narrative" ("The Concept" 136). For Thompson, cinema is first and foremost a storytelling medium. To fulfill this purpose, any given film needs to "'contain' the diverse elements that make up its whole system" within the "unifying structures" that render the narrative comprehensible and endow it with a sense of thematic unity and coherence ("The Concept" 134). "Excessive elements," Thompson argues, "do not form relationships beyond those of coexistence" and refuse to let films blend into unified wholes (135). Instead, such elements effect "a movement away from [. . .] direct progression" and cause a "skidding [of] perception" that calls undue attention to aspects of form and style (132). Thompson's discussion of cinematic excess illuminates some of the reasons for the largely negative critical reception of *Suicide Squad*. Viewed from the perspective of a film critic invested in values such as narrative coherence and efficient plotting, *Suicide Squad*'s frequent analepses seem to be, at least in part, without an obvious narrative function; accordingly, the film's tendency to jump between timeframes resulted in reviews that emphasized the film's stuttering story flow and lack of "logistical" sense.

For several reviewers, the film's pop-music soundtrack produced a similar "skidding of perception" as well. In his review of the film, *io9*'s Germain Lussier, for example, noted that . . .

> Ayer uses a copious amount of pop songs in *Suicide Squad*. Too many pop songs, if we're being honest. From the Animals and Kanye West, to Eminem and the White Stripes, these songs are certainly nice to hear, but in almost every single case they've obviously been picked for very literal reasons. For example, "Seven Nation Army" is played when the team comes together as an army. "Come Baby Come" by K7 is played almost solely so the line "Swing batter batter batter batter swing" can play in a key moment. By themselves, each song is enjoyable, but together they just clash with each other. In that sense, the music ends up being almost the perfect microcosm of the film – the pieces are good, but together they somehow end up making less than the sum of their parts. ("Movie Review")

Lussier's view was echoed by other critics. *The Wrap*'s Alonso Duralde, for example, deemed the soundtrack "a parade of the most on-the-nose music cues since 'Forrest Gump,'" while LaSalle's review for the *San Francisco Chronicle* described the film's use of pop songs as "terrible" and distracting (LaSalle).[26] In her discussion of cinematic excess, Thompson suggests that the frequent repetition of a device with a clearly established given function can generate an impression of redundancy on the part of the viewer ("The Concept" 136). If overdone, such redundancies might draw attention away from other, narratively more important aspects and thereby "invite the partial disintegration of a coherent reading" (134). In criticizing *Suicide Squad*'s soundtrack, the critics cited above made a similar argument, framing the film as disorganized and insufficiently coherent. *Suicide Squad*'s problems are not limited to the film's excessive use of pop-songs and analepses. Arguably, the film's large cast of iconic characters (of which some get only little screen time), its over-reliance on voice-over narration, and the extensive use of expository dialogue during the drawn-out showdown (1:32:40–46:00), for example, also contributed to its negative reception. Ayer's film thus layered excess upon excess, thereby fragmenting its narrative into a series of tenuously connected moments that refused to combine into a unified whole.

But *Suicide Squad*'s formal tics alone do not sufficiently explain the critical response to the film. After all, *Deadpool* was hardly less excessive and employed many of the same devices as Ayer's film. Interestingly, however, most reviewers framed *Deadpool*'s over-the-top violence, abundance of coarse language, non-linear narrative structure, and hyper-active pop-cultural commentary as strengths rather than as weaknesses. *Deadpool*'s foregrounded self-reflexivity constituted a key reason for these divergent responses: By offering a sarcastic commentary on the superhero genre and breaking the fourth wall, Miller's film managed to balance its excesses with a performative display of fannish expertise that preempted an easy dismissal by critics. *Suicide Squad*, however, played it straight. As result, the film's idiosyncratic style aggravated a failure of fan management that had begun months before. Likewise, *Suicide Squad*'s already disadvantageous positioning within fan-cultural discourses made its formal excesses stand out even more. Ayer's film thus had the odds stacked against it, as the emerging critical consensus about the film was articulated against the backdrop of a fan discourse that already framed the *DCEU* as problematic.

Notably, however, *Suicide Squad*'s excesses did not disqualify the film for all its viewers. In her essay on excess, Thompson notes that non-motivated or non-functional elements can sometimes produce "strange, unfamiliar, and striking" moments that yield a fascination of their own (134). *Suicide Squad* possesses a similar kind of "strangeness" – one that, while difficult to put into words, does register in the reviews of some fan-cultural critics. Lussier's review for *io9*, for example, likens *Suicide Squad* to an "action-packed B-movie" and points out that its first twenty minutes are quite effective in capturing the viewer's attention: "It's disjointed, for sure, and things get a bit monotonous because the story isn't really advancing, but there's a certain energy to much of it. With this much set-up, you definitively want to see what's next" (Lussier, "Movie Review"). Lussier's review here frames the film's redeeming qualities in contradictory terms, suggesting that *Suicide Squad* is both monotonous and action-packed, tedious but also full of energy. In his own review of the film, *AICN*'s Harry Knowles is at a similar loss for words, but stresses that the film's lack of order and coherence make it actually quite appealing:

> It's a mess, but it's a mess like playing in the mud when you're a kid. Or that crazy mismatched quilt your grandmother made for you that felt so fucking good. It's a mess like eating BBQ without a napkin. . . . As a DC/ MARVEL/IMAGE/CHARLETON/EC/GOLD KEY/CLASSICS ILLUSTRATED/UNDERGROUND comic fan, I came away wanting to see it again, soon [. . .]. There's so much disconnected awesome here that fans can have a great time. But know – you'll leave wanting desperately. . . MORE. ("Harry Says")

Knowles's and Lussier's observations point to the generic conventions of superhero narratives, whose fast-paced plots often subordinate questions of narrative coherence to the need to provide ever-new variations on familiar motifs, characters, and situations.[27] Their references to B-movies and comic books are thus more than apt for a film like Ayer's, whose narrative logic is no less flimsy than that of many superhero comics. *Suicide Squad*, in other words, offers the same kind of sensational, easily accessible, and pleasantly inconsequential entertainment that can also be found in the pages of superhero comics. Despite *Suicide Squad*'s failure to resonate with the online fan public's gatekeepers, its "energy" and "disconnected awesomeness" arguably hew closely to the spirit of the source material – just not in a manner appreciated by most professional critics.

CONCLUSION

The contrast between *Deadpool* and *Suicide Squad* highlights the different degrees of success with which both films managed to position themselves within the discourses of the online fan public. The favorable reception of Miller's film was centrally connected to its foregrounded hyper-referentiality, self-reflexive moments, and familiarity with fan-cultural discourses – elements which catered to the interpretive habits of professional consumers. Crucially, however, the leaked *Deadpool* test footage and subsequent marketing campaign also played up these aspects, thereby laying the groundwork for a favorable reception of the film. *Suicide Squad*, however, offered fannish commentators fewer things to talk about, as its indebtedness to superhero comics manifested itself in formal excesses that were not accompanied by self-reflexive commentary. Lacking the positive advance publicity of the *Deadpool* leak, *Suicide Squad*'s online marketing campaign also suffered from the need to position the film within a discourse that was already critical of Warner's *DCEU*. As a result, the online fan public of late 2016 proved to be a less than hospitable environment for Ayer's movie. The fan management practices at work in *Logan*, *Deadpool* and *Suicide Squad* also left their mark on subsequent releases in the genre. For example, *Deadpool 2* (Fox 2018; Dir. David Leitch) – which premiered two years after the first film and one year after *Logan* – opens with a scene in which the protagonist attempts suicide and bemoans the death of Jackman's Wolverine via voice-over: "Fuck Wolverine. First, he rides my coattails with the R-rating. Then the hairy motherfucker ups the ante by dying. What a dick. Well, guess what, Wolvie? I'm dying in this one, too" (*Deadpool 2* 0:02:19–31). In moments such as these, *Deadpool 2* not only takes the viewers' familiarity with the recent history of the genre for granted, but also articulates a self-reflexive commentary on superhero blockbusters' tendency to create increasingly inventive stories out of the same narrative building blocks.

A similar sensibility informed *Deadpool 2*'s marketing campaign, which tried to both repeat and outdo the success of the first film's campaign. Echoing the low-fidelity aesthetics of the test footage leaked in 2014, one of the teaser trailers for the sequel featured a voice-over that commented on the clip's conspicuously unfinished visual effects and an "action scene" staged with the help of plastic figures, toy cars, and cardboard boxes ("Deadpool 2 Official Teaser"). This time around, however, marketing efforts did not pre-empt the emergence of a negative pre-release buzz, as rumors about poorly received test screenings surfaced on Twitter shortly before *Deadpool 2*'s premiere. Responding to these rumors, 20th Century Fox soon threatened legal action against the authors of the tweets and eventually managed to get the respective posts removed from the platform (see Palmer, Havran). Fox's response can be understood as a particularly aggressive form of fan management that sought to re-establish control over an online discourse threatening to turn sour. Usually, however, fan management practices proceed in less confrontational ways. Feedback loops between production and consumption are important here as well: *Deadpool*'s and *Suicide Squad*'s failures and successes also informed the production of 2020's *Birds of Prey (and the Fantabulous Emancipation of One Harley Quinn)*, which had Margot Robbie's Harley Quinn teaming up with a group of female vigilantes. The R-rated *Birds of Prey* featured similar excesses as *Suicide Squad*, but countered *Deadpool*'s implicit masculinism with an ensemble cast of female protagonists. Crucially, however, it also mimicked Miller's film by including more explicit depictions of graphic violence, a similarly focused non-linear structure, and a self-reflexive voice-over narration by Robbie's character. In 2021, Robbie's Harley returned for a second time to star in the James Gunn-directed *The Suicide Squad*, which not only brought back several other characters from Ayer's take on the property, but also offered similarly irreverent (and even more violent) excesses as *Deadpool* and *Birds of Prey*. The poor reception of Leto's Joker, however, played a role in the production of the Joaquin Phoenix-starring *Joker* (2019): The latter featured a strikingly different version of the titular villain and told a self-contained story set outside of the *DCEU*'s established continuity. The above examples demonstrate an acute awareness of fan-cultural discourses on the part of screenwriters, directors, film producers, and studio executives, as well as their readiness to course-correct once films appear to underperform commercially. The fan management practices discussed in this chapter thus illustrate the adaptability of the contemporary culture industry, which, as I have argued in Chapter 1, can itself be understood as a highly dynamic social system that evolves in response to shifts in its cultural, medial, and social environments.

The films and marketing practices discussed above also illustrate the extent to which recent superhero blockbuster cinema is informed by industrial efforts to monitor and interact with audience discourses online. Such efforts hinge on the potentially symbiotic (but also potentially conflicting) relationship between studios, filmmakers, and marketers, on the one hand, and fan-oriented publications, media platforms, and (professional as well as non-professional) fans, on the other. In the era of cognitive capitalism, the commercial success of cultural commodities ultimately hinges on their ability to interface with online discursive environments – and the fan management practices discussed in this chapter demonstrate how such projects play out in practice.

NOTES

1. The usage of Johnny Cash's cover version of the Nine Inch Nails song "Hurt" in the first trailer underscored the somber tone of the then-unreleased film ("Logan | Official Trailer"). The film's graphically violent action scenes were showcased in a longer "Redband" trailer released soon after.
2. Posted on the fan-oriented websites *TheMarySue*, *io9*, and *ComingSoon*, the reviews cited above echo those published in mainstream publication such as *The New York Times* (see Dargis, "Review: In *Logan*"), *The LA Times* (Turan), or *The Guardian* (Bradshaw). For user reviews of the film that express similar opinions, see "Logan Reviews."
3. For interviews with the actor that thematize his positioning as a fan, see Weintraub; Keyes, "Hugh Jackman." In a 2017 *Hollywood Reporter* piece, Jackman furthermore characterizes *Logan* as a "love letter to the Wolverine fans" (Roxborough).
4. Commentary and analyses published on sites such as *io9* have thematized industrial attempts to co-opt fan culture quite explicitly (for an example, see Bricken, "Does Appeasing"). On the idea of consumers' realist attitude towards cultural commodities, see Chapter 1.
5. For critiques of this binary view – which informs Henry Jenkins's work and much of the research in the tradition of the Birmingham Centre for Contemporary Cultural Studies – see the first chapter of Hills's *Fan Cultures* and Kelleter, "Einführung."
6. For an overview on *Deadpool*'s production history, see Kit, "Did Deadpool."
7. Rumors about the test footage had circulated since the summer of 2013, when Deadpool creator Rob Liefeld confirmed its existence in an appearance at San Diego Comic Con (Van Winkle, "Deadpool"). A Reynolds-starring *Deadpool* film had been in development since 2003 and received intermittent media attention in the following years (see Marshall; "Ryan Reynolds"; Connelly; Keyes, "Rob Liefeld"; Venable). The test footage released in July 2014 was not the first leak associated with the production, as a 2010 draft of Reese and Wernick's screenplay had begun circulating on the Internet several months before.
8. Reese and Wernick's 2010 screenplay closely prefigures the plot of the 2016 film, which indicates that even finer details had been worked out by the time of the leak. In a 2013 interview, Ryan Reynolds also characterized the film as having "been developed to high heaven" (Venable).
9. For a (non-academic) overview of the characters' development across titles, see Lussier, "The Unlikely Origins."
10. After *X-Men Origins*' 2009 premiere, users of sites such as *AICN*, for example, complained about Deadpool's lack of screen-time, non-canonical powers, and apparent demotion to the status of a run-of-the-mill super-villain. For exemplary responses of this kind, see *AICN*'s non-review of *X-Men Origins* (which quotes several negative reviews by fans and other publications instead of reviewing the film itself) and the user commentary below it (Knowles, "Harry's Official Position").
11. For more examples of this reception, see Garcia; Perry, "Update"; Oliver; Romano.
12. For exemplary coverage of the image, see Carle.

13. The promotional videos released in this context proved to be particularly effective at generating the attention of the fan-oriented online public and included a first video released on April 1, which affirmed the film's rumored R-rating (see Shirey, as well as "Is Deadpool Going to be PG-13?"), a clip titled "How Deadpool spent Halloween" in which the protagonist berates a group of children dressed in X-Men costumes, and a public service announcement about the dangers of testicular cancer narrated by the red-suited anti-hero ("Deadpool – Gentlemen").
14. For exemplary coverage of the San Diego Comic Con panel and reporting on the trailer that emphasizes the film's fan appeal, see Oldham; McMillan, "Why"; Rivera.
15. On comics reading as a practice that is less intense that film reception, see my discussion in the preceding chapter. My observations here are also based on Vivian Sobchack's suggestion that "grand displays of industrial light and magic" (like the ones on display in *Deadpool*'s opening sequence) involve a "decentered subjectification of *special effects*" that distances the spectator from the film image (282).
16. For an illustrative example of this tendency, see author Joe Kelly's *Deadpool* story "With Great Power comes Great Coincidence" (*Deadpool* #11, 1997).
17. For additional overviews of *Suicide Squad*'s critical reception, see Wickman and Canfield; Finger; for an exemplary piece, see LaSalle.
18. The *Metacritic* and *RottenTomatoes* scores referenced here were recorded in the early morning hours of August 17, 2016, (a week after the film's theatrical premiere) and remain accessible via *The Internet Archive*'s Wayback Machine. At the time of writing in early 2021, aggregate user scores on both had shifted to 6.0 on Metacritic and 59 per cent on RottenTomatoes. The disconnect between critical opinions and user ratings also played out across other platforms. In late 2017, 71 per cent of the more than 428,000 users who rated the film on *The Internet Movie Database*, for example, awarded six or more out of ten stars; similarly, most of the user reviews shared via the US-American versions of Apple's iTunes and Amazon's PrimeVideo granted the film a four- or five-star rating (both services used five-star rating systems at the time) (see "Suicide Squad – Customer Reviews"; "Suicide Squad (2016) – User Ratings").
19. For some exemplary comments along these lines, see the commentary section below Lussier's *Suicide Squad* review for *io9* (Lussier, "Movie Review"). Recurring claims about *io9*'s alleged bias towards Marvel movies eventually prompted site editor Rob Bricken to write a sarcastic "Confession" about his connection to a far-flung "Conspiracy to Destroy DC's Live-Action Movies." The *change.org*-petition by DC movies fan Abdullah Coldwater soon prompted criticism by other fans; as result, Coldwater first changed the petition's goals (demanding that audiences ignore film criticism altogether) and then abandoned it completely (see Coldwater; Couch).
20. Ayer's film generated a total worldwide gross of $745 million, but its production budget of $175 million made it less profitable than Mangold's and Miller's films.
21. Plans for a *Suicide Squad* movie date back to 2009. For reporting on the film's early development stages, see McNary, "Warner Bros."; Kit, "Scribe In." For reporting on Warner's initial announcement of the *DCEU*, see Franich, "Justice League," "Warner Bros." For early reporting on the film after its official announcement, see Sneider; Trendacosta, "Just How Insane"; Holmes.
22. Principal production for *Suicide Squad* began in early April 2015 (see "Suicide Squad Will Officially Start Filming"). For the first images released through Ayer's Twitter account, see Ayer "Cast Read through"; Trendacosta, "Finally a Look."
23. For reporting and commentary on the state of the franchise in the aftermath of *Batman V. Superman*'s release, see Child; Chipman; McCarthy; Schwerdtfeger; Collin. The reception

of the *DCEU* took a particularly negative turn after the release of *Batman V. Superman*, but contributors to fan-sites had voiced skepticism about Warner's plans in the years before (see Clark; Bricken, "If This Is"; Woerner).

24. For the *THR* piece, see Masters; for *io9*'s recirculation of the story, see Whitbrook.
25. These elements of *io9*'s coverage followed a longer engagement with the *DCEU* that, for the most part, occurred in the site's ongoing coverage of entertainment news. This coverage occasionally included subtle (and usually skeptical) evaluations of the *DCEU*'s future potential (for an example, see Lussier, "A Major Shake Up").
26. For an overview on the film's many songs and the order of their appearance, see Campbell.
27. See my discussion in Chapter 2.

CHAPTER 5

Cinematic Populism and the Political Superhero Blockbuster

On the eve of the US presidential elections on November 3, 2020, *Stephen Colbert's Election Night* special on the Showtime television network opened with an animated segment that appropriated the iconography of Batman movies to cast President Donald Trump as a cartoonish supervillain and his challenger Joe Biden as an aloof, but heroic defender of the democratic process. Titled "Election Knight Rises," the segment derived much of its humor from the fact that it depicted the events of the day as a dramatic confrontation between a Batman-like Biden and a Joker-like Trump. In doing so, the segment mapped key categories of the superhero genre onto the 2020 election and portrayed the latter as pivotal moment in an epic battle between exceptional people whose outcome would decide the fate of the American nation. Simultaneously, the segment used this construction as basis for a series of highly intertextual jokes about both candidates. The election day special's opening was neither the first nor the only example of this kind of joke on late night television. In fact, it followed similar segments on Stephen Colbert's *Late Show* (CBS, since 2015) which, earlier that year, had used mash-ups of television news footage and scenes from *Avengers: Endgame* (2019) to depict prominent Democrats and Republicans as superheroes or super-villains ("America: Endgame," "America: Endgame [RNC Edition]"). The resonance of these send-ups was heightened by the fact that the election campaigns of both parties occasionally used similar references to the genre to advance their causes. In December 2019, for example, one of the Twitter accounts operated by the Trump campaign posted a short video with a doctored scene from *Endgame* that superimposed Trump's face onto the head of the super-villain Thanos. In the clip, Trump/Thanos uses the magical Infinity Gauntlet to turn Democrats such as Nancy Pelosi and Adam Schiff into dust – a depiction that soon not only prompted outrage on

Twitter and other social media, but also inspired mockery by users who noticed that the footage implicitly depicted Trump as a genocidal madman whose plans were bound to fail (@TrumpWarRoom; see also Einwächter, Ossa, Sina, and Stollfuss 148–49). But Republican campaigners were not the only ones inspired by superhero narratives. In the summer of 2020, a YouTube ad titled "Team Biden" funded by the Democratic super PAC NextGen America used mock pencil drawings and captions in faux comics lettering to portray former Vice President Biden and left-wing Democrats such as Bernie Sanders and Alexandria Ocasio-Cortez as part of a team that was diverse in opinion, but united in the goal of defeating Trump. Interviewed by *The Atlantic*, NextGen America spokesperson Ben Wessel explained the ad as an attempt to attract younger voters by presenting moderate and progressive members of the party as a group of "Democratic Avengers" who combined their powers in a heroic struggle against evil (Khazan). Racking up a few thousand views on *YouTube*, the "Team Biden" clip did not make much of a contribution to the eventual success of the Biden campaign. Its existence nonetheless gives testament to the discursive productivity and allegorical resonance of what Chapter 2 has discussed as the superheroic political imaginary: a flexible, serially reiterated, and latently political narrative framework that centers on Manichean struggles between exceptional heroes and villains. Mapped onto real-world situations, this framework imparts easily legible meanings, assigns clear-cut roles, goals, and motivations; more than anything else, it makes politics entertaining (or at least more exciting than, say, broadcasts on C-SPAN or commentary pieces in the *New York Times*).

The above appropriations of motifs, characters, and tropes from superhero movies speak to the extent to which the genre has become entrenched within what sociologist Niklas Luhmann calls the "latent everyday culture" of the contemporary United States.[1] For Luhmann, the modern mass media's unending stream of ever-new and yet familiar forms provides a readily available general "background knowledge" that lends itself "as a starting point for [further] communication" (*The Reality* 66). In doing so, the mass media also provide memory functions for the societies in which they operate, as they keep recognizable forms and topics in cultural circulation (see 95–102). By the late 2010s and early 2020s, the many-decade-long proliferation of superhero narratives in film, comics, and other media had firmly anchored the genre within the cultural memory of the United States. It is because of this entrenchment that the invocation of the genre's well-worn tropes and figures could bestow a surplus of meaning on political ads and late-night comedy routines, making a range of follow-up responses (such as likes, shares, re-tweets, and posts on social media) possible.

But the enduring prominence of superhero narratives alone does not sufficiently explain the contemporary prominence of politicized references to the genre. Until the end of the 1990s, the colorful spectacles of superhero blockbuster cinema's first wave were frequently dismissed as mindless popcorn cinema and only rarely invoked in political contexts. Subsequent years, however, have witnessed a significant shift in the genre's public reception. Writing in 2012, Dan Hassler-Forest observed that "superhero movies are now often interpreted as social and/or political allegories, and discussed in full earnestness in terms of 'what they teach us' about ourselves" (*Capitalist Superheroes* 45). After the September 11, 2001, attacks on the World Trade Center, the post-9/11 context was frequently invoked as reference point for such readings, but reviewers and films have since moved on to other topics.[2] More recent superhero movies have been read as commentaries on political issues that ranged from the United States' endless War on Terror and workings of the military industrial complex, over the 2008 financial crisis and left-wing protest movements in the United States, as well as questions of gender equality and feminist empowerment, to debates about the legitimacy of political violence in the face of racial injustice, for example.[3] Given the genre's roots in a culture of cheap and ephemeral print media for children and adolescents, the valuation of superhero movies as a form of political commentary seems an unlikely development – one that is worth exploring, as it contributes to the contemporary prominence and commercial success of the genre. After all, reviews that frame superhero blockbusters as political allegories not only increase the cultural visibility of these films, but also legitimize them as a type of smart (though not necessarily serious) popular entertainment.

This chapter explores recent superhero blockbusters' ability to invite, encourage, and solicit such readings and examines the means they employ towards this end. It argues that superhero movies' reception as political allegories and appropriations, such as the ones discussed at the beginning of the chapter, respond to a cinematic populism prominently on display in recent entries of the genre. This populism can be understood as a politically charged variant of the hyper-referential style that combines the genre's penchant for good-versus-evil stories with references to real-world politics and an affectively powerful cinematic presentation. Films that subscribe to this mode of storytelling foreground the otherwise latent political themes that are implicit in the genre's shared conventions. These themes include the tension between the extralegal activities of superheroes and the authority of state actors, the contrast between super-powered figures and regular people, as well as the idea that violence is the best means to combat threats to the social order. Earlier, I have suggested that adherence to these conventions not only allows for the continued iteration of similar plots, but also constrains the genre's ability to address political subject-matter. Building on these ideas, I argue below that the categories of the superheroic imaginary are structurally similar to the basic building blocks of what political scientist Cas Mudde and sociologist Cristóbal

Rovira Kaltwasser describe as the "thin-centered ideology" of political populisms. The latter can be understood as a schematic, but inherently flexible worldview that "considers society to be ultimately separated into two homogeneous and antagonistic camps, 'the pure people' versus 'the corrupt elite,' and which argues that politics should be an expression of the volonté générale (general will) of the people" (5). Mudde and Kaltwasser stress that political populisms by themselves "can offer neither complex nor comprehensive answers to the political questions that modern societies generate" (6). Instead, populisms need to borrow ideas from other, "at times contradictory," ideologies – such as "fascism, liberalism, or socialism," for example (5). Superhero blockbusters, I suggest, exhibit a similar propensity to borrow motifs and ideas from a variety of discourses. More precisely, I argue that recent entries of the genre perform their relevance to real-world issues by importing concepts and concerns from contemporary political discourses. But in doing so, these films remain committed to the categories of the superheroic political imaginary and present their conflicts as antagonistic struggles between exceptional heroes and villains – a framing that, more often than not, precludes a nuanced exploration of complex subject-matter and results in a superficial engagement with contemporary politics. I note in the second chapter that this superficiality should be understood as competitive advantage rather than as flaw, since it allows reviewers to read their own (at times quite different) concerns and beliefs into the films in question. The genre's penchant for simple good-versus-evil plots thus makes a range of follow-up responses possible, thereby contributing to the media buzz that often surrounds individual releases. What I call cinematic populism combines this ideological malleability with a kinetic film style and state-of-the-art effects that frame superheroes as alluring, affectively engaging, more-than-human figures, a presentation that further adds to the genre's cross-partisan appeal.

To make this case, this chapter examines three films that offer particularly clear articulations of the genre's cinematic populism – 2014's *Captain America: The Winter Soldier*, its 2016 sequel *Captain America: Civil War*, and 2018's *Black Panther*, all part of Disney's *Marvel Cinematic Universe* (*MCU*). All three films focus on the adventures of what Jason Dittmer has termed "nationalist superheroes," which is to say that each of their protagonists is identified as "representative and defender of a specific nation-state" through "name, uniform and mission" (7). In the case of the first two films, this hero is the titular Captain America (Chris Evans), a superpowered American soldier who wears variations of a red, white, and blue outfit for significant parts of each movie. *Black Panther*'s eponymous hero (portrayed by Chadwick Boseman and introduced as a supporting character in *Civil War*) is king and defender of the fictional African nation of Wakanda. In the films discussed in this chapter, both protagonists are globetrotting adventurers who use their superpowers to advance their respective country's interests at home and abroad. But all three films also tell stories about their hero's ambivalent relationship to the state. The two *Captain America*-films, for instance, pit their protagonist against representatives of the state and its agencies: In *The Winter Soldier*, the hero takes on his employer S.H.I.E.L.D. (a fictionalized amalgamation of the NSA, CIA, and military special forces), which has been corrupted by the agents of a sinister conspiracy. In the 2016 sequel *Civil War*, Captain America and a few of his colleagues rebel against a US-backed UN effort to regulate superheroic activity, a move that brings him into conflict with Iron Man and other members of the Avengers. In *Black Panther*, the protagonist's status as the ruler of Wakanda is challenged by the villain Killmonger (Michael B. Jordan), who claims the throne for himself and seeks to use the country's resources to advance a project of international Black liberation. Each of the three films establishes its relevance to real-world events by incorporating elements of different political discourses: state surveillance, conspiracist ideology, a host of other issues in the case of *The Winter Soldier*, American geopolitics and partisan strife in the case of *Civil War*, and Black radicalism in the case of *Black Panther*. *The Winter Soldier*, *Civil War*, and *Black Panther* furthermore demonstrate superhero blockbusters' ability to invite a reception as political allegories, as all three films were favorably reviewed as such at the time of their theatrical run, a reception that was shared by reviewers and critics with different (and, at times, diametrically opposed) partisan orientations.

In what follows, I suggest that this reception is not an accident; all three films encourage allegorical interpretations as a "preferred reading" (Fiske 16). In making this case, I follow in the footsteps of other scholars who have written about the often-vague politics of blockbuster films and superhero narratives. Richard Maltby, for example, has argued that Hollywood productions generally "are constructed to accommodate, rather than predetermine, their audiences'" reactions (43). For Maltby, this political "ambiguity and textual uncertainty" is related to the commodity status of Hollywood films (42). "Hollywood's commercial aesthetic," so Maltby suggests, ultimately "concedes the authority to decide what a movie's content means to the individual viewer, who is provided with a host of opportunities to exercise that authority" (43). Matt Yockey makes a parallel case about Marvel's superhero comics of the 1960s, which "generally steered clear of overt political statements," but nonetheless incorporated "affective tropes of resistance to appeal to a countercultural sensibility without being 'counter' to anything specifically" ("Introduction" 23). In doing so, the company's titles managed to convey a vague sense of relevance to real-world debates without offending the political sensibilities of their readers. Likewise, David Bordwell argues that superhero movies such as *Iron Man* or *The Dark Knight* are "*strategically ambiguous* about politics" because they seek to solicit affirmative readings from opposing political camps ("Superheroes," emphasis in the original; see also Burke 38–39). The ability to invite divergent interpretations,

Bordwell notes, allows blockbuster films to encourage discussion and debate and to thereby "create a cultural event" around their own reception (Bordwell, "Superheroes").

In this chapter, I also consider the vagueness and ambiguity of superhero movies as culturally productive and as closely related to their capacity to inspire follow-up conversations. But I furthermore want to suggest that the genre's populism at times generates political effects beyond and apart from the media buzz that films need to generate within the attention economy of twenty-first-century popular culture. By engaging with political subject-matter and by staging affectively powerful moments, superhero blockbusters put images and ideas into cultural circulation and make them available to viewers – and viewers, in turn, occasionally appropriate these contents for their own (implicitly or explicitly) political purposes. In early 2018, for example, *Black Panther*'s engagement with Black radicalism and its depiction of Wakanda as an Afrofuturist utopia was not only positively commented on by reviewers and critics, but also informed expressions of Black solidarity on Twitter and other social media. Around the same time, groups of online activists from different ends of the political spectrum tried to use the film's popularity as a springboard for their own campaigns. I discuss these responses in more detail towards the end of this chapter. But I want to emphasize here that superhero movies not only tell stories about political subject-matter, but also possess a potential to participate in broader cultural debates and ongoing social conflicts. While highly ambiguous, the genre's cinematic populism thus occasionally yields a surplus of political productivity that interacts, contrasts, or aligns itself with responses that one could consider to be intended effects (such as positive reviews) in potentially counter-intuitive ways.[4] Moreover, what is true of *Black Panther* – which in many ways constitutes an exceptional superhero movie that produced responses more explicitly political than other films – is also true of the genre in general, even if the political effects of superhero blockbusters' populism are not always obvious. I argue in the conclusion of this chapter that superhero blockbuster films, by keeping variations of populism's core ideas and motifs in cultural circulation, participate in the perpetuation of a discursive and cultural environment where political populisms continue to resonate. The thematic and stylistic echoes between political populisms and superhero blockbuster films thus are politically significant, even though individual entries of the genre tend to negotiate politics in a notoriously vague and ambivalent fashion.

CINEMATIC POPULISM

In the first chapter of their short volume on the subject, Mudde and Kaltwasser stress populism's status as a "contested concept" that has been defined in a number of different ways: (1) as ideology or type of political movement, for example, but also as shorthand for "a democratic way of life built through popular engagement in politics"; (2) as vehicle for a type of radical emancipatory politics; (3) as label for a redistributive economic policies; (4) as strategy of governance that builds on the direct support of a mass following; or (5) as style of political campaigning that seeks to mobilize a base of supporters against a social, political, or cultural elite (see 2–4). To counter this profusion of competing meanings, Mudde and Kaltwasser suggest that populism is most usefully conceptualized as "a discourse, an ideology, or a worldview" that, to different degrees and in different ways, informs all the phenomena noted above (5). Populism in this sense is a phenomenon of liberal democratic societies (even though its stated goals often run counter to such orders) and usually tied to other, more fully developed ideologies. Taken on its own terms, however, populism is built around the core concepts of the people, the elite, and the general will, which, taken together, allow for a schematic mapping of society and its conflicts. Central to this worldview is what Ernesto Laclau terms the "people/power bloc contradiction" (see Laclau; Mudde and Kaltwasser 9; Bonikowski and Gidron 1594). Following Laclau, Mudde and Kaltwasser stress that the populist category of "the people" is best understood as an "empty signifier" that can be filled with different meanings. This conceptual emptiness not only endows populism with the "capacity to frame 'the people' in a way that appeals to different constituencies," but also enables the generation of "a shared identity between different groups and facilitate their support for a common cause" (9). Populism uses such constructions of "the people" as basis for a moral argument against society's (alleged or actual) domination by self-interested elites, which are imagined as "one homogeneous corrupt group that works against the 'general will' of the people" (11). The general will, in turn, is understood as the political expression of the people's shared interests and often conflated with the notion of "common sense." Accordingly, populist leaders and parties tend to style themselves not only as true and authentic representatives of the general will, but also as committed to shared values and traditions that are attributed to the people – which, in right-wing populisms, are often understood to be ethnically or culturally homogeneous (16–18).

Mudde and Kaltwasser's conception of populism productively overlaps with approaches that use the term as label for a particular style of political agitation. Along these lines, sociologists Bart Bonikowski and Noam Gidron discuss populism as a style of "claims-making" that political actors employ to mobilize support against existing power structures (1593). Bonikowski and Gidron also stress the centrality of the "moral opposition between the people, which are viewed as the only legitimate source of power, and the elites, whose interests are perceived as inherently contrary to those of the populace" (1596). Importantly, however, the authors point out that the production of "visceral emotional reactions" is a central element of populist rhetoric (1598). Populism, so Bonikowski and Gidron note, is effective because it employs "emotionally charged frames" that stoke anger against elites – by emphasizing the elite's immorality, for example, or by overstating the danger that they pose to the common good (1598). Such fear-mongering is particularly openly on display in the "paranoid style" of right-wing populisms, which, as Richard Hofstadter argues, often fuse a Manichean worldview with a "crusading mentality" and an alarmist rhetoric about an impending "social apocalypse" (xii; see Bonikowski and Gidron 1599).

Against this background, the cinematic populism of superhero blockbusters can be understood as a combination of shared thematic preoccupations and common formal tendencies that echo the ideology and affectively charged style of political populisms. Unlike its political counterparts, however, the genre's populism does not seek to mobilize voters or induce social or political change. It also does not engage in the explicit condemnation of actually existing elites or social groups, even though superhero narratives often tell stories about literal strongmen that defend communities against great evils or corrupted power structures. Rather, its central goal is the production of publicity effects. Superhero blockbusters' cinematic populism is thus best understood as a strategy for the mobilization of affirmative audience discourses. It thus serves a similar purpose as the fan management practices discussed in the preceding chapter, although it targets a broader media public and not just the discourses of online fandom. Informed by commercial imperatives, cinematic populism seeks to foster the cultural visibility of superhero movies – and it does so by relying on a set of carefully calibrated themes, figures, and stylistic devices that encourage allegorical interpretations and attribute political significance to entries of the genre.

The overlap between superhero blockbuster cinema's populism and its political counterparts becomes obvious if one compares the thematic building blocks of the superheroic political imaginary with the core concepts of populism's thin-centered ideology. As I argue in Chapter 2, the superheroic political imaginary can be understood as a loosely defined and serially reiterated narrative framework that delineates how political subject-matter can be addressed within the genre. This framework comprises a few basic concepts – exceptional heroes and villains, less powerful regular people, a fundamentally good but corruptible state, a perpetually threatened social order, and the idea that violence is the best means of solving social problems and political conflicts – which entries of the genre bring into ever-new, but often familiar constellations. Read against Mudde and Kaltwasser's work, the categories of the superheroic political imaginary turn out to be closely analogous to the core elements of populism's thin-centered ideology. The genre's villains, for instance, correspond to the elites of political populisms, as both are imagined as self-interested and socially corrupting evil-doers who are ready to accept the loss of innocent civilians as cost of doing business. Just as importantly, the villains' plans often spell doom for the lives of regular people and frequently usher in literal apocalypses. Superheroes, by contrast, dedicate their lives to the fight against such threats and fulfill a similar function as populist leaders (who, in the real-world, often stylize themselves as heroic defenders of a common good). Moreover, the superheroic political imaginary and populist ideologies both tend to frame the people as a collective united in its interest in a just, stable, and functioning social order. In addition, both types of populism treat the category of the people as an "empty signifier" whose exact meaning is often left vague. But the people in the populist sense of the term – that is, the people as a collective actor or subject – only rarely take center stage in superhero narratives. Instead, entries of the genre tend to represent the "people" metonymically, through the inclusion of non-super-powered supporting characters that get caught up in the heroes' adventures – as family members, friends, love interests, bystanders, victims, supporters of the protagonist, or villainous henchmen, for example. The concept of the general will, in turn, finds its equivalent in the prosocial mission of most superheroes. The latter usually manifests itself in efforts to save non-super-powered individuals from harm, but almost never in proactive projects that would benefit all people (such as attempts to remedy structural social problems or reform unjust political orders).[5] In its classical configuration, the superheroic political imaginary is thus structurally conservative, which is why the politics of superhero narratives often lean towards the right as well.

Entries of the genre employ this basic storytelling framework in a variety of variations and permutations, often infusing it with novel ideas or backgrounding some of its elements in favor of others (an adaptability that echoes the malleability of political populisms). The films discussed in this chapter, for example, derive their central conflicts from the ambivalent relationship between a nationalist hero and the state. In such narratives, the state is usually imagined as essentially benevolent yet easily corrupted. As result, the task of defending the state falls to figures such as Captain America and Black Panther, who are presented as personifications or embodiments of the common good.

But the categories of the superheroic political imaginary are only one component of the genre's cinematic populism. The other is a kinetic filmmaking style that combines state-of-the-art visual effects with affectively powerful action sequences that frame superheroes as alluring, more-than-human figures. Just like political populisms, the populism of superhero movies thus attains much of its mobilizing power from its affective charge.[6] As action and adventure films, superhero blockbusters stage spectacular moments that move or excite us, thereby enabling an affective and/or emotional as well as cognitive investment. The films discussed in this chapter connect such moments to the staging of vistas that echo politicized images circulating elsewhere in the contemporary media environment – images of terrorist attacks and urban warfare, of policemen and other representatives of the state meting out violence, and of bodies engaged in physical altercations or performing amazing feats, for example. The staging of extraordinary superheroic bodies is a central element of this strategy. Endowed with impossible agility, levity, endurance, and strength, the heroes of superhero blockbuster cinema leap across large distances, jump from tall buildings and speeding cars without bruising themselves, defeat skilled opponents in hand-to-hand-combat, and quickly recover from injuries that would kill anyone else. While the work of stunt performers, the muscular physique of actors such as Chris Evans and Chadwick Boseman, elaborate fight choreographies, and aspects of cinematography and editing help to convey these abilities, a significant part of this work is also done by computer-generated animation (CGA) technologies that allow for the seamless blending of live-action footage and digitally generated imagery. Crucially, these technologies also allow for the replacement of human actors with computer-generated doubles who can perform in sequences that are too dangerous, expensive, or impractical to shoot otherwise.[7] Dan North suggests that such digitally (re-)created figures make a significant difference for the way in which audiences relate to superhero characters: Virtually indistinguishable from their flesh-and-blood counterparts but extraordinarily capable, digital doubles enable "the indulgence of fantasies of power [. . .], with the digital body standing in for our selves as a surrogate corporealisation of such desire" (171; see also 166–73; Gilmore). In *The Winter Soldier*, *Civil War*, and *Black Panther*, such corporealizations of desire occur in narratives that center on nationalist superheroes and conflicts over state power, a constellation that connects the affective charge of digitally enhanced bodies to vaguely political subject-matter. But the kinetic appeal of cinematic superheroes is not completely contained by political significations or interpretations. Discussing the use of CGA in *Iron Man* (2008), Steen Christiansen notes that digital doubles also are "alluring cinematic object[s]" that, precisely because of their larger-than-life nature, are "not necessarily subsumed to narrative logic, emotional character investment or any other human concern" (33). The protagonists of superhero blockbuster cinema thus oscillate between their function as characters (with more or less clearly established abilities, backstories, and commitments to the state, the people, or the nation) and an existence as affectively intense spectacles. This double character further adds to the broad appeal of the films in which these figures appear, as it allows for a number of different responses on the part of the audience: They might enjoy these films for their staging of cinematic attractions, for their performance of real-world relevance, or for their combination of both.

In summary, the cinematic populism of superhero movies can be understood as a vaguely political assortment of themes, figures, and stylistic devices that endows entries of the genre with the capacity to invite allegorical readings from different partisan standpoints. Reading superhero blockbusters as political allegories, in turn, means adopting a perspective that filters the world through the conceptual framework of superhero narratives. This perspective casts political conflicts as Manichean confrontations, political figures and factions as heroes or villains, and the state as fundamentally benign or a tool of nefarious powers. Expressed within the categories of the superheroic imaginary, even complex political issues and conflicts become simple good versus evil stories that can be resolved through physical confrontations between heroes and villains. However, since the storyworlds of superhero narratives tend to deviate significantly from the world of the viewers, some interpretative work is needed to read entries of the genre as commentaries on specific political issues. Depending on who performs it, this work might yield different results, as not all observers of the genre draw the same parallels. A figure like Captain America, for example, has traditionally been read as both left-leaning defender of the disenfranchised and right-wing champion of conservative values (DiPaolo ix). To a certain extent, such diverging interpretations are made possible by the fact that superhero blockbusters tend to present their heroes (and most of their villains) as "flat" types rather than as rounded, psychologically complex characters.[8] As result, heroes such as Captain America and Black Panther often turn out to be curiously underdefined yet strangely alluring figures that can remain situated above partisan divides. This does not mean that just anything can be read into any given example of the genre. Yet, generally, superhero movies tend to treat political subject-matter in schematic terms that are compatible with different standpoints on the American political spectrum. 2014's *Captain America: The Winter Soldier* provides a good example of this tendency.

THE WINTER SOLDIER BETWEEN CONSPIRACY NARRATIVE AND REAL-WORLD POLITICS

Directed by Anthony and Joe Russo and released in 2014, *Captain America: The Winter Soldier* is the ninth entry of Disney's *Marvel Cinematic Universe* and the second entry of the franchise to focus on Captain America (also known as Steve Rogers; the character also stars in 2011's *Captain America: The First Avenger* and, in a supporting role, in 2012's *The Avengers*). Like other entries of the franchise, *The Winter Soldier* connects to various parts of the *MCU*, but its central storyline encompasses a relatively self-contained conspiracy plot that is introduced and (almost completely) resolved within the film's running time.[9] This plot revolves around a sinister scheme by the evil terrorist organization HYDRA, which has managed to infiltrate the spy agency S.H.I.E.L.D. and seeks to assassinate thousands to impose a new world order. To this end,

HYDRA – which was introduced as a fascist secret society with roots in Nazi Germany in *The First Avenger* – has hijacked S.H.I.E.L.D.'s sophisticated surveillance and weapons technologies. Around the time of its premiere, many reviewers read *The Winter Soldier*'s themes as commentary on recent world events. In part, this response was informed by the timing of the film's release, which occurred less than a year after the 2013 NSA scandal and Edward Snowden's disclosures about the United States' global surveillance capabilities. In an article titled "Captain America and the Age of Snowden," *Buzzfeed*'s Alison Willmore, for example, suggests that the film addressed "contemporary fears about surveillance, secrecy, and the fundamental untrustworthiness of large institutions." Sharing this view, *Film Inquiry*'s David Kahen-Kashi celebrates the film for its "political discussion" of "mass surveillance, monitoring by secret organizations, and censorship." More openly partisan commentators offered similar interpretations: Writing for the far-right website *Breitbart.com*, John Nolte, for example, reads *The Winter Soldier* as "a blatant 175 million 'screw you' to Barack Obama's surveillance state," suggests that villain Alexander Pierce (Robert Redford) embodied a "left-wing ethos," and notes the film's apparent references to "President Obama's kill lists, his drones and dishonest ramping up of the surveillance state" ("Hollywood"). Around the same time, blogger Josh Bell, in a piece for the website of the American Civil Liberties Union, likewise commends the film as a "commentary on targeted killing" and "dragnet surveillance."

The shared tenor of these reviews is hardly a coincidence, as *The Winter Soldier*'s opening moments already foreground the film's potential as political allegory. *The Winter Soldier* begins with a scene that shows an abnormally fast Steve Rogers and the less agile Sam Wilson (also known as The Falcon; portrayed by Anthony Mackie) jogging around the Tidal Basin in downtown Washington DC during their morning workout routine. Over the course of the next minute, the characters pass several historical landmarks, including the Jefferson Memorial, the Washington Monument, the World War II Memorial, and the Reflecting Pool. Eventually, both heroes end up in front of the Capitol building (Figure 5.1), where Rogers is picked up for a mission by his colleague Natasha Romanoff (also known as Black Widow; played by Scarlett Johansson) (*The Winter Soldier* 0:00:32–03:18).[10] The next scene then depicts Rogers, Romanoff, and a team of black ops soldiers aboard a jet-plane speeding through the sky above the Arabian Sea. After some banter, Rogers and his S.H.I.E.L.D. colleagues jump off the plane and board a freighter whose crew has been taken hostage by a group of international terrorists. The ensuing rescue mission unfolds as an extended sequence during which Captain America and Black Widow use their exceptional martial arts skills to overwhelm their opponents (0:03:19–12:56). Afterwards, the film cuts back to Washington DC, where a digitally created aerial establishing shot lets the camera circle around

Figure 5.1 Early in *Captain America: The Winter Soldier* (2014), Steve (Chris Evans) and Sam (Anthony Mackie) work out in front of Washington DC's Capitol building and other political landmarks. Screengrab from Amazon Prime Video.

the Triskelion, S.H.I.E.L.D.'s skyscraper-like headquarters on the shore of the Potomac (0:12:56–13:13). Mapping a trajectory from the heart of American politics onto a foreign battlefield and back home to one of the centers of the nation's security apparatus, these opening minutes associate Captain America with iconic national landmarks, present a kinetic display of military might, and ultimately frame S.H.I.E.L.D. (whose headquarters tower over a tiny capitol visible in the distant background) as the true locus of American power. In doing so, the first few minutes of *The Winter Soldier* already invite interpretations that map the film's concerns onto real-world politics.

Over the course of the next hour, *The Winter Soldier* includes multiple other scenes that encourage such readings. The first of these moments follows directly after the establishing shot of the Triskelion and occurs in a dialogue scene between Rogers and his commanding officer Nick Fury (Samuel L. Jackson). Fury introduces Cap to the agency's newly constructed fleet of networked and partly automated flying fortresses, which are designed to track and kill terrorists to "neutralize [. . .] threats before they even happen" – a plot element that reviewers such as Willmore and Kahen-Kashi connected to the politics of preventive strikes and drone warfare. The scene ends with an argument between the two characters, as Rogers objects to the project on moral grounds (*The Winter Soldier* 0:13:20–16:28). Shortly afterwards, another scene depicts a meeting between Fury's superior Pierce and the members of the "World Security Council," who are tasked with overseeing S.H.I.E.L.D.'s actions. Here, dialogue establishes the agency's status as an American world police (0:22:19–24:11). The film then cuts to a meeting of military veterans chaired by Sam Wilson, who, in this iteration of the *Captain America* property, works for the Department of Veteran's Affairs. At the meeting, a young veteran talks about the difficulty of reintegrating into civilian life (0:24:12–26:00). Directly afterwards, the film cuts to a tense exchange between Fury and two white police officers who have stopped his car for no apparent reason, thereby evoking the specters of racial profiling and police violence against Black men. The moment escalates into a failed attempt on Fury's life, a firefight involving a dozen participants, and a suspenseful car chase through downtown DC (0:26:00–31:55). Later in the film, it is revealed that S.H.I.E.L.D. possesses the technological capability to access anyone's "bank records, medical histories, voting patterns, emails [. . . and] SAT scores," and that HYDRA has developed an algorithm that uses these data to predict future behavior – a theme that allowed the film to be read as commentary on the debates about surveillance and the NSA scandal noted earlier (1:12:04–13:10). In all these instances, references to real-world politics remain brief and quickly give way to action scenes or other confrontations between characters. As result, the film does not really offer substantial engagement with any of the issues raised. Instead, *The Winter Solider* name-checks a variety of political topics – from the ethics of military action, over the re-integration of veterans into society, to police violence against Black men and the dangers of domestic surveillance – so as to perform a sense of relevance to current debates and invite politicizing interpretations (which, in turn, could reference these moments as evidence of the film's political significance).

The above allusions work in conjunction with the film's conspiracy plot. In his book *Conspiracy Theories*, Mark Fenster suggests that narratives about nefarious conspiracies and powerful elites secretly plotting to orchestrate world events are not simply the preserve of fringe groups on the margins of society, but constitute an "integral aspect of American, and perhaps modern and postmodern life" (9). On the one hand, this is so because such narratives are frequently articulated by representatives of the "populist strain in American political culture" who use the motif of conspiracy to rally support against (real or imagined) opponents (9). On the other hand, popular crime and adventure fiction often uses the notion of a far-reaching and powerful conspiracy as a "recurring explanatory and organizational logic" (123). As such, the motif of a hidden conspiracy plays "an integral role in the cause and effect that propel a narrative forward" and provides "a particular set of challenges for the central protagonist" (123). In fact, conspiracy fiction usually revolves around the protagonists' efforts to uncover and stop a wide-ranging, but secret plot that has thrown (or threatens to throw) the world into turmoil, and it often sends central characters on a heroic quest to uncover the truth behind a series of suspicious events (Fenster 122–36).

In *The Winter Soldier*, this quest begins with the attempt on Fury's life, which becomes the starting point for an investigation by Captain America and Black Widow. Around the one-hour mark, the two heroes trace a piece of intelligence back to its source in an abandoned Army camp in rural New Jersey. Here, Rogers and Romanoff find artificial intelligence modeled after the mind of Arnim Zola, one of the villains of the first Captain America film. True to his character as a comic book supervillain, the digitized Zola tells Rogers and Romanoff that S.H.I.E.L.D. had been infiltrated by HYDRA sleeper agents since the agency's early days (0:58:50–1:04:00). The film illustrates these revelations with a diegetic montage sequence that intercuts shots from *The First Avenger* with fictional newspaper clippings, historical newsreel footage, and video of more recent world events – including, among other things, images of Churchill, Roosevelt, and Stalin at the 1945 Yalta conference, Muammar Gaddafi during the 1990s, and a shot of Julian Assange on a balcony of the Ecuadorian Embassy in London in 2012. By including this montage, the film presents a "melding of fact and fiction" that, as Fenster notes, is typical of conspiracy narratives in general (120). In addition, *The Winter Soldier* here stages what Fenster discusses as the "narrative pivot" of conspiracy narratives: a "moment in which the central character, through investigative skill or sheer luck, uncovers convincing evidence of a conspiracy" (124). Here, the true actors and motivations behind the events of the film's first hour are revealed, and the line between good and bad characters is clearly demarcated. Zola's revelations usher in a change in "the pace and tone of the narrative," which now comes to focus on the resolution of the conspiratorial plot. The rest of *The Winter Soldier* then depicts how the conflict between the heroes and HYDRA plays out in a string of escalating confrontations that eventually culminate in a violent showdown during which most of HYDRA's agents are either killed or otherwise incapacitated. Accordingly, the second hour of the film is dominated by fast-paced action set-pieces that include car chases, shoot-outs, fistfights, explosions, and gigantic airships crashing into skyscrapers. In effecting this shift towards spectacular action, the narrative pivot ultimately directs the narrative away from the references to real-world politics featured in other parts of *The Winter Soldier*, thereby allowing the film to avoid a clear stance on any of the issues raised before.

On another level, however, the film's conspiratorial narrative logic added to *The Winter Soldier*'s allegorical potential. Focusing on the revelations of the film's conspiracy plot, *Entertainment Weekly*'s Darren Franich, for example, reads the film as a critique of the American surveillance apparatus. According to Franich, *The Winter Soldier* "basically says that the NSA was invented by Nazis [. . .] and that we let it happen, *insisted* even, giving up our freedom because we were too afraid to do anything else" ("The Real"). For *The Washington Post*'s Alyssa Rosenberg, by contrast, the inclusion of a conspiratorial outside enemy "undermine[s] the movie's critique of the intelligence community," as it presented HYDRA's evil plans – rather than the project of mass surveillance as such – as the central problem. Rosenberg thus suggests that the film ultimately absolves the US government of any wrongdoing. It would be wrong to consider any of these two opinions (or any of the other reviews cited so far) as a misreading of the film's politics, since Rosenberg's and Franich's reviews each argue for their respective interpretations in similarly convincing ways – arguably, however, the film itself is ambiguous enough to make both readings appear equally plausible. But not every critic shared the opinion that *The Winter Soldier*'s best qualities were to be found in its political message. Writing for the popular science-fiction blog *io9*, Charlie Jane Anders characterizes the film as a "brilliant action movie" but "mediocre political thriller" whose "intensity and cleverness [. . .] vanish during moments where [characters] are discussing the plot" (*"Captain America 2"*). In particular, Anders criticizes *The Winter Soldier*'s setting in "a world where everything is black and white" and its failure to deliver meaning political commentary, noting that the latter would be "a natural consequence of building a murky conspiracy thriller around Steve Rogers, the one guy for whom everything is never that complicated" (Anders, *"Captain America 2"*). Anders's assessment points to the limitations of the superheroic political imaginary, which, in its classical configuration, is generally ill-equipped to address problems that cannot be solved through knock-outs and gunfights.

Ultimately, however, *The Winter Soldier*'s combination of conspiratorial plot, vague references to real-world politics, and escalating spectacle proved to be an effective means to encourage a politicized reception. To this end, the film tells a story largely devoid of depictions of "regular" people and instead focuses on a conflict between two camps of powerful elites: Captain America and his allies, on the one hand, and HYDRA's conspirators, on the other. But its narrative about a hero marshalling an armed resistance against a secret plot to overthrow a just political order still revolves around the populist categories of the leader, the elites, and the common good, a construction that resonated with critics, invited allegorical interpretations, and endowed the film with an added layer of political significance. Two years later, the next Captain America-Film, the portentously titled *Civil War*, repeated this exercise with notable variations.

CIVIL WAR, GEOPOLITICS, AND PARTISAN STRIFE

Compared to *The Winter Soldier*, *Civil War* tells a more convoluted story in which confrontations no longer unfold only between superheroes and villains. After an Avengers mission in Lagos, Nigeria, goes awry and results in the death of innocent bystanders, the team is confronted by the newly appointed US Secretary of State General Ross (William Hurt; reprising his role from 2008's *The Incredible Hulk*), who announces that their future activities have to be brought under UN monitoring and control. Ross's demands ultimately split the Avengers into two groups, one led by Captain America, who opposes the regulation, and the other by Iron Man (also known as Tony Stark, portrayed by Robert Downey Jr.), who sees the need for more supervision.[11] This division coincides with the reappearance of Captain America's childhood friend Bucky Barnes (Sebastian Stan), who – after having been outed as a brainwashed super-assassin during the second act of *The Winter Soldier* – now seems to be implicated in a terror attack on a UN summit that kills T'Chaka (John Kani), king of the isolationist African nation of Wakanda. While Captain America and the Falcon go off-grid to prove Bucky's innocence, Iron Man and T'Chaka's son T'Challa (Chadwick Boseman) – heir to the Wakandan throne and, in his identity as the Black Panther, superheroic defender of his homeland – set out to capture Bucky and bring him to justice. The film eventually reveals that the conflicts between Captain America, Iron Man, Bucky, and Black Panther were artificially engineered by the villainous Baron Zemo (Daniel Brühl); the latter blames the Avengers for the death of loved ones who perished when the fictional European country of Sokovia was destroyed during the climax of 2015's *Age of Ultron*. *Civil War* also plays out on a much grander scale than *The Winter Soldier*: Whereas the earlier film covered only a few days of story-time and largely remained confined to a domestic American setting, *Civil War* includes several different timeframes (among them flashbacks set in the early 1990s) and takes its characters to multiple locales around the globe – including the urban settings of Lagos, Manhattan, London, Vienna, Berlin, and Bucharest, as well as the Avengers' compound in upstate New York, an airport outside of Leipzig, and an abandoned military base in Siberia. *Civil War* also features a much larger cast of central and supporting players, as it brings back characters from preceding entries of the *MCU*, including War Machine (Don Cheadle), Black Widow, fellow Avengers Hawkeye (Jeremy Renner), Scarlet Witch (Elizabeth Olsen), and The Vision (Paul Bettany), as well as the less obviously affiliated Ant-Man (Paul Rudd). Finally, the film also introduces a new incarnation of Spider-Man (Tom Holland) into the franchise.

Given its themes and global scope, it is tempting to read *Civil War* as an engagement with what Fredric Jameson terms the "geopolitical unconsciousness" – that is, as an allegorical "attempt to think the world system as such" (4). Writing in the early 1990s, Jameson associates this idea with the "geopolitical aesthetic" of films that, in one way or another, negotiate the effects of an increasingly globalized capitalist order and the rise of a "computerized media technology which eclipses [the world system's] former spaces and faxes an unheard-of simultaneity across its branches" (10). Understood in these terms, *Civil War* invites an allegorical reading as commentary on the fallout of American military interventions around the world, a reading which casts Captain America and his fellow superheroes as stand-ins for the American military and Zemo as an analogue to international terrorism. This view is further supported by the globetrotting trajectory of *Civil War*'s narrative, which appears to collapse or erase any sense of geographical distance, allows characters to quickly and easily move from one location to the next, and presents state actors (such as American intelligence agencies and the German federal police) as operating without regard for national borders and jurisdictions.

Around the time of its theatrical release, many reviewers picked up on these themes and explicitly framed the film as commentary on the United States' ability to project its power around the globe. The *Minneapolis Star Tribune*'s Colin Covert, for example, reads the film as "a smart political allegory" about "civilian body counts," "security procedures that feel more invasive than protective," and "uses of power as the means to an uncertain end." Making a similar case, *The Washington Post*'s Michael Canva, in an interview with the film's directors Anthony and Joe Russo, notes that *Civil War* operates against a "backdrop of geopolitical terror" and suggests that the film "illustrate[s] the impact of violent missions across national borders." In the same piece, Anthony Russo emphasizes that this interpretation resonates with the intentions of the directors, who sought to "correlate superpowers and superheroes with the idea that if you go where you want to in the world, and if you do what you want to do when you go there [. . .] you're going to create a pushback." As was to be expected, however, not all critics were equally convinced of *Civil War*'s political significance. Writing for *The New York Times*, A. O. Scott argues that the film's "aura of vague topical importance" would not make up for its "cumbersome and not very original narrative." Scott also took issue with the "rampant misuse of allegorical interpretation" by "hard-pressed, click-seeking cultural journalists and political pundits" who would predictably find "echoes, resonances and subtexts in a big pop-cultural pseudo-event" such as *Civil War*. Scott's review thus gestures towards the synergistic effects that exist between the publicity goals of filmmakers and the practices of journalists who also need to generate attention within the competitive online discourses of digital-era capitalism – even though his own take on the film, which performed an attitude of contrarian opposition to a mainstream response, was arguably informed by the same imperatives.

Despite Scott's protestations, other critics also saw political concerns reflected in the film, even though many focused on apparent parallels to domestic (rather than international) matters. For these reviewers, the film's focus on regulatory efforts and in-group conflict thus read like an allegory about the ambivalences of state power and the dangers of political polarization. *Wired* reviewer Angela Watercutter, for instance, understands *Civil War* as a commentary on "the struggle between consent and dissent" with governmental authority; likewise, *PopMatters*' Daniel Rasmus sees it as a film about "relationships threatened by politics and circumstance." Writing for *The Daily Beast*, reviewer Nick Schager similarly considers *Civil War* a "conservative manifesto" that celebrates "opposition to imperious federal oversight." Reading Captain America as a quintessentially Republican hero and Iron Man as representative of the "self-critical, dove-ish, nanny-state advocating Left," Schager suggests that the film ultimately sides with its nominal protagonist to tout the virtues of "self-governance." Jim Geraghty, blogging for the website of the traditionally conservative *National Review*, however, sees *Civil War* as "a thought-provoking examination of power, authority, and who watches the watchmen" that "doesn't fit comfortably on either side of the partisan divide." Responding directly to Schager's piece, Geraghty shares the former's reading of the characters' politics, but argues that the film presents Iron Man's position as the more sensible one in a world populated by superheroes and villains.

In foregrounding the themes of governmental oversight and in-group conflict, critics such as Watercutter, Rasmus, Schager, and Geraghty respond to motifs that are most obviously present during the first half of *Civil War*. In a scene around the twenty-minute mark, for example, General Ross stresses the challenge that superheroes pose to the authority of nation states:

> What would you call a group of US-based, enhanced individuals who routinely ignore sovereign borders and inflict their will wherever they choose, and who, frankly, seem unconcerned about what they leave behind? [. . .] For the past four years, you've operated with unlimited power and no supervision. That's an arrangement the governments of the world can no longer tolerate. (*Civil War*, 0:21:58–23:18)

Foregrounding the extralegal status of superheroes, the film here presents the fallout of the Avengers' activities as a political problem that inspires an international regulatory effort. Subsequent scenes then explore the heroes' differing positions on the subject, presenting Captain America's actions as informed by his refusal to yield to superiors with an unclear agenda and explaining Iron Man's deference to the state as motivated by feelings of remorse about lost civilian lives (*Civil War* 0:27:56–31:58; 0:57:37–1:10:06). Interestingly, the film ends without resolving the conflict between the two heroes: Even though Captain America defeats Iron Man during a climactic showdown (Figure 5.2), the final minutes of *Civil War* leave Rogers' half of the Avengers as fugitives from the law and the group around Tony receiving (but ignoring) orders from General Ross. *Civil War* thus avoids siding with either Iron Man or Captain America and keeps their disagreements suspended until the next film brings both figures together again.[12] This open ending presents both characters' positions as equally viable (an ambiguity that registers in a review such as Geraghty's) and lays the groundwork for a further elaboration of the conflict in future installments.

Figure 5.2 *Captain America: Civil War* ends with a showdown between Captain America (Chris Evans) and Iron Man (Robert Downey Jr.). Screengrab from Amazon Prime Video.

Even more importantly, however, *Civil War* eventually reveals that much of the conflict between the heroes was artificially engineered by Baron Zemo. The film thus identifies the real culprit behind the titular civil war as a foreign third party that sowed discord among the (mostly American) group of heroes. On the one hand, this turn of events re-affirms the need for superheroes (and, implicitly, the need for American military interventions abroad). On the other hand, the actions of the villainous Zemo are presented as an almost proportional response to the collateral damage caused by the Avengers; in addition, Zemo's grief over dead family members renders him a more sympathetic villain than previous *MCU* bad guys. In *Civil War*, the lines between good and evil are thus much more diffuse and permeable than in *The Winter Soldier*. Unlike most entries of the genre, the film also does not end with the death of the villain at the hands of the hero, but with Zemo's capture and arrest by Black Panther, the film's other nationalist superhero. This ending seems to affirm the alignment of the superhero and the nation state. Simultaneously, Captain America's continued refusal to yield to a higher authority also allows for a diametrically opposed reading. Ultimately, however, *Civil War* refuses to articulate a clear-cut message and delegates the task of meaning-making to viewers and reviewers.

The comparison between *The Winter Soldier* and *Civil War* reveals interesting differences and similarities: In the first film, a conspiratorial threat to the established order is ultimately averted by the protagonist and his sidekicks; in the second, the solution of a central conflict is deferred to the future of the series. But both films share a focus on alluring, more-than-human figures whose powers rival or outstrip the powers of the state and who confront each other in a series of spectacular action scenes. Both films furthermore present themselves as vaguely political projection screens onto which recipients could cast different meanings.

The last film discussed in this chapter, 2018's *Black Panther*, exhibited a similar openness to divergent interpretations – but it also engendered a much more significant cultural response.

BLACK PANTHER AND THE POLITICS OF AMBIVALENCE

By the time of its theatrical release in February of 2018, the Ryan Coogler-directed *Black Panther* had already become a highly anticipated cultural phenomenon. Garnering significant attention from both fan-oriented media and the mainstream press, *Black Panther* set a record for advance ticket sales in January of the same year (Stewart 4; McNary, "'Black Panther'") – a remarkable development for a movie about a hero that, before Marvel's plans for the film were made public in 2014, was not well known outside of comics fandom. To compensate for the character's relative obscurity, the studio and its marketing partners used the time between the film's announcement and its premiere to release a steady feed of production and casting news, concept art, and other promotional materials, all of which were quickly circulated through social media and picked up by fan-sites and entertainment news outlets. The emerging marketing narrative positioned Black Panther as an emphatically Black superhero movie steeped in an Afrofuturist aesthetic, helmed by a Black director and lead by an ensemble cast of Black actors. In October of 2017, a newly released trailer showcased *Black Panther*'s looks to the tune of a soundtrack that sampled Gil Scott-Heron's "The Revolution Will Not Be Televised," a presentation that readied the ground for politicizing readings of the film. Buoyed by a wealth of entertainment news coverage and reporting, the marketing campaign generated, as Ann Hornaday later noted in her *Washington Post* review, an atmosphere of "breathless hype" that accompanied the run-up to the film's eventual release. For Hornaday, this hype turned out to be well-founded, as *Black Panther* deserved to be celebrated for its engagement with "the legacy of colonialism; [. . .] the tension between autonomy and social conscience; and the need for solidarity within an African diaspora at political and cultural odds with itself." Making a similar case, *Time*'s Jamil Smith suggested that the film was centrally about "what it means to be black in both America and Africa – and, more broadly, in the world." Smith also stressed *Black Panther*'s cultural significance as . . .

> . . . the first megabudget movie – not just about superheroes, but about anyone – to have an African-American director and a predominantly black cast. Hollywood has never produced a blockbuster this splendidly black. [. . .] *Black Panther* is poised to prove to Hollywood that African-American narratives have the power to generate profits from all

audiences. And, more important, that making movies about black lives is part of showing that they matter.

Smith's views were echoed by many other critics. *The Atlantic*'s Vann R. Newkirk II, for example, praises the film's "incredible gains in representation" and characterizes it as a "fantasy about black power" that grapples with "the idea of a global revolution by black peoples" (for reviews along similar lines, see Brody; Barber). But not all reviewers shared these positive impressions. *The Guardian*'s Kenan Malik, for example, dismisses *Black Panther* as a "mediocre film" that lacks deeper engagement with the themes of political radicalism and resistance. But even Malik agrees that the film reflects a utopian "need for hope in gloomy post Obama times."

In light of the film's release against the backdrop of the Black Lives Matter protests and the hard right turn of American politics during the years of the Trump presidency, it is perhaps inevitable that *Black Panther* was received as "an ideologically charged affirmation of Black pride," as literary scholar Jarrel De Matas puts it (120). But *Black Panther* also invited such readings openly, as it not only included much lauded performances by Black actors but staged Wakanda as an Afrofuturist utopia characterized by a mix of traditional African fashions and architectures, science-fictional high technology, and computer-generated cityscapes – a combination which itself generated considerable media attention.[13] The film further encouraged politicizing readings by centering on the conflict between the eponymous hero and the villainous Killmonger – characters who, as *The New Yorker*'s Jelani Cobb notes, could be read as "dueling responses to five centuries of African exploitation at the hands of the West." As the recently ascended king of Wakanda, Boseman's T'Challa is the ruler of a never colonized yet technologically advanced isolationist nation-state whose exceptional status is based on an abundance of the mystical metal vibranium. Over the course of *Black Panther*, T'Challa's rule over Wakanda is challenged by – and temporarily lost to – his long-lost cousin Eric Stevens (née N'Jadaka, also known as Killmonger), who, due to the country's laws of succession, also has a rightful claim to the throne. However, where T'Challa pursues a policy of non-interference in the domestic affairs of other countries, Killmonger seeks to use Wakanda's resources to arm insurgents and to support a campaign of international Black liberation. The film presents this conflict as both personal and political, as Killmonger is at least in part motivated by the death of his father N'Jobu (Sterling K. Brown) at the hands of T'Challa's late father T'Chaka (again portrayed by John Kani and, in flashbacks, also Atandwa Kani). The ensuing confrontation between T'Challa and Killmonger is furthermore framed as a battle of contrasting temperaments that pits the calm and regal T'Challa against the ruthless and unrestrained

Killmonger, who is prone to violent outbursts and does not hesitate to kill even close associates.

Black Panther's short-circuiting of political and personal conflicts registered prominently in the many reviews that celebrate Killmonger as sympathetic villain: *Vulture*'s Kyle Buchanan, for example, argues that the character's quest was "rooted in more provocative real-world issues than any Marvel villain thus far" ("How"). Noting *Black Panther*'s resonance with real-world injustices, *The New Yorker*'s Doreen St. Félix likewise suggests that "Killmonger's rage and rashness are more coherent" than T'Challa's position ("On Killmonger"). But some critics – and those more explicitly situated on the left in particular – also take issue with the film's depiction of Black radicalism. Writing for the website *Africa Is a Country*, Russel Rickford, for example, dismisses *Black Panther* as "a counterrevolutionary film" that seeks to delegitimize more radical forms of activism by portraying Killmonger's project as "a bitter crusade for vengeance rather than as a rational response to the horrors of white supremacy and imperialism." Making a similar case, Charles Athanasopoulos, in his contribution to the volume *Why Wakanda Matters*, suggests that Killmonger ultimately represents "a caricature" that serves to "demonize Black radicalism" (138). Fittingly, *Black Panther* was positively reviewed by *Breitbart*'s John Nolte, who advances an affirmative interpretation from the right that commends the film's apparent endorsement of isolationism, frames T'Challa as an analogue to Donald Trump, and identifies Killmonger as stand-in for the Black Lives Matter movement ("'Black Panther'").

Nolte's review was an outlier in a larger field of (mostly negative) responses from the American right – but, like the other reviews cited thus far, his reading nonetheless points to the range of allegorical interpretations afforded by the film. Like *Civil War* before it, *Black Panther* refuses to articulate a clear-cut political message and instead offers a set of carefully layered ambiguities. Writing about these ambiguities, media scholar Derilene Marco notes that, on the one hand, the film exploited the "affectivity" of hypercompetent Black superheroes and super-villains for commercial gain. On the other hand, *Black Panther*'s "exceptional positive portrayals of black characters" generated "awareness and readings of blackness beyond the film" (9) – a development that was especially noteworthy as it occurred within a genre that has traditionally construed whiteness as the norm (see 1–2). This discursive productivity was closely related to the depiction of Killmonger as a charismatic villain who is more than a match for the titular hero. In *Black Panther*, Killmonger and his father N'Jobu both articulate radical assessments of the long history of slavery and oppression in the United States. One hour into the film, for example, a flashback sequence set in 1992, the year of the Los Angeles riots, shows N'Jobu confronting his brother about

Wakanda's refusal to intervene in the domestic affairs of countries that oppress Black people:

> I observed for as long as I could. Their leaders have been assassinated. Communities flooded with drugs and weapons. They are overly policed and incarcerated. All over the planet, our people suffer because they don't have the tools to fight back. (*Black Panther* 1:03:09–37)

Later in the film, Killmonger similarly vows to provide "black folks" with the "firepower" needed to "fight their oppressors" (1:26:11–20). In his final scene, Killmonger even situates his own actions within a long history of African-American resistance that reaches back to the Middle Passage of the Atlantic slave trade: "Just bury me in the ocean. With my ancestors that jumped from the ships. Cause they knew death was better than bondage" (*Black Panther* 1:53:04–15; Figure 5.3). Killmonger's goal of overthrowing oppressive social orders and the rootedness of his struggle in a very real history of violence against Blacks render him a sympathetic figure – a characterization that played no small part in the positive critical reception of Jordan's character. But, as Athanasopoulos points out, the film also presents Killmonger as an exaggerated and violent embodiment of "toxic masculinity" who is at least in part driven by a lust for revenge (143; see 143–45). Effectively painting Killmonger as a ruthless villain whose actions cannot be excused, *Black Panther* thus remains indebted to a conventional configuration of the superheroic political imaginary that frames attacks on existing social and political orders as inherently dangerous.

This inherently conservative worldview also informs *Black Panther*'s central conflict, which pits Killmonger against the idealized representative of a nation-state with a fundamentally just social order. Crucially, however, T'Challa's

Figure 5.3 With his last words, Killmonger (Michael B. Jordan) situates his actions within a longer history of African-American struggle. Screengrab from Amazon Prime Video.

conflict with Killmonger is not only a struggle over the kingdom of Wakanda, but also a fight for the continued existence of an established international order – after all, T'Challa repeatedly refuses to use Wakandan weapons to arm insurrectionists abroad. Not coincidentally, this conflict comes to a head during a drawn-out battle sequence towards the end of the film, in which the hero and his army face off against Killmonger and his allies, while the villain's planes try to get a shipment of weapons out of the country (*Black Panther* 1:37:40–49:15). The sequence ends with Killmonger's troops surrendering to T'Challa's authority and the planes being shot out of the sky by CIA agent Everett Ross (Martin Freeman) – and thus with a return to order that re-affirms pre-existing Wakandan and international states of affairs. The film's depiction of Killmonger as a sympathetic (if seriously flawed) villain is thus counter-balanced by the structural conservatism of *Black Panther*'s overall narrative trajectory.

In producing such ambiguities, Coogler's film offered reviewers plenty of material to interpret. Depending on reviewers' political leanings, these interpretations produced different results. For some critics, the film presents itself as an uplifting and inspiring celebration of Black power; for others, it represents an essentially conservative dismissal of radical politics; for yet others, it amounts to an affirmation of Trumpist policies. All these readings capture some aspects of the film's politics while backgrounding, downplaying, or ignoring others – and all of them are based on the idea that *Black Panther* is a meaningful political allegory in the first place. The widespread acceptance of this view attests to the textual productivity of allegorical interpretation as a journalistic and critical practice that offers reviewers a ready-made template for the discussion of superhero blockbuster films. Critics who answered *Black Panther*'s ambivalent messaging with allegorical interpretations ultimately contributed to the media hype about the film. In doing so, these reviewers participated in the phenomenon they set out to comment on, adding their voices to a diverse choir of critical opinions, marketing efforts, and promotional materials that also insisted on the film's cultural and political significance.

The cultural phenomenon of *Black Panther*, however, extends well beyond marketing narratives and the responses of professional critics. In the days and weeks around its premiere, *Black Panther* inspired an unprecedented number of posts on Twitter, where the use of the hashtags #Black Panther and @BlackPanther first set a new record for unique posts in a single day and eventually made Coogler's film the most tweeted about movie of 2018 (D'Alessandro; Peris). The Twitter traffic about the film also included several hashtags under which users stressed the need for Black representation within popular culture in general – such as the posts published under #WhatBlackPantherMeansToMe (Diaz). The positive audience response to the film took on other forms as well. In her contribution to the volume *Why Wakanda Matters*, Stewart discusses the Wakandan salute – "the crossing of the arms over one's chest as a greeting" – and the phrase "Wakanda Forever" as expressions of Black solidarity that were inspired by the film (10). Stewart suggests that the salute and the exclamation, which were performed on social media and elsewhere, expressed a utopian "desire to live in a different world – one that demolishes the oppression of Black people" (8). As Stewart puts it, . . .

> When people say "Wakanda Forever," they are celebrating a place where they can live in harmony. For them, Wakanda, represents
> - a place where Black people create and sustain their own;
> - a place where Black people can serve as a leader without someone demanding his – or her – birth certificate again and again;
> - a place where when Black people, put their hands up, nobody shoots; or better yet,
> - a place where Black people never have to put their hands up;
> - a place where Black people can drink tea, eat skittles, and walk home in peace;
> - a place where Black people can ride a train on New Year's Eve and not be shot while handcuffed;
> - a place where Black people can breathe;
> - a place where the strength and beauty of a Black woman is the norm;
> - and a place where no one ever has to say "Me Too." (9)

Arguably, not everyone using the Wakandan salute or the phrase "Wakanda Forever" invested the gestures with these exact meanings. But Stewart's response itself demonstrates the film's capacity to latch onto and mobilize, as she puts it, the "fantasy of living in a better place." In light of the United States' long and continued history of white supremacy and institutionalized racism, this fantasy inevitably took on a political dimension as it challenged a view of the US as a fundamentally just and well-ordered society. By inspiring such expressions of Black solidarity and utopian longing, *Black Panther* thus generated latently political effects that extended beyond the media buzz which the film and its marketers sought to produce. This political surplus productivity became tangible on Twitter and other platforms – but its significance could not be easily measured, as it manifested itself not only in tweets, but also in subjective affects and feelings that were more difficult to quantify.

Notably, however, *Black Panther* also prompted more explicitly political audience responses. In the days and weeks before the film's premiere, far-right online activists organized on Facebook to drive down the film's rating on *Rotten Tomatoes* by posting negative user reviews to the site – efforts which were quickly shut down by both platforms and ultimately did not significantly impact the film's public reception (Van Winkle, "Absurd Trolls"; Smith, "Revolutionary"). After the start of *Black Panther*'s theatrical run, activists from the same spectrum also started a disinformation campaign on Twitter that, among other things, circulated false claims about attacks on white moviegoers (see Muncy, "Twitter Trolls"; Parker). This second campaign also proved to be relatively unsuccessful, as most of its posts were quickly drowned out by satirical retorts and fact-checking tweets that generated a higher volume of responses (for an analysis, see Babcock, Villa Cox, and Kumar). But these far-right activities nonetheless attest to the affective power of the film – which, in addition to inspiring expressions of Black solidarity and longing, also inspired a reactionary backlash that sought to counter the apparent gains in representation.

Around the same time, activists from the other side of the political spectrum sought to channel the hype around the film into more constructive purposes as well. In February of 2018, the activist group Electoral Justice Project launched the #WakandaTheVote campaign on Twitter, which encouraged users to register for the then-upcoming mid-term elections via text message and promoted efforts to "set up voter registration events" at movie theaters (Lockhard; see also Muncy, "These Activists"). Using imagery from Marvel's *Black Panther* comics to promote its cause, the campaign's message was quickly picked up by fan-oriented websites and other online news outlets. Other activists adopted a more critical stance towards the Disney conglomerate. Shortly before the film's premiere, a Change.org-campaign titled #BreakBreadMarvel protested *Black Panther*'s perceived cooptation of Black identity politics and called on Disney and Marvel Studios to invest "*25% percent of their WORLDWIDE profit* [. . .] in black communities" (Gormley; for coverage of this campaign, see Pimentel). The campaign's statement of purpose justified these ambitious goals by pointing to the studios' targeting of Black audiences and argued that these had little to gain in supporting the film:[14]

> As black communities across the United States continue to grapple with issues such as gentrification, police brutality, and substandard living conditions we cannot continue to recklessly support these conglomerates, allowing them to profit off of us without demanding something more than just their products in return. (Gormley)

Like other activist responses to the film, the #BreakBreadMarvel campaign ultimately did not make a significant difference for the film's box-office performance or the distribution of its profits. While the campaign generated some coverage by fan-oriented websites and other news outlets, its petition eventually garnered less than 12,000 signatures. Thus, the project eventually faded into the background noise of a ceaselessly busy online media public. Before doing so, however, the campaign had highlighted the tensions between *Black Panther*'s themes of Black radicalism and self-sufficiency, the expressions of

Black solidarity it inspired, and the commercial interests of the Disney conglomerate – which sought to capitalize on the film's Blackness but did not intend to share its profits with anyone.

From the interpretations of reviewers and critics, over the reactions of Twitter users, to the campaigns of political activists, the diverse responses to *Black Panther* demonstrate the film's ability to mobilize what Chapter 1 has discussed as cultural externalities: discursive activities in the environment of superhero blockbuster films that add to (or detract from) their public visibility and positive critical reception. Either boosting or trying to counter the hype around *Black Panther*, these responses contributed to the multi-faceted discourse about the film and further invested it with political meaning. In doing so, the activities that clustered around the film expressed concerns that were not identical with the commercial goals of the producers. The activist campaigns discussed above, for instance, ultimately pursued their own political agendas; likewise, the allegorical readings of critics were informed by the need to produce content, to meet deadlines, and to generate clicks. Similarly, the profits of the Disney conglomerate probably were not the primary concern of the movie-goers who shared their enthusiasm about the film on social media. But in latching onto the film and by circulating online, the responses of these audiences invariably contributed to the cultural visibility of *Black Panther*. These reactions also demonstrated the curious logics of a digital capitalism that can turn even radical political gestures into economically productive externalities. This does not mean that the political and cultural significance of *Black Panther* was completely absorbed or counter-acted by commercial interests. First and foremost, latently political affects and individual responses to the film belonged to the viewers and were not necessarily subjected to the valorization mechanisms of cognitive capitalism. However, the textualized expressions of such responses – in social media posts, reviews published by online publications, and the campaigns of online activists, for example – inevitably added to the vast amount of online activity that, in early 2018, ensured *Black Panther*'s medial omnipresence.

CONCLUSION

Like its political counterparts, the populism of superhero blockbuster cinema can be understood as tool for the mobilization of popular support – albeit a tool that targets influential voices within the media environment (such as reviewers, critics, and users of social media) instead of voters. In fact, the genre's populism is curiously disinterested in the articulation of unambiguous political statements or the production of political effects. Contemporary superhero blockbusters generally keep their references to real-world politics superficial and couch their messages in an ambiguity that, as scholars such as Richard Maltby argue, is typical for Hollywood cinema. This superficiality and ambiguity endow superhero movies with an unusual capacity to solicit a positive reception from critics with diverse partisan identifications. Despite this, most entries of the genre articulate a relatively uniform worldview. *The Winter Soldier*, *Civil War*, and *Black Panther*, for example, all divide their casts of characters into two groups: superheroes and villains, on the one hand, and regular people, one the other. More precisely, the everyday realities of ordinary people here provide the staging grounds for conflicts between the heroes and the villains, which occupy the narrative center of each movie. Because the threats posed by the villains tend to be enormous, their containment is best left to hyper-competent and morally superior elites – other actors (such as organs of a state, for example) are not up the task and easily corrupted anyway. The villains, in turn, are occasionally supplied with tragic backstories, but usually seek to overthrow or destroy established orders. Yet, heroes and villains are united in their penchant for violence, which is presented as the best means to defend or challenge the social order. The emphasis on violence resonates with the fact that ordinary people are rarely given much screen-time in superhero blockbusters – and with the fact that more democratic or egalitarian kinds of political activity (such as grassroots activism or community organizing) do not appear to exist in the world of Marvel movies. Despite the opinions of reviewers, the films discussed in this chapter thus are poor vehicles for the exploration of political subject-matter, as their basic conceptual framework is simply too limited to represent complex social relationships, conflicts, and modes of settling them.

That does not mean that the genre is politically insignificant, only that its significance manifests itself on a more abstract level, one that is somewhat removed from the interpretations of professional critics or the responses of individual viewers. In Chapter 1, I noted that the products of the culture industry should not be understood as tools for direct ideological interpellation. After all, consumers are free to reject or question cultural commodities and the messages that they articulate. In fact, consumers have to assume a critical distance to the objects of their recreational consumption practices, if they want to successfully navigate the vast entertainment landscapes of the early twenty-first century. But superhero blockbusters, like other popular entertainment, still put messages, ideas, narratives, and concepts into cultural circulation. In *The Reality of the Mass Media*, Luhmann suggests that the production of widely known "topics," conversational "objects," and other "condensates of meaning" is a central function of the mass media as a social system (37). Drawing on Luhmann's work, Elena Esposito similarly argues that the mass media provide a commonly accepted repertoire of conceptual distinctions which informs the ways in which societies observe and describe themselves – precisely because the ongoing character and wide reach of mass medial communication allows for "the repeated use of the same concepts in different situations" (21, translation mine; see 213–39). Likewise, the political significance of superhero blockbuster's cinematic populism lies not so much in its overt messages, but rather in the inventory of conceptual distinctions that these films make available. Taken together, these distinctions provide a ready-made pattern for the mapping of a social reality that imagines the world as battleground for Manichean struggles between exceptional people while regular folks observe from the sidelines. As I have shown at the beginning of this chapter, this pattern also circulates outside of the superhero genre. Sketches on late night television, political advertising, and allegorizing film reviews, for example, all disseminate elements of the genre's populism further, thereby preparing the ground for its continued appropriation by other actors. In this manner, superhero blockbuster cinema participates in an ongoing serialization of populist ideologies.

This does not mean that superhero blockbuster cinema can be blamed for the rise of right-wing populism in the US and elsewhere, which is rooted in political and economic realities quite distinct from (though not unrelated to) the operations of popular entertainments. But the continued popularity of superhero blockbusters still contributes to the perpetuation of a latent everyday culture in which political populisms can continue to resonate and appear as meaningful responses to existing social conditions.

NOTES

1. See my discussion of the mainstreaming of fandom and superhero narratives as "unfree symbolic commons" in Chapter 1. Einwächter, Ossa, Sina, and Stollfuss similarly note that the Trump campaign's Thanos-tweet gives testament to the fact that "comic book narratives" have become "part of a mainstream cultural repertoire that is easily accessible" (152). Arguably, however, this observation is more accurate for superhero narratives than it is for comics in general.
2. My usage of allegory here follows Dietmar Peil's understanding of the term; he uses it as shorthand for any "complete text or larger text-segment whose meaning can only be accessed through reference to another level of significance, while its foregrounded literal meaning remains largely irrelevant" (12, translation mine). In the years after 2001, reviewers and critics have read films such as *Superman Returns* (2006), *V for Vendetta* (2005), or *The Dark Knight* (2008) as allegories on post-9/11 American culture and politics (for examples, see Stanford; Simonpillai; Corliss; Davidson; Stevens, "The Dark Knight"). This tendency was prominent among scholarly engagements with the genre as well (for examples, see Kellner, *Cinema Wars*; Hassler-Forest, *Capitalist Superheroes*; DiPaolo; for a nuanced take on such approaches, see Packard).
3. For reviews that read the *Iron Man* films (2008, 2011, 2013) as allegories on American military engagements in the Middle East, see Stevens, "Iron Man"; Hunter; Suebsaeng; Darius. For a discussion of Nolan's *The Dark Knight Rises* (2012) as a conservative commentary on left-wing protest movements such as Occupy, see Graeber.

4. It is important to note here that audience responses (of any kind) exceed the direct control influence of creative actors (producers, screenwriters, directors) involved in the making of these films. As I have suggested in the Introduction, the behavior of audiences is never simply the mere result of film reception, but complexly entangled with the actions and affordances of innumerable actors and agencies. Similarly, the discursive resonance and excess political productivity of superhero movies is a product of countless different agencies joining forces under contingent circumstances – of larger political climates, of the conventions of superhero narratives reiterated by individual films, of filmic images and moments that take on political meaning accidentally or coincidentally, of journalists faced with the need to meet word counts and deadlines, of critics who write about politics and popular culture for a living, and of lay audiences who see their own politics reflected in or challenged by superhero movies, for instance.
5. Due to the serial character of the genre's unfolding, exceptions to this rule do, in fact, exist. James McTeigue's *V for Vendetta* (2005), for example, presents itself as an overtly anti-fascist superhero narrative in which the hero manages to bring down the authoritarian government of a dystopian near-future Britain with the support of a mass populist uprising (on *V for Vendetta*, see Beer; Kohns). See the Conclusion.
6. Drawing on the work of Gilles Deleuze and Félix Guattari, Brian Massumi defines affect as "a pre-personal intensity corresponding to the passage from one experiential state of the body to another" ("Notes" xvi). Shouse similarly discusses affect as "a non-conscious experience of intensity, [. . .] a moment of unformed and unstructured potential." Affect in this sense is to be distinguished from feeling (that is, "a sensation that has been checked against previous experiences and labelled") and emotion ("the projection/display of a feeling") (Shouse). What I discuss as "affective charge" thus refers to films' ability to affect viewers – that is, films' capacity to provide intense experiences that are registered on a bodily level and that, subsequently, can be qualified in terms of feeling and cognition (or meaning).
7. For overviews of the visual effects shots and detailed technical discussions of the CGA technologies used in the films discussed in this chapter, see Duncan, "Captain's Orders," "A Family Affair"; Edwards, "Afrofuture." *The Winter Soldier*, *Civil War*, and *Black Panther* all not only made extensive use of digital doubles, but also relied on digital visual effects technologies to render virtual environments and combine them with footage shot in studios and on location.
8. Jared Gardner notes that the flat characters of serial fiction generally tend to invite a more intense attachment on the part of recipients than the more rounded characters of self-contained literary works (57–58).
9. *The Winter Soldier*'s conspiracy plot ties into an ongoing storyline of the ABC television series *Agents of S.H.I.E.L.D.* (2013–20; see Chapter 3), but most of the film's central conflicts are resolved by the end of its last act.
10. All times according to the German Amazon Video release of *The Winter Soldier*, titled, like the German theatrical release, *The Return of the First Avenger* (see Filmography: Feature Films).
11. Iron Man's readiness to accept such regulatory efforts is the result of a confrontation with the mother (played by Alfre Woodard) of a civilian casualty who, in an example of retroactive continuity, is said to have died offscreen during the events of *Age of Ultron*. Woodard's character (which only receives a few minutes of screen-time) represents one of the few instances in which regular people play a crucial part in the unfolding of the conflicts between heroes and villains.

12. Accordingly, the conflict between Captain America and Iron Man resurfaces as a minor plot point in 2018's *Avengers: Infinity War*, where the differences are quickly set aside, as more pressing problems need to be addressed.
13. For news media coverage of costume designer Ruth E. Carter's work on *Black Panther* and its adaptation of traditional fashions from a variety of African cultures, see Ryzik; Frederick; St. Félix, "Ruth"; on the film's Afrofuturist cityscapes and architecture, see Edwards, "Afrofuture."
14. Notably, the marketing efforts for the film included a pre-release campaign that, as Disney marketing executive Asad Ayaz explains to the *Hollywood Reporter*, aimed to "super-serv[e] black moviegoers while also making [the film] the broadest moviegoing event" (McClintock). To this end, marketing efforts for *Black Panther* included "heavy ad buys for sports that deliver big African American audiences, [. . .] a music tie-in led by rapper Kendrick Lamar, as well as a stop at New York Fashion Week," with the latter featuring designs inspired by Ruth E. Carter's work for the film.

Conclusion: Superhero Blockbusters as Entertainment for the Age of Cognitive Capitalism

> Hollywood remains trapped in old ideas and stale forms – in narrative paradigms that look increasingly dubious in the light of current events. The dominant genre of the 21st century so far has been the superhero movie, with an ethos (and often a fan base) that is fundamentally antidemocratic. The institutions of government (with the occasional and ideologically significant exception of the municipal police department) are venal and incompetent. Their civic functions are better left to rich guys, ultrapowerful mutants or off-the-books paramilitaries made up of industrialists, military officers and demigods. Meanwhile, the public is entirely disempowered, cowering in fear of evil intruders or whipped up into a frenzy by unscrupulous demagogues. The hero alone can save them.
>
> (A. O. Scott, in: Dargis and Scott, "One Nation Under a Movie Theater? It's a Myth." *The New York Times*, September 7, 2017)

> Whenever Adeline attended a comic book convention and encountered *cosplay*, she was sure that she was witnessing the ultimate state of late period capitalism. People who spent their leisure time *tweeting* and creating intellectual property for Twitter were going out into the world and dressing themselves as the intellectual properties of major international corporations. They had performed their bodies into walking advertisements for entities in which they had no economic stake. These advertisements would later appear in photographs on Facebook and Twitter and Tumblr and Pinterest and Flickr and be collated on advertising supported websites like *Newsarama* and *io9* and *The Mary Sue*. Brand identity was complete.
>
> (Jarett Kobek, *I Hate the Internet* [2016], 149)

Asked about the company's competitors at Netflix's earnings call, [CEO Reed] Hastings said that he isn't really concerned about Amazon and HBO "because the market is just so vast." "You know, think about it, when you watch a show from Netflix and you get addicted to it, you stay up late at night. We're competing with sleep, on the margin. And so, it's a very large pool of time." The company and its more traditional competitors, he said, are like "two drops of water in the ocean of both time and spending for people"

(Alex Hern, "Netflix's Biggest Competitor? Sleep." *The Guardian*, April 18, 2017)

Taken together, the above quotes – two from widely-read mainstream newspapers, the third from a formally experimental novel about the Internet age – address three aspects of superhero blockbusters' contemporary prominence that are central to the argument developed in this book. In the first quote, *New York Times* film critic A. O. Scott connects a complaint about superhero blockbuster cinema's perceived lack of innovation to an argument about the political significance of the genre. Superhero movies, he suggests, are not only devoid of aesthetic value and narrative innovation, but also prime examples of a morally bankrupt, latently anti-democratic, crowd-pleasing cinema in the age of Trump. In the second quote, comics artist Adeline, one of the protagonists of Kobek's short novel, reflects on digital-era capitalism and its tendency to harness the cultural activities of media audiences for commercial gain. In the eyes of Adeline, user activity on social media and practices like cosplay are little more than fuel for a culture-industrial machinery that avails itself of the free labor of fans and then sells the products of this labor back to the audience. In this scenario, media fans appear as naive cultural producers who are subjected to forces beyond their control, and online fan culture is presented as the appendix of an entertainment industry that only cares about consumers if their practices increase its bottom-line. Finally, in the third quote, Netflix CEO Reed Hastings articulates a vision of his company's potential for future growth that echoes Jonathan Crary's notion of a 24/7 culture. According to Hastings, viewers' need to reconstitute their bodily capacities constitutes a cap for further market growth. This boundary could be overcome, however, if consumers could be convinced to sleep less and stream more. On the one hand, this vision is relevant here because video-on-demand platforms such as Netflix, Amazon Video, Disney+, or HBO Max have become the most important distribution nodes for all kinds of filmic and televisual content during the COVID-19 pandemic. On the other hand, Hastings's musings are especially instructive if we consider the business model of such services, which are built around the sale of access to streaming libraries and the valorization of user activity. For a company such as Netflix, serialized television dramas and hyper-referential superhero franchises are ideal tools to maximize the time and attention that users dedicate to the platform, especially if getting hooked on a series means ignoring the offerings of other providers. If we accept these three statements, superhero blockbusters must appear as embodiments of contemporary popular culture's worst tendencies: as form of unoriginal entertainment whose stories are, at best, politically dubious; as tool for the exploitation of unpaid fan labor; and as type of media content designed to chain media users to a "global infrastructure for continuous work and consumption" (as Crary puts it in *24/7*) (3).

The preceding chapters of this book have argued that twenty-first-century superhero blockbusters embody all these tendencies to some extent. But it would nonetheless be wrong to reduce superhero movies to the status of mere vehicles of an oppressive culture-industrial apparatus. In fact, all the claims made above need to be taken with a healthy grain of salt. Superhero blockbusters' narrative mechanics and political allegiances, for example, are not as uniform and transparent as Scott implies. As serial narratives, superhero blockbusters must balance repetition with variation. As result, old ideas and stale forms are bound to be modified by narrative twists and stylistic innovations sooner rather than later. The evolution of the hyper-referential style since 1978's *Superman* gives testament to the radical changes that have occurred within superhero blockbuster cinema, as this early superhero blockbuster differs significantly from the extravagant spectacles of, say, *Zack Snyder's Justice League* (2021). Most entries of the genre nonetheless remain indebted to the categories of a structurally conservative worldview that frames the world as a realm of good-versus-evil conflicts between exceptional elites. I have argued in the preceding chapter that the basic categories of this worldview echo the ideologies of populists who try to mobilize support for a struggle against elites which are imagined as corrupt. Scott's remarks thus identify a particularly troubling aspect of superhero blockbuster cinema. But entries of the genre usually couch their political messages in layers of ambiguity – and sometimes perform interesting revisions or inversions of the genre's storytelling formula.

James McTeigue's *V for Vendetta* (2005), for example, sides with a figure that, in most other entries of the genre, would be classified as a villain rather than a hero. Haunted by traumata suffered in the past and driven by a lust for revenge, the film's faceless protagonist V (Hugo Weaving) stages a terror campaign against the government of a dystopian England and eventually overthrows said government with the help of a mass insurrection. Towards the end of the film, the people of London, clad in identical costumes that resemble the get-up of the film's hero, march towards the Houses of Parliament. Confronted with masses that easily outnumber them, the security forces assembled to stop the protesters surrender their guns and let them pass. Viewed in 2021, the sequence seems to premediate the storming of the United States Capitol by supporters of President Trump on January 6 of that year. This reading resonates with the film's focus on a conflict between a fundamentally good people (who, awoken by a populist leader, eventually take their protest to the streets) and a small cabal of nefarious elites. But, in other moments, *V for Vendetta* leaves little doubt that fascist leaders, hate-spewing television pundits, and the systematic oppression of minorities are the real enemy of the people. Early in the film, the protagonist V also justifies his actions as a struggle for "fairness, justice, and freedom." In including such moments, *V for Vendetta* performs an operation typical of superhero blockbusters: It evokes seemingly universal (but only vaguely defined) ideals, avoids adopting a too controversial stance on concrete political subject-matter, and ultimately affirms a populist worldview. Arguably, it was precisely this vagueness which made the film appealing to viewers who sought to invest it with their own meanings.

And invest they did. In the years after 2006, the Guy Fawkes-mask, which the protagonist V uses as part of his costume, quickly became popular as an all-purpose symbol for street protests of various stripes and eventually came to be used by activists around the world (on the mask as a protest symbol, see Beer; Call; Sonçul). In the process, the mask was worn by activists with diverse political backgrounds and agendas: libertarian defenders of capitalism and anarchists facing off on the streets of Manhattan in 2006 (see Launder); members of the international Hacktivist collective Anonymous in 2008 (see Kushner); participants of the 2011 Occupy protests in New York and elsewhere; protesters in Istanbul's Gezi Park in 2013 (see Sonçul 1; Kohns 90; Beer 96); and far-right autonomous nationalists in Germany in 2016 (see Diesing). The iconography of *V for Vendetta* thus turned out to be as versatile and adaptable to new situations as the storytelling engine at the heart of the superhero genre. The drive of this engine is populist, but its parts can swing into different directions – and sometimes, they seem to be moving into different directions at the same time.

It is worth emphasizing, however, that the ability to articulate nuanced and cogent political commentary on messy real-world issues generally does not count among the strengths of superhero blockbuster cinema. As examples of an action- and special-effects-driven genre, superhero blockbusters generally paint in broad strokes, focusing on cinematic attractions, fast-paced plots, and clear-cut conflicts. Accordingly, superhero blockbusters' political significance lies not so much in their overt ideological messages – which usually are purposefully ambivalent anyway – but rather in their capacity to inspire a range of reactions within their immediate cultural and medial environments. In prompting responses from reviewers and journalists, professional and non-professional critics, fans, activists, and (last, but not least) scholars, superhero movies turn themselves into centerpieces of larger cultural phenomena. Occasionally, as in the case of *V for Vendetta* or the example of *Black Panther* discussed in the preceding chapter, these audience responses are explicitly political and interface with ongoing political struggles and debates. But the activities that unfold in response to the reception of superhero movies invariably also generate medial exposure for the genre, thereby yielding a definite impact within the attention economy of the contemporary online public. Ultimately, superhero blockbusters present themselves as the products of a culture industry that is disinterested in the indoctrination of consumers but seeks to capitalize on their cultural and textual productivity.

I Hate the Internet's vision of twenty-first-century fan culture as a reservoir of unpaid labor nonetheless does not quite capture the implications of this situation. While Adeline's thoughts accurately represent how audience practices might be valorized by media corporations, most fans are probably aware of such processes. In general, fan audiences are hardly oblivious of the entertainment industries' commercial imperatives. Likewise, the mechanisms of the contemporary attention economy – which translates cultural visibility into clicks, likes, followers, shares, re-tweets, and other measurable activities carried out within the digital enclosure of the Internet – are hardly opaque to an audience versed in the use of social media. After all, users who seek to gain a following on Twitter, Instagram, or TikTok need to position themselves carefully within competitive discursive environments, must produce content that is reliably interesting and innovative, have to build relationships with their followers, and so on. Highly active users of social media thus tend to perform activities that are analogous to those carried out by the producers and marketers of commercial entertainments. Rather than being ignorant of corporate attempts to capitalize on the free labor of media users, a significant part of the audience arguably accepts this dimension of contemporary popular culture as a given. This does not mean that fans are uncritical. But fannish criticism of popular culture is usually based on a basic affinity for the criticized object and only rarely involves a complete rejection of the culture-industrial system. One might call this disposition fannish realism and acknowledge that the practices of contemporary fan culture are neither necessarily naive, nor always in opposition to those of the media industry. Moreover, fannish engagements with commercial entertainments usually involve strong emotional investments and a sense of ownership on the part of consumers. Such personal stakes inform many passionate debates in the commentary sections of fan-oriented websites; yet, in rarer cases, fans might also be able to translate their expertise into a profitable career on YouTube or other social media. The practices of media fans should thus not be understood as something that is external to the operations of the entertainment industries, as both fields have become inextricably entangled. Crucially, however, the practices of non-professional media fans are not the only – and perhaps not even the most important – source of immaterial labor for contemporary media franchises. Superhero blockbusters are successful, not only because they appeal to a small group of die-hard fans, but also because they mobilize a broad range of economically productive activities on the part of their audiences – from the viewing practices of consumers who follow the genre's narrative over longer periods of time, over the discourses on fan-sites and social media, to the responses of professional reviewers and critics.

Finally, Hastings's suggestion that streaming services compete over the last chunks of consumers' free time also reads like an overstatement. Culture-industrial products generally try to maximize the time, money, and attention that consumers can dedicate to them, and serial narratives are particularly effective in that regard. For consumers, the use-value of such commodities is determined by the pleasures and distractions these can offer. But Adorno's work on the culture industry reminds us that the leisure practices of consumers must also be productive for their integration into larger social orders. Once recreational activities cease to contribute to the reproduction of individuals' capacity to work, attend school, or participate in other forms of sanctioned social interaction, such practices quickly become the target of regulatory discourses. Not coincidentally, the last few decades have seen the rise of a public health debate about the dangers of Internet addiction, video game addiction, porn addition, and other (real or imagined) pathologies that revolve around an excessive use of digital and networked consumer electronics. Hastings's goal of maximizing the Netflix users' daily hours of engagement with the platform is thus bound to run into obstacles beyond and apart from the bodily capacities of consumers.

I have shown in Chapter 3 that the strategies of serial storytelling at work in recent superhero blockbuster cinema nonetheless encourage a time-consuming and culturally productive engagement with ongoing film series, transmedial extensions, and related paratexts. Once they become available for home video consumption, the entries of franchises such as Disney's *Marvel Cinematic Universe* (*MCU*) or Warner's *DC Extended Universe* (*DCEU*) furthermore invite the kind of physically demanding "binge-watching" practices that are often associated with video-on-demand services such as Netflix. And the technological infrastructure of the digital era – with its multiplying options to access media content and its expanding archives of material – generally enables a type of audience engagement that is more extensive than even the most dedicated fan practices of earlier decades. But most contemporary superhero blockbusters still feature plots whose central causal chains do not extend beyond the end credits. Entries of the genre also offer cinematic spectacles that remain appealing and accessible to viewers who are unaware of, or uninterested in larger narrative architectures. Finally, platforms such as Netflix allow us to consume films and TV series at our own pace. For some viewers, such user-directed media consumption might indeed result in the loss of sleep; for others, it might offer the opportunity to compartmentalize the reception of streaming content and interweave it with other everyday practices in a manner previously impossible. In the digital era, commercially produced entertainment can thus insert itself into the most private spaces and times. The culture industry's hold over the time and attention of viewers still remains limited, as consumers also have to attend to other matters.

Recent superhero blockbuster films still are ideally suited to operate in the "always on" media environment of the digital age. Multi-linear franchises such as the Disney's *MCU* or Warner's slate of superhero films (which, by 2021, encompasses the films of the *DCEU* as well as titles set in separate narrative continuities) invite viewers to explore vast clusters of interrelated related movies, comics, and other materials. In doing so, these franchises present themselves as continually expanding entertainment environments that invite short-term forays and partial explorations as much as long-term stays and detail-obsessed expeditions. In the process, superhero blockbuster franchises demand and inspire a host of consumer activities that play out across different locales within our digitized and networked media environment, from movie theaters and video-streaming platforms, over social media, fan-oriented websites, and the mainstream press, to offline (but thoroughly mediated) events such as comic conventions. The user activity generated within this media environment not only raises the cultural profile of cultural commodities and corporate producers, but it is also directly productive for capitalist valorization processes based on the sale of movie tickets and subscriptions to streaming services, advertising, the algorithmic analysis of user data, and so on. Some of the implications of the increasingly complex relationships between commercial entertainments, their consumers, and the online public are captured by the idea that commercial popular culture has transitioned from a consumption-based model to an engagement-centric one. But this transition is best understood as part of a larger transformation within the capitalist mode of production that economists such as Carlo Vercellone and Yann Moulier Boutang discuss as the emergence of capitalism's "cognitive" phase. This phase sees the ascendance of a sector of the economy that is built on the valorization of culturally, textually, and informationally productive work; such work is carried out within digital and networked media environments and performed by workers who might not be paid for their efforts (and who might not even understand themselves as workers in any traditional sense).

This new economic regime exerts pressure on existing business models within the entertainment industry and the cultural forms connected to them. The evolution of superhero blockbuster cinema since 1978 offers an illustrative example of the impact of such pressures. Starting in the late 1990s and early 2000s, superhero blockbusters began to absorb the lessons of a reconfigured spirit of capitalism (Boltanski and Chiapello) that touts the virtues of participatory online media, celebrates serial storytelling as an effective tool for audience mobilization, and re-imagines the figure of the informed and highly engaged media fan as the ideal kind of consumer. Informed by this ideology, superhero movies are transformed into a type of entertainment whose profitability hinges on its ability to capture and valorize the productive capacities that exist within their cultural and medial environment. This transformation entails two closely significant shifts. Firstly, the superhero movie is re-tooled into a more explicitly serialized form of entertainment. Secondly, the superhero blockbuster is turned into a format that seeks to maximize the overall volume of related discursive activity within the online public. Informed by these objectives, the genre reconfigures its shared politics of audience engagement. The genre's hyper-referential style of storytelling, for example, eventually embraces increasingly fragmented plots that demand more than a passing familiarity with fan discourses, online paratexts, and preceding entries of the genre. The genre's changing storytelling strategies are paralleled by fan management practices that seek to prefigure the reception of films by fan-cultural critics and influential online publications. Finally, the genre comes to adopt a cinematic populism that invites allegorical readings and allows films to latch onto current political debates. Together, these three components of superhero blockbusters' politics of engagement result in a remarkable capacity to set people, things, discourses, and practices into motion.

That does not mean that these means always produce the desired effects. My discussion of *Suicide Squad* in Chapter 4 has shown that fan management practices fail occasionally. Likewise, some superhero movies generate less-than-stellar box-office returns; similarly, few entries of the genre garner an unambiguously positive reception by critics. Moreover, the public response to superhero blockbusters at times includes unintended spill-over effects – such as activist campaigns that try to latch on to the hype around popular releases – that are not always compatible with the public relations goals of producers. However, as products of an evolutionary social system, superhero blockbusters are more than able to adapt to changes within their cultural and medial environments. In other words, negative models are models, too, and even films that fail will eventually leave their mark on subsequent entries of the genre.

The phenomena discussed in this book are not entirely unique to superhero blockbuster cinema. The genre's serialization practices, for instance, bear more than a passing resemblance to contemporary television drama series, which also often feature large ensemble casts and developing character relationships, a balancing of self-contained plots and ongoing storylines, and escalations of increasingly baroque narrative and visual appeals.[1] Because of these parallels, Peter Vignold argues that recent superhero franchises offer a "remediation of television's serial structures" within the blockbuster format (11, my translation). However, while Vignold's observation alerts us to the significant parallels between these two popular narrative formats, the idea that cinema's competition with television is a primary driver for the evolution of superhero movies also obfuscates the larger economic and medial transformations that have affected

CONCLUSION 189

both media. The contemporary prominence of explicitly serialized modes of storytelling in film and television is thus better understood as the product of a culture-industrial regime organized around the idea of ongoing, culturally productive engagement. This regime has remodeled other popular media franchises as well. In its most recent configuration, Disney's *Star Wars* franchise, for example, also presents it as a multi-linear cinematic universe that encompasses several different subseries and modes of serialization. The latter include three trilogies of "proper" *Star Wars* films (with *The Force Awakens*, 2015, *The Last Jedi*, 2017, and *The Rise of Skywalker*, 2019, as the most recent entries), a more loosely connected anthology series of films set in other timeframes (*Rogue One*, 2016; *Solo*, 2018), several serialized TV dramas on Disney+ (*The Mandalorian*, since 2019; *The Book of Boba Fett*, 2021; *Andor*, 2022), as well as numerous animated television series, tie-in comics, novels, and digital games. Moreover, recent additions to the *Star Trek* franchise – such as *Discovery* (since 2018), *Picard* and *Lower Decks* (since 2020), or *Prodigy* (since 2021) – have been marketed as part of an expanding *Star Trek Universe* since 2019 (Staff). Toho and Legendary Entertainment have similarly re-booted the Godzilla series as a cinematic universe that encompasses 2014's *Godzilla*, 2017's *Kong: Skull Island*, 2019's *Godzilla: King of the Monsters*, and 2021's *Godzilla vs. Kong*. Other long-running franchises – such as the *Fast and the Furious* films or the *Harry Potter/Fantastic Beasts* series – have also spawned commercially successful spin-offs in different media during the third and fourth waves of superhero blockbuster cinema.

The operations of these other entertainment franchises parallel the practices of superhero blockbuster cinema not only with regards to their obvious serialization practices. The most recent *Star Wars* and *Star Trek* installments, for example, are saturated with references to many-decade-old series and source materials – a type of intertextuality that capitalizes on the existence of a "diffuse intellectuality" (Vercellone) and the recipients' ability to navigate complex systems of cultural reference. As properties with long histories of previous serial unfolding, both *Star Wars* and *Star Trek* rely on practices of fan management not unlike those discussed in Chapter 4. Recent entries of both franchises have furthermore inspired activist campaigns that echo some of the politicized responses to Disney's *Black Panther*.[2] All of these parallels indicate that the aesthetic practices of superhero blockbuster cinema are expressive of a larger paradigm and not just coincidental. Developments in other media appear to follow a similar logic, too. By adding new downloadable content or online-only expansions on a regular basis, triple-A digital games such as Rockstar Games' *GTA 5* (2013) and Sony Interactive's *Marvel's Spider-Man* (2018) also enable modes of serial engagement that keep users involved over longer periods of time. Similar dynamics are also on display on video-based social media platforms such as YouTube and TikTok, which more directly capitalize on the valorization of user activity. Like superhero blockbuster cinema, the externality-driven popular culture of cognitive capitalism has hardly exhausted all its options.

When I began this project in the summer of 2012, superhero movies seemed destined to dominate Hollywood's production slates and the international box-office charts for some time to come. Almost ten years later, it still seems apt to call superhero film the dominant Hollywood genre. Yet, at the time of writing, the future of this genre arguably seems more uncertain than before. In the summer of 2021, superhero blockbuster cinema – and the world, for that matter – seems desperate to go back to its pre-COVID-19 ways, but the lasting effects of the pandemic (and the certain future of global climate change) are likely to make this endeavor more difficult than one might think. At the very least, the immediate future of superhero blockbuster cinema will probably play out in the same places as much of the rest of our increasingly screen-mediated lives – in our living rooms and on our laptops, tablets, or TV screens, far away from crowded theaters and public exhibition spaces. It seems safe to assume, however, that superhero blockbuster cinema will not go away anytime soon. Likewise, the critical and scholarly engagement with the genre is far from complete. But my own paratextual production about superhero movies stops here, at least for the time being.

NOTES

1. On the narrative strategies of complex television, see Mittell, *Complex TV*; Kelleter, "Whatever Happened"; Kelleter and Jahn-Sudmann; Brinker, "On the Formal Politics," "NBC's Hannibal."
2. In 2017, right-wing activists staged social media campaigns to protest the alleged "misandry" and liberal slant of *Star Wars: The Last Jedi* (Disney, 2017) and *Star Trek: Discovery*.

Works Cited

TEXT-BASED SOURCES (PRINT, DIGITAL, ONLINE, AND COMICS)

Action Comics, vol. 1, no. 1, DC Comics, 1938.
@TrumpWarRoom. "House Democrats can push their sham impeachment all they want. President Trump's re-election is inevitable.' *Twitter*, December 10, 2019, twitter.com/trumpwarroom/status/1204503645607333888.
Adorno, Theodor W. *The Culture Industry: Selected Essays on Mass Culture*. Edited by J. M. Bernstein. Routledge, 2005.
---. "Culture Industry Reconsidered." *The Culture Industry: Selected Essays on Mass Culture*. Edited by J. M. Bernstein, Routledge, 2005, pp. 98–106.
---. "Free Time." *The Culture Industry: Selected Essays on Mass Culture*. Edited by J. M. Bernstein. Routledge, 2005, pp. 187–97.
---. "Thesen über Bedürfnis." *Gesammelte Schriften, Band 8: Soziologische Schriften I*. Edited by Rolf Tiedemann. Suhrkamp, 1972, pp. 392–96.
"All Time Box Office. Worldwide Grosses." *Box Office Mojo*, www.boxofficemojo.com/alltime/world/.
Anders, Charlie Jane. "Captain America 2 Is One of The Best Action Movies I've Ever Seen." *io9*, December 16, 2015, io9.gizmodo.com/captain-america-2-is-one-of-the-best-action-movies-ive-1558076828.
---. "Deadpool Is Brutal in the Best Possible Way." *io9*, February 12, 2016, io9.gizmodo.com/deadpool-is-brutal-in-the-best-possible-way-1758665475.
Andrejevic, Mark. *iSpy: Surveillance and Power in the Interactive Era*. University Press of Kansas, 2007.
Askwith, Ivan. "Television 2.0: Reconceptualizing TV as an Engagement Medium." *Massachusetts Institute of Technology*, 2007, cmsw.mit.edu/television-2-0-tv-as-an-engagement-medium.
Athanasopoulos, Charles. "Black Radical Thought as a Pathology in *Black Panther*." *Why Wakanda Matters. What* Black Panther *Reveals About Psychology, Identity, and Communication*. SmartPop, 2020, pp. 137–47.

Auger, Andrew. "DCEU Isn't Franchise's Official Name." *Screen Rant*, September 29, 2017, screenrant.com/dceu-movie-universe-official-name/.
Babcock, Matthew, Ramon Alfonso Villa Cox, and Sumeet Kumar. "Diffusion of Pro- and Anti-False Information Tweets: The Black Panther Movie Case." *Computational and Mathematical Organization Theory*, vol. 25, no. 2, 2019, pp. 72–84.
Backman, Russell. "In Franchise: Narrative Coherence, Alternates, and the Multiverse in *X-Men*." *Superhero Synergies. Comic Book Characters Go Digital*. Edited by James N. Gilmore and Matthias Stork. Rowman & Littlefield, 2014, pp. 201–19.
Balio, Tino. *Hollywood in the New Millennium*. BFI, 2013.
Barber, Nicholas. "Black Panther: The Most Radical Hollywood Blockbuster Ever?" *BBC.com*, February 6, 2018, www.bbc.com/culture/article/20180206-black-panther-the-most-radical-hollywood-blockbuster-ever.
Barla, Josef, and Fabian Steinschaden. "Kapitalistische Quasi-Objekte: Zu einer Latour'schen Lesart Marx' Ausführungen zur Maschine." *Crossing Borders: Grenzen (Über)Denken | Thinking (across) Borders: Beiträge zum 9. Kongress der Österreichischen Gesellschaft für Philosophie*. Edited by Alfred Dunshirn et al. Österreichische Gesellschaft für Philosophie, 2012, pp. 361–70.
Barnes, Brooks, and Nicole Sperling. "Warner Bros. Says All 2021 Films Will Be Streamed Right Away." *The New York Times*, December 3, 2020, www.nytimes.com/2020/12/03/business/media/warner-brothers-movies-hbo-max.html.
Beer, Andreas. "Ein neues Gesicht der Revolte? Die Ästhetik der V-Maske zwischen Comic, Film und *Occupy*-Protesten." *Kritische Berichte*, vol. 1, 2016, pp. 96–106.
Behrens, Roger. *Krise und Illusion: Beiträge zur kritischen Theorie der Massenkultur*. Lit Verlag, 2003.
---. *Verstummen: Über Adorno*. Wehrhahn, 2004.
Bell, Josh. "What Captain America Has to Say About the NSA." *American Civil Liberties Union*, April 18, 2014, www.aclu.org/blog/national-security/secrecy/what-captain-america-has-say-about-nsa.
Bell, Amanda. "Here's What Fans Want to Happen to Wolverine in His Last Stand." *MTV News*, July 27, 2015, www.mtv.com/news/2225132/hugh-jackman-the-wolverine.
Berger, Richard. "'Are There Any More at Home Like You?' Rewiring *Superman*." *Journal of Adaptation in Film & Performance*, vol. 1, no. 2, 2008, pp. 87–101.
Berman, Eliza. "Deadpool Just Broke a Significant Box Office Record." *Time*, March 29, 2016, www.time.com/4274867/enums.
Bolin, Göran. "The Labor of Media Use." *Information, Communication, & Society*, vol. 15, no. 6, 2012, pp. 796–814.
Boltanski, Luc, and Ève Chiapello. *The New Spirit of Capitalism*. Verso, 2007.
Bonikowski, Bart, and Noam Gidron. "The Populist Style in American Politics: Presidential Campaign Discourse 1952–1996." *Social Forces*, vol. 94, no. 4, 2016, pp. 1593–621.
Booth, Paul. "Narractivity and the Narrative Database: Media-Based Wikis as Interactive Fan Fiction." *Narrative Inquiry*, vol. 19, no. 2, 2009, pp. 372–92.
Bordwell, David, Kristin Thompson, and Jeff Smith. *Film Art: An Introduction*. 12th Edition. McGraw-Hill, 2020.
Bordwell, David. *Narration in the Fiction Film*. Methuen, 1985.
---. "Superheroes for Sale." *Observations on Film Art*. David Bordwell, August 16, 2008, www.davidbordwell.net/blog/2008/08/16/superheroes-for-sale.
---. *The Way Hollywood Tells It: Stories and Style in Modern Movies*. University of California Press, 2006. Kindle ebook.
Boutang, Yann Moulier. *Cognitive Capitalism*. Translated by Ed Emery. Polity Press, 2011.

Bradshaw, Peter. "Logan Review – Hugh Jackman's Wolverine Enters a Winter of X-Men Discontent." *The Guardian*, Guardian News and Media, February 17, 2017, www.theguardian.com/film/2017/feb/17/logan-review-hugh-jackmans-wolverine-enters-a-winter-of-x-men-discontent.

Brasch, Ilka, and Felix Brinker. "Opening Gambits: Cross-Media Self-Reflexivity and Audience Engagement in Serial Cinema, 1936–2008." *Exploring Seriality: From Early Cinema to Transmedia*. Edited by Ariane Hudelet and Anne Crémieux. Routledge, 2021, pp. 19–36.

Breznican, Anthony. "'Marvel One-Shot: Agent Carter' – FIRST LOOK at Poster and Three Photos from the New Short!" *EW.com*. Entertainment Weekly, July 11, 2013, ew.com/article/2013/07/11/marvel-one-shot-agent-carter-first-look/4.

Bricken, Rob. "Confession: I Am Part of a Sinister Conspiracy to Destroy DC's Live-Action Movies." *io9*, August 11, 2016, io9.gizmodo.com/confession-i-am-part-of-a-sinister-conspiracy-to-destr-1785146565.

---. "Does Appeasing Nerds Actually Make a Movie More Successful?" *io9*, April 21, 2016, io9.gizmodo.com/does-appeasing-nerds-actually-make-a-movie-more-success-1772353627.

---. "If This Is the DC Superhero Movie Schedule Through 2018, It's Insane." *io9*, June 12, 2014, *io9*.gizmodo.com/if-this-is-wbs-dc-movie-schedule-through-2018-its-insa-1590109688.

---. "Ryan Reynolds' Deadpool Movie Test Footage Is Heartbreakingly Perfect." *io9*, July 28, 2014, io9.gizmodo.com/ryan-reynolds-deadpool-movie-test-footage-is-heartbreak-1612017335.

Brinker, Felix. "NBC's *Hannibal* and the Politics of Audience Engagement." *Transgressive Television: Politics and Crime in 21st-Century American TV Series*. Edited by Birgit Däwes, Alexandra Ganser, and Nicole Poppenhagen. Winter, 2015, pp. 303–28.

---. "On the Formal Politics of Narratively Complex Television Series: Operational Self-Reflexivity and Audience Management in *Fringe* and *Homeland*." *Poetics of Politics: Textuality and Social Relevance in American Literature and Culture*. Edited by Sebastian M. Herrmann, Carolin Alice Hoffmann, Katja Kanzler, Stefan Schubert, and Frank Usbeck. Winter, 2015, pp. 41–62.

---. "On the Political Economy of the Contemporary (Superhero) Blockbuster Series." *Post-Cinema: Theorizing 21st Century Film*. Edited by Shane Denson and Julia Leyda. Reframe Books, 2016, reframe.sussex.ac.uk/post-cinema/4-2-brinker/.

---. "Reader Mobilization and the Courting of Fannish Consumption Practices in 1970s Marvel Superhero Comic Books." *Participations: Journal of Audience and Reception Studies*, vol. 17, no. 2, 2020, pp. 245–73.

---. "Transmedia Storytelling in the 'Marvel Cinematic Universe' and the Logics of Convergence-Era Popular Seriality." *Make Ours Marvel. Media Convergence and a Comics Universe*. Edited by Matt Yockey. University of Texas Press, 2017, pp. 207–33.

Brody, Richard. "The Passionate Politics of 'Black Panther.'" *The New Yorker*, February 16, 2018, www.newyorker.com/culture/richard-brody/the-passionate-politics-of-black-panther.

Brooker, Will. *Hunting the Dark Knight: Twenty-First Century Batman*. I. B. Tauris, 2012.

Brown, Jeffrey A. *The Modern Superhero in Film and Television: Popular Genre and American Culture*. Routledge, 2017.

Bruns, Axel. *Blogs, Wikipedia, Second Life and Beyond: From Production to Produsage*. Peter Lang, 2008.

Buchanan, Kyle. "How *Black Panther* Crafted Erik Killmonger's Compelling Arc." *Vulture*, February 20, 2018, www.vulture.com/2018/02/how-black-panther-crafted-erik-killmongers-compelling-arc.html.

Burke, Liam. *The Comic Book Film Adaptation*. University Press of Mississippi, 2015.

Burlingame, Ross. "Ryan Reynolds Says Deadpool Movie Got Greenlit Within 24 Hours After Footage Leaked." *Comicbook.com*, January 30, 2016, comicbook.com/2016/01/30/ryan-reynolds-says-deadpool-movie-got-greenlit-within-24-hours-a.

Call, Lewis. "A is for Anarchy, V is for Vendetta: Images of Guy Fawkes and the Creation of Postmodern Anarchism." *Anarchist Studies*, vol. 16, no. 2, 2008, pp. 154–72.

Campbell, Christopher. "Here Are All the Songs in 'Suicide Squad.'" *Fandango*, August 8, 2016, www.fandango.com/movie-news/here-are-all-the-songs-in-suicide-squad-751181.

Canby, Vincent. "Superman (1978): It's a Bird, It's a Plane, It's a Movie." Rev. of *Superman*. *The New York Times*, December 15, 1978.

Canva, Michael. "'Captain America: Civil War' Directors Reveal How Their Movie Flexes These Political Meanings." *The Washington Post*, May 8, 2016, www.washingtonpost.com/news/comic-riffs/wp/2016/05/08/captain-america-civil-war-directors-explain-the-movies-political-meaning.

Carle, Chris. "Deadpool Costume Revealed." *IGN*, March 27, 2015, www.ign.com/articles/2015/03/27/deadpool-costume-revealed.

Castoriadis, Cornelius. "The Greek and the Modern Political Imaginary." *Salmagundi*, vol. 100, 1993, pp. 102–29.

Cerny, Alan. "Logan Review #1 at ComingSoon.net." *ComingSoon.net*, ComingSoon.net, February 17, 2017, www.comingsoon.net/movies/reviews/815505-logan-review-2.

---. "Suicide Squad Review at ComingSoon.net." *ComingSoon.net*, August 2, 2016, www.comingsoon.net/movies/reviews/752953-suicide-squad-review-2.

Chabon, Michael. "Fan Fictions: On Sherlock Holmes." *Maps and Legends: Reading and Writing along the Borderlands*. McSweeney's, 2008, pp. 35–57.

Child, Ben. "Where Does Batman v Superman's Mauling Leave Warner's Plan for a DC Comics Cinematic Universe?" *The Guardian*, March 24, 2016, www.theguardian.com/film/filmblog/2016/mar/24/batman-v-superman-warner-dc-comics-zack-synder-dawn-of-justice.

Chitwood, Adam. "Deadpool Review." *ComingSoon.net*, February 7, 2016, www.comingsoon.net/movies/reviews/654595-deadpool-review.

---. "Wolverine 3 Has Started Filming; Simon Kinberg Confirms R-Rating, Says It's a Violent, Different Wolverine." *Collider*, May 9, 2016, www.reddit.com/r/comicbookmovies/comments/4ijrzx/wolverine_3_has_started_filming_simon_kinberg.

Chipman, Bob. "Batman V Superman & The DCEU: Now What?" *Screen Rant*, April 10, 2016, screenrant.com/batman-v-superman-changes-dceu-whats-next.

Christiansen, Steen Ledet. *Drone Age Cinema: Action Film and Sensory Assault*. I. B. Tauris, 2017.

Clark, Noelene. "Superman and Batman Will Unite on Film, Warner Confirms at Comic-Con." *Hero Complex. Los Angeles Times*, July 24, 2013, herocomplex.latimes.com/movies/superman-batman-movie-comic-con/.

Cobb, Jelani. "'Black Panther' and the Invention of 'Africa.'" *The New Yorker*, February 20, 2018, www.newyorker.com/news/daily-comment/black-panther-and-the-invention-of-africa.

Coffin, Lesley. "Review: Deadpool Is True to the Comic, So Apparently, I Don't Like Deadpool." *The Mary Sue*, February 10, 2016, www.themarysue.com/deadpool-movie-review/.

Coggan, Devan. "Hugh Jackman Teases 'Wolverine 3' as 'Very Different in Tone'." *EW.com*. Time Inc, October 4, 2016, ew.com/article/2016/10/04/hugh-jackman-teases-wolverine-3-different-tone.

Coldwater, Abdullah. "Don't Listen to Film Criticism." *Change.org*, www.change.org/p/don-t-listen-to-film-criticism.

Collin, Robbie. "8 Lessons DC Must Learn from the Batman V Superman Beatdown." *The Telegraph*, March 26, 2016, www.telegraph.co.uk/film/batman-v-superman-dawn-of-justice/spoilers-ending-dc-extended-universe.

Collura, Scott. "Logan Was Influenced by the Classic Western Shane." *IGN*, December 14, 2016, www.ign.com/articles/2016/12/14/how-logan-was-influenced-by-the-classic-western-shane.

Connelly, Brendon. "Movie Deadpool to Break Fourth Wall, Talk to The Audience." *Slashfilm*, July 3, 2009, www.slashfilm.com/movie-deadpool-to-break-fourth-wall-talk-to-the-audience/7.

Coogan, Peter. "Comics Predecessors." *The Superhero Reader*. Edited by Charles Hatfield, Jeet Heer, and Kent Worcester. University of Mississippi Press, 2013, pp. 7–15.

Couch, Aaron. "'Suicide Squad' Fans Petition Rotten Tomatoes to Shut Down After Poor Reviews." *The Hollywood Reporter*, August 2, 2016, www.hollywoodreporter.com/heat-vision/suicide-squad-rotten-tomatoes-asked-916787.

Corliss, Richard. "Can A Popcorn Movie Also Be Political? This One Can." Rev. of *V for Vendetta*. *Time*, vol. 167, no. 11, March 13, 2006, pp. 58–59.

Covert, Colin. "'Captain America: Civil War' A Smart Political Allegory." *Minneapolis Star Tribune*, May 5, 2016, www.pressdemocrat.com/article/entertainment/captain-america-civil-war-a-smart-political-allegory/?sba=AAS:

Crary, Jonathan. *24/7: Late Capitalism and the Ends of Sleep*. Verso, 2014.

Cucco, Mario. "The Promise Is Great: The Blockbuster and the Hollywood Economy." *Media, Culture & Society*, vol. 31, no. 2, 2009, pp. 214–30.

D'Alessandro, Anthony. "'Black Panther' Goes Wild: At $242M Superhero Owns Best 4-Day Opening & Defeats 'Last Jedi' – Update." *Deadline.com*, February 20, 2018, deadline.com/2018/02/black-panther-thursday-night-preview-box-office-1202291093/.

Daniels, Les. *Superman: The Complete History*. Chronicle, 1998.

Dargis, Manohla, and A. O. Scott. "One Nation Under a Movie Theater? It's a Myth." *The New York Times*, September 7, 2017, www.nytimes.com/2017/09/07/movies/movies-politics-conservatives-liberals.html.

Dargis, Manohla. "Courage, Loyalty, Honor, Kablooey." Rev. of *Captain America: The Winter Soldier*. *The New York Times*, April 3, 2014, www.nytimes.com/2014/04/04/movies/hero-returns-in-captain-america-the-winter-soldier.html.

---. "Review: In 'Logan,' a Comic-Book Stalwart Turns Noirish Western." *The New York Times*, March 2, 2017, www.nytimes.com/2017/03/02/movies/logan-review-hugh-jackman-wolverine-x-men.html.

Darius, Julian. "Why *Iron Man 3* is the Best *Iron Man* Film to Date." *Sequart.org*, May 6, 2013, sequart.org/magazine/21937/why-iron-man-3-is-the-best-iron-man-film-to-date.

Dath, Dietmar. *Superhelden: 100 Seiten*. Reclam, 2016.

Daum, Timo. *Das Kapital sind wir: Zur Kritik der digitalen Ökonomie*. Nautilus, 2017.

Davidson, Rjurik. "Vagaries & Violence in *V for Vendetta*." Rev. of *V for Vendetta*. *Screen Education*, vol. 46, March 2007, pp. 157–62.

De Kosnik, Abigail. "Fandom as Free Labor." *Digital Labor. The Internet as Playground and Factory*. Edited by Trebor Scholz. Routledge, 2013, pp. 98–111.

De Matas, Jarrel. "More Than Movies: Reconceptualizing Race in *Black Panther* and *Get Out*." *The Popular Culture Studies Journal*, vol. 8, no. 1, 2020, pp. 120–38.

Deleuze, Gilles, and Félix Guattari. *Anti-Oedipus: Capitalism and Schizophrenia*. University of Minnesota Press, 1983.

Delwiche, Aaron, and Jennifer Jacobs Henderson. *The Participatory Cultures Handbook*. Routledge, 2013.

Denson, Shane, and Andreas Sudmann. "Digital Seriality: On the Serial Aesthetics and Practice of Digital Games." *Media of Serial Narrative*. Edited by Frank Kelleter. Ohio State University Press, 2017, pp. 261–83.

Denson, Shane, and Julia Leyda. "Perspectives on Post-Cinema: An Introduction." *Post-Cinema: Theorizing 21st Century Film*. Edited by Shane Denson and Julia Leyda. Reframe Books, 2016, reframe.sussex.ac.uk/post-cinema/introduction.

Denson, Shane, and Julia Leyda, editors. *Post-Cinema: Theorizing 21st Century Film*. Reframe Books, 2016, reframe.sussex.ac.uk/post-cinema.

Denson, Shane, and Ruth Mayer. "Grenzgänger: Serielle Figuren im Medienwechsel." *Populäre Serialität. Narration – Evolution – Distinktion. Zum seriellen Erzählen seit dem 19. Jahrhundert*. Edited by Frank Kelleter. Transcript, 2012, pp. 185–203.

Denson, Shane. "Marvel Comics' Frankenstein: A Case Study in the Media of Serial Figures." *Amerikastudien – American Studies*, vol. 56, no. 4, 2011, pp. 531–53.

---. "Seriality." *The Bloomsbury Handbook of Literary and Cultural Theory*. Edited by Jeffrey R. Di Leo. Bloomsbury, 2018, pp. 684–85.

Diaz, Eric. "The Story Behind the 'What BLACK PANTHER Means to Me' Hashtag." *Nerdist*, February 10, 2018, nerdist.com/article/what-black-panther-means-to-me-hashtag/.

Diesing, Richard. "Anonymous.Kollektiv: Hetze unterm Anonymous-Deckmantel." *Zeit Online*, June 6, 2016, www.zeit.de/digital/internet/2016-06/anonymous-kollektiv-rechte-hetze.

DiPaolo, Marc. *War, Politics, and Superheroes: Ethics and Propaganda in Comics and Film*. McFarland, 2011.

Dittmer, Jason. *Captain America and the Nationalist Superhero: Metaphors, Narratives, and Geopolitics*. Temple University Press, 2013.

Dornbush, Jonathon. "Deadpool Trailer Trailer." *EW.com*, August 3, 2015, ew.com/article/2015/08/03/deadpool-trailer-tease.

Dowd, Tom, Michael Fry, Michael Niederman, and Joseph Steiff. *Storytelling Across Worlds: Transmedia for Creatives and Producers*. Taylor & Francis, 2013.

Duncan, Jody. "Captain's Orders." *Cinefex*, vol. 138, June 2014, [n. p, digital magazine].

---. "A Family Affair." *Cinefex*, vol. 138, June 2016, [n. p, digital magazine].

Duralde, Alonso. "'Suicide Squad' Review: Margot Robbie, Viola Davis, Stand out in Overstuffed Spectacle." *The Wrap*, August 2, 2016, www.thewrap.com/suicide-squad-review-dc-extended-universe.

Dyer-Witheford, Nick. *Cyber-Marx: Cycles and Circuits of Struggle in High-Technology Capitalism*. University of Illinois Press, 1999.

Ebert, Roger. "Superman Movie Review & Film Summary (1978)." *RogerEbert.com*, December 15, 1978, www.rogerebert.com/reviews/great-movie-superman-1978.

Eco, Umberto. "*Casablanca*: Cult Movies and Intertextual Collage." *SubStance*, vol. 14, no. 2, 1985, pp. 3–12.

---. "Innovation and Repetition: Between Modern and Post-Modern Aesthetics." *Daedalus* vol. 114, no. 4, 1985, pp. 161–84.

---. "The Myth of Superman." *Diacritics* vol. 2, no. 1, 1972, pp. 14–22.

Eddy, Cheryl. "Jared Leto's New Joker Already Has an Epic Set Of Memes." *io9*, April 25, 2015, io9.gizmodo.com/jared-letos-new-joker-already-has-an-epic-set-of-memes-1700176400.

Edwards, Jason. "The Materialism of Historical Materialism." *New Materialisms. Ontology, Agency, and Politics*. Edited by Diana Coole and Samantha Frost. Duke University Press, 2010, pp. 281–98.

Edwards, Graham. "Afrofuture." *Cinefex*, vol. 158, April 2018, [n. p., digital magazine].
Einwächter, Sophie, Vanessa Ossa, Verónique Sina, and Sven Stollfuss. "On the Intersection of Fan Studies and Comics Studies: Contextualization and Introduction." *Participations: Journal of Audience and Reception Studies*, vol. 17, no. 2, 2020, pp. 148–60.
Esposito, Elena. *Soziales Vergessen: Formen und Medien des Gedächtnisses der Gesellschaft*. Suhrkamp, 2002.
Evans, Elizabeth. *Understanding Engagement in Transmedia Culture*. Routledge, 2020.
Felski, Rita. "Context Stinks!" *New Literary History*, vol. 42, no. 4, 2011, pp. 573–91.
Fenster, Mark. *Conspiracy Theories: Secrecy and Power in American Culture*. University of Minnesota Press, 2008.
Finger, Bobby. "The Reviews for Suicide Squad Are in, and They Aren't Pretty." *The Muse*, August 2, 2016, themuse.jezebel.com/the-reviews-for-suicide-squad-are-in-and-they-arent-pr-1784708757.
Fiske, John. *Television Culture*. Routledge, 1992.
Flanagan, Martin, Mike McKenny, and Andy Livingstone. *The Marvel Studios Phenomenon: Inside a Transmedia Universe*. Bloomsbury, 2016.
Foucault, Michel. *The Birth of Biopolitics. Lectures at the Collège de France, 1978-79*. Edited by Michel Senellart. Palgrave, 2008.
Franich, Darren. "'Justice League,' 'Wonder Woman,' 'Green Lantern'? Thoughts on DC Films." *EW.com*, October 15, 2014, ew.com/article/2014/10/15/wonder-woman-dc-movies-justice-league-green-lantern.
---. "The Real, Subversive Politics of 'Captain America: The Winter Soldier'." *EW.com*, April 6, 2014, ew.com/article/2014/04/06/captain-america-the-winter-soldier-hydra-shield-paranoia.
---. "Warner Bros. Announces 10 DC Movies, including 'Wonder Woman'." *EW.com*, October 15, 2014, ew.com/article/2014/10/15/justice-league-green-lantern-wonder-woman-flash-movies.
Frederick, Candice. "*Black Panther*'s Ruth E. Carter on Designing for the Revolution." *Harper's Bazaar*, February 18, 2019, www.harpersbazaar.com/culture/film-tv/a26344844/ruth-e-carter-black-panther-costume-designer-oscars-2019-interview/.
Fuchs, Christian. *Social Media: A Critical Introduction*. Sage, 2017.
Gabilliet, Jean-Paul. *Of Comics and Men: A Cultural History of American Comic Books*. Translated by Bart Beaty and Nick Nguyen. University of Mississippi Press, 2010.
Gaines, Jane. "Superman and the Protective Strength of the Trademark." *Logics of Television: Essays in Cultural Criticism*. Edited by Patricia Mellencamp. Indiana University Press, 1990, pp. 173–92.
Gallio, Niccolò. "The Immersive Marketing Campaign for *X-Men: Days of Future Past*." *The X-Men Films: A Cultural Analysis*. Edited by Claudia Bucciferro. Rowman & Littlefield, 2016, pp. 17–30.
Garcia, James. "Deadpool Movie Test Footage Has Leaked, Watch It Here." *Flickering Myth*, July 28, 2014, www.flickeringmyth.com/2014/07/deadpool-movie-test-footage-leaked-watch.
Gardner, Jared. *Projections: Comics and the History of Twenty-First-Century Storytelling*. Stanford University Press, 2012.
Geraghty, Jim. "*Captain America: Civil War* Is No 'Conservative Manifesto.'" *National Review*, May 9, 2016, www.nationalreview.com/2016/05/captain-america-civil-war-not-conservative.
Gettell, Oliver. "'Logan' Screens Extended Preview, Early Reactions Praise Gritty Tone." *EW.com*, December 8, 2016, ew.com/article/2016/12/08/logan-early-reactions-praise-gritty-tone.

Gilman, Greg. "Hugh Jackman '99.9 Percent' Sure 'Wolverine' Sequel Will Be His Last 'X-Men' Movie." *TheWrap*, April 30, 2014, www.thewrap.com/hugh-jackman-99-9-percent-sure-wolverine-sequel-will-last-x-men-movie.

Gilmore, James N. "Will You Like Me When I'm Angry? Discourses of the Digital in *Hulk* and *The Incredible Hulk*." *Superhero Synergies: Comic Book Characters Go Digital*. Edited by James N. Gilmore and Matthias Stork. Rowman & Littlefield, 2014, pp. 11–26.

Goodman, Jessica. "'Suicide Squad' Director Shares Photo of Jared Leto as The Joker." *The Huffington Post*, April 10, 2015, www.huffingtonpost.com/2015/04/10/jared-leto-the-joker-photo-n_7040042.html?guccounter=1.

Gormley, Chaz. "25% of Marvel Studios Profits from the 'Black Panther' Film Invested in Black Communities." *Change.org*, www.change.org/p/the-walt-disney-company-25-of-marvel-studios-profits-from-the-black-panther-film-invested-in-black-communities.

Graeber, David. "Super Position." *The New Inquiry*, October 8, 2012, thenewinquiry.com/super-position.

Grainge, Paul. *Brand Hollywood: Selling Entertainment in a Global Media Age*. Routledge, 2008.

Graves, Michael. "The Marvel One-Shots and Transmedia Storytelling." *Make Ours Marvel: Media Convergence and a Comics Universe*. Edited by Matt Yockey. University of Texas Press, 2017, pp. 234–47.

Gray, Jonathan. *Show Sold Separately: Promos, Spoilers, and other Media Paratexts*. New York University Press, 2010.

---. "New Audiences, New Textualities: Anti-Fans and Non-Fans." *International Journal of Cultural Studies*, vol. 6, no. 1, 2003, pp. 64–81.

Groves, Don. "Why the U.S. Studios Need to Get Much Smarter in Their Marketing Strategies." *Forbes Magazine*, September 19, 2016, www.forbes.com/sites/dongroves/2016/09/19/why-the-u-s-studios-need-to-get-much-smarter-in-their-marketing-strategies.

Hagedorn, Roger. "Technology and Economic Exploitation: The Serial as a Form of Narrative Presentation." *Wide Angle*, vol. 10, no. 4, 1988, pp. 4–12.

Harman, Graham. *Bruno Latour: Reassembling the Political*. Pluto Press, 2014.

Harvey, David. *A Brief History of Neoliberalism*. Oxford University Press, 2007.

---. "From Fordism to Flexible Accumulation." *The Condition of Postmodernity: An Inquiry into the Conditions of Cultural Change*. Blackwell, 1989, pp. 141–72.

Hassler-Forest, Dan. *Capitalist Superheroes: Caped Crusaders in the Digital Age*. Zero Books, 2012.

---. *Science Fiction, Fantasy, and Politics: Transmedia Worldbuilding Beyond Capitalism*. Rowman & Littlefield, 2016.

Hatchett, Keisha. "Review: Logan Is the Brutal, Yet Wonderfully Authentic X-Men Film We Don't Deserve." *The Mary Sue*, 17 Feb. 2017, www.themarysue.com/review-logan-movie/.

Hatfield, Charles, Jeet Heer, and Kent Worcester, editors. *The Superhero Reader*. University of Mississippi Press, 2013.

Hatfield, Charles. "Jack Kirby and the Marvel Aesthetic." *The Superhero Reader*. Edited by Charles Hatfield, Jeet Heer, and Kent Worcester. University of Mississippi Press, 2013, pp. 136–54.

Havran, Annemarie. "Miserabel oder Exzellent? Verwirrung um 'Deadpool 2'-Testvorführungen." *FILMSTARTS.de*, March 13, 2018, www.filmstarts.de/nachrichten/18517660.html.

Hayes, Gary P. *How to Write a Transmedia Production Bible: A Template for Multiplatform Producers*. Australian Government/Screen Australia, 2011.

Hayward, Jennifer. *Consuming Pleasures: Active Audience and Serial Fictions from Dickens to Soap Opera*. The University Press of Kentucky, 1997.

Heer, Jeet, and Kent Worcester, editors. *A Comics Studies Reader*. University of Mississippi Press, 2009.
Hern, Alex. "Netflix's Biggest Competitor? Sleep." *The Guardian*, April 18, 2017, www.theguardian.com/technology/2017/apr/18/netflix-competitor-sleep-uber-facebook.
Hill, Libby. "Critics Deem 'Suicide Squad' a 'Disappointing Disaster'." *Los Angeles Times*, August 2, 2016, www.latimes.com/entertainment/herocomplex/la-et-hc-suicide-squad-critic-roundup-20160802-snap-htmlstory.html.
---. *Fan Cultures*. Taylor & Francis, 2002.
Hofstadter, Richard. *The Paranoid Style in American Politics and Other Essays*. Alfred A. Knopf, 1965.
Holmes, Adam. "5 Big Reveals About Jared Leto's Joker in Suicide Squad." *Cinemablend*, March 13, 2015, www.cinemablend.com/new/5-Big-Reveals-About-Jared-Leto-Joker-Suicide-Squad-70299.html.
Holub, Christian. "Boyd Holbrook's 'Logan' Villain Revealed." *EW.com*, October 10, 2016, www.ew.com/article/2016/10/10/wolverine-boyd-holbrook-logan-villain-revealed.
---. "Hugh Jackman's Wolverine Is Battle-Scarred in Latest 'Logan' Photo." *EW.com*, October 26, 2016, ew.com/article/2016/10/26/logan-hugh-jackman-wolverine-photo.
---. "'Logan' Director Teases Artsy New Set Photos from Wolverine Movie." *EW.com*, October 10, 2016, www.ew.com/article/2016/10/10/logan-wolverine-movie-set-photos.
Hornaday, Ann. "'Black Panther' Is Exhilarating, Groundbreaking and More than Worth the Wait." *The Washington Post*, February 9, 2018, www.washingtonpost.com/goingoutguide/movies/black-panther-is-exhilarating-groundbreaking-and-more-than-worth-the-wait/2018/02/09/5bff1d4c-0916-11e8-94e8-e8b8600ade23_story.html?noredirect=on&utm_term=.999845bcb456.
Hoppeler, Stephanie, and Gabriele Rippl. "Continuity, Fandom und Serialität in anglo-amerikanischen Comic Books." *Populäre Serialität: Narration – Evolution – Distinktion: Zum seriellen Erzählen seit dem 19. Jahrhundert*. Edited by Frank Kelleter. Transcript, 2012, pp. 367–79.
Horkheimer, Max, and Theodor W. Adorno. *Dialectic of Enlightenment. Philosophical Fragments*. Edited by Gunzelin Schmid Noerr. Stanford University Press, 2002.
"Hugh Jackman Asks for Ideas from Fans for His Final Outing as Wolverine." *BBC News*, July 28, 2015, www.bbc.co.uk/newsbeat/article/33688933/hugh-jackman-asks-for-ideas-from-fans-for-his-final-outing-as-wolverine.
Hughes, Jamie A. "Who watches the Watchmen? Ideology and 'Real World' Superheroes." *The Journal of Popular Culture* vol. 39, no.4, 2006, pp. 546–57.
Hunter, Jack. "Tony Stark Battles the Military-Industrial Complex." Rev. of *Iron Man 2*. *Charleston City Paper*, May 19, 2010, www.charlestoncitypaper.com/charleston/tony-stark-battles-the-military-industrial-complex/Content?oid=1992017.
Huyssen, Andreas. *After the Great Divide: Modernism, Mass Culture, Postmodernism*. Macmillan, 1986.
Jackman, Hugh. "WOLVERINE . . .ONE LAST TIME. HJ." *Instagram*, March 28, 2015, www.instagram.com/p/0x7TKcihJw.
Jahn-Sudmann, Andreas, and Frank Kelleter. "Die Dynamik serieller Überbietung: Amerikanische Fernsehserien und das Konzept des Quality TV." *Populäre Serialität. Narration – Evolution – Distinktion. Zum seriellen Erzählen seit dem 19. Jahrhundert*. Edited by Frank Kelleter. Transcript, 2012, pp. 205–24.
Jameson, Fredric. *The Geopolitical Aesthetic: Cinema and Space in the World System*. Indiana University Press, 1995.

Jeffries, Dru. "Spotting Stan: The Fun and Function of Stan Lee's Cameos in the Marvel Universe(s)." *Make Ours Marvel: Media Convergence and a Comics Universe.* Edited by Matt Yockey. University of Texas Press, 2017, pp. 297–318.

Jenkins, Henry. *Convergence Culture: Where Old and New Media Collide.* New York University Press, 2006.

---. *Fans, Bloggers, and Gamers: Exploring Participatory Culture.* New York University Press, 2006.

---. "Revenge of the Origami Unicorn: The Remaining Four Principles of Transmedia Storytelling." *Confessions of an AcaFan: The Official Weblog of Henry Jenkins.* Henry Jenkins, December 12, 2009, henryjenkins.org/blog/2009/12/revenge_of_the_origami_unicorn.html.

---. *Textual Poachers: Television Fans and Participatory Culture.* Routledge, 1992.

---. "The Reign of the 'Mothership': Transmedia's Past, Present, and Possible Futures." *Wired TV: Laboring Over an Interactive Future.* Edited by Denise Mann. Rutgers University Press, 2014, pp. 244–68.

---. "Transmedia 202: Further Reflections." *Confessions of an AcaFan: The Official Weblog of Henry Jenkins.* Henry Jenkins, August 1, 2011, henryjenkins.org/blog/2011/08/defining_transmedia_further_re.html.

Jenkins, Henry, Sam Ford, and Joshua Green. *Spreadable Media: Creating Value and Meaning in a Networked Culture.* New York University Press, 2013. Kindle ebook.

Jewett, Robert, and John Shelton Lawrence. "Crowds of Superheroes." *The Superhero Reader.* Edited by Charles Hatfield, Jeet Heer, and Kent Worcester. University of Mississippi Press, 2013, pp. 80–83.

Johnson, Derek. "Cinematic Destiny: Marvel Studios and the Trade Stories of Industrial Convergence." *Cinema Journal*, vol. 52, no. 1, 2012, pp. 1–24.

---. "Learning to Share: The Relational Logics of Media Franchising." *FOE: Futures of Entertainment Conference.* MIT Convergence Culture Consortium, June 29, 2010, www.convergenceculture.org/weblog/2011/06/c3_white_paper_learning_to_sha.php.

---. *Media Franchising: Creative License and Collaboration in the Culture Industries.* New York University Press, 2013. Kindle ebook.

---. "Will the Real Wolverine Please Stand up? Marvel's Mutation from Monthlies to Movies." *Film and Comic Books.* Edited by Ian Gordon, Mark Jancovich, and Matthew P. Allister. University of Mississippi Press, 2007, pp. 64–85.

Jones, Gerard. "Men of Tomorrow." *The Superhero Reader.* Edited by Charles Hatfield, Jeet Heer, and Kent Worcester. University of Mississippi Press, 2013, pp. 16–22.

Kahen-Kashi, David. "'Captain America: The Winter Soldier' Discusses Political Paranoia." *Film Inquiry*, May 5, 2014, www.filminquiry.com/captain-america-winter-soldier-2014.

Khazan, Olga. "Is This the Secret to Selling Joe Biden?" *The Atlantic*, September 14, 2020, www.theatlantic.com/politics/archive/2020/09/joe-biden-youth-vote-turnout/616168/.

Kelleter, Frank. "Five Ways of Looking at Popular Seriality." *Media of Serial Narrative.* Edited by Frank Kelleter. Ohio State University Press, 2017, pp. 7–34.

---, editor. *Media of Serial Narrative.* Ohio State University Press, 2017.

---, editor. *Populäre Serialität: Narration – Evolution – Distinktion: Zum seriellen Erzählen seit dem 19. Jahrhundert.* Transcript, 2012.

---. "Populäre Serialität: Eine Einführung." *Populäre Serialität: Narration – Evolution – Distinktion: Zum seriellen Erzählen seit dem 19. Jahrhundert.* Edited by Frank Kelleter. Transcript, 2012, pp. 12–46.

---. *Serial Agencies: The Wire and its Readers.* Zero Books, 2014.

---. "Whatever Happened, Happened: Serial Character Constellation in *Lost*." *Amerikanische Fernsehserien der Gegenwart: Perspektiven der American Studies und der Media Studies*. Edited by Christoph Ernst and Heike Paul. Transcript, 2015, pp. 57–87.

Kelleter, Frank, and Daniel Stein. "Autorisierungspraktiken seriellen Erzählens: Zur Gattungsentwicklung von Superheldencomics." *Populäre Serialität: Narration – Evolution – Distinktion: Zum seriellen Erzählen seit dem 19. Jahrhundert*. Edited by Frank Kelleter. Transcript, 2012, pp. 259–90.

Kelleter, Frank, and Kathleen Loock. "Remaking as Second-Order Serialization." *Media of Serial Narrative*. Edited by Frank Kelleter. Ohio State University Press, 2017, pp. 125–47.

Kellner, Douglas. *Cinema Wars: Hollywood Film and Politics in the Bush-Cheney Era*. Wiley-Blackwell, 2010.

---. "Theodor W. Adorno and the Dialectics of Mass Culture." *Adorno: A Critical Reader*. Edited by Nigel C. Gibson and Andrew Rubin. Blackwell, 2002, pp. 86–109.

Kelly, Joe, and Pete Woods. "With Great Power Comes Great Coincidence." *Deadpool*, vol. 1, no. 11, Marvel Comics, 1997.

Kendrick, Ben. "'Suicide Squad': Jared Leto Recreates 'Killing Joke' Joker Photo." *Screen Rant*, April 9, 2015, screenrant.com/jared-leto-joker-killing-joke-photo-suicide-squad.

Keyes, Rob. "Exclusive Logan Video Interview with Hugh Jackman." *Screen Rant*, February 23, 2017, screenrant.com/logan-hugh-jackman-interview/.

---. "Rob Liefeld Concerned for 'Deadpool' Movie." *Screen Rant*, December 15, 2010, screenrant.com/deadpool-movie-concerns-directors.

Kit, Borys. "Did 'Deadpool' Director Tim Miller Leak the Test Footage That Launched a Franchise?" *The Hollywood Reporter*, February 15, 2016, www.hollywoodreporter.com/heat-vision/did-deadpool-director-tim-miller-865307.

---. "Scribe in for 'Suicide Squad' Pact." *The Hollywood Reporter*, February 25, 2009, www.hollywoodreporter.com/news/scribe-suicide-squad-pact-79891.

Klock, Geoff. *How to Read Superhero Comics and Why*. Bloomsbury, 2002.

Knowles, Harry. "Harry's Official Position on WOLVERINE." *Aint It Cool News*, May 1, 2009, www.aintitcool.com/node/40937.

---. "Harry Says SUICIDE SQUAD Is Like a Jackson Pollock Comic! A MisMatched Quilt to Wrap Yourself up in!" *Aint It Cool News*, August 5, 2016, www.aintitcool.com/node/75896.

Kobek, Jarett. *I Hate the Internet*. We Heard You Like Books, 2016.

Kocharekar, Sangeeta. "'What Do You Want to See Happen?' Hugh Jackman Calls on X-Men Fans to Suggest Ideas for Final Wolverine Movie as He Marks the Last Time He Will Be 'Putting on the Claws.'" *Daily Mail Online*, July 29, 2015, www.dailymail.co.uk/tvshowbiz/article-3178158/Hugh-Jackman-asks-Twitter-fans-weigh-Wolverine-movie.html.

Kohns, Oliver. "Guy Fawkes in the 21st Century: A Contribution to the Political Iconography of Revolt." *Image & Narrative*, vol. 14, no. 1, 2013, pp. 89–104.

Kozinets, Robert V. "Fan Creep: Why Brands Suddenly Need 'Fans.'" *Wired TV: Laboring Over an Interactive Future*. Edited by Denise Mann. Rutgers University Press, 2014, pp. 161–75.

Kuhn, Annette, and Guy Westwell, editors. "Cycle," "Film Style," "New Hollywood (Post-Classical Hollywood)," "Superhero Film." *Oxford Dictionary of Film Studies*. Oxford University Press, 2012. Kindle ebook.

Kushner, David. "An Inside Look at Anonymous, the Radical Hacking Collective." *The New Yorker*, September 8, 2014, www.newyorker.com/magazine/2014/09/08/masked-avengers.

Laclau, Ernesto. "Towards a Theory of Populism." *Politics and Ideology in Marxist Theory: Capitalism, Fascism, Populism.* NLB, 1977, pp. 143–99.

Landow, George P. "Hypertext in Literary Education, Criticism, and Scholarship." *Computers and the Humanities*, vol. 23, 1989, pp. 173–89.

LaSalle, Mick. "'Suicide Squad' Offers 2 Hours of Soul-Sickening Sensory Torment." *SFGate*, August 4, 2016, www.sfgate.com/movies/article/Suicide-Squad-is-two-hours-of-9067798.php.

Latour, Bruno. *Reassembling the Social: An Introduction to Actor-Network-Theory.* Oxford University Press, 2007.

---. *The Pasteurization of France.* Translated by Alan Sheridan and John Law. Harvard University Press, 1988.

Launder, William. "'V' Stands for Very Bad Anarchist Movie." *Columbia News Service*, May 2, 2006, https://web.archive.org/web/20080211185604/http://jscms.jrn.columbia.edu/cns/2006-05-02/launder-anarchistfight/story_syndication.

Lazzarato, Maurizio. "Immaterial Labour." *Radical Thought in Italy.* Edited by Paolo Virno and Michael Hardt. University of Minnesota Press, 1996, pp. 132–46.

Lee, Stan, and Steve Ditko. "Spider-Man!" *Amazing Fantasy*, vol. 1, no. 15, Marvel Comics, 1962, pp. 1–11.

Lévy, Pierre. *Collective Intelligence: Mankind's Emerging World in Cyberspace.* Basic Books, 1999.

Lockhard, P. R. "#WakandaTheVote: How Activists Are Using Black Panther Screenings to Register Voters." *Vox*, February 21, 2018, www.vox.com/policy-and-politics/2018/2/21/17033644/black-panther-screenings-voter-registration-wakanda-the-vote.

"Logan Reviews – What Did You Think?!" *SuperHeroHype*, March 9, 2017, www.superherohype.com/features/391995-logan-reviews-what-did-you-think.

Loock, Kathleen, and Constantine Verevis. "Introduction: Remake | Remodel." *Film Remakes, Adaptations, and Fan Productions: Remake | Remodel.* Edited by Kathleen Loock and Constantine Verevis. Palgrave-Macmillan, 2012, pp. 1–15.

Loock, Kathleen. "Adaption und Serialität." *Grundthemen der Literaturwissenschaft: Adaption.* Edited by Rainer Emig and Lucia Krämer. De Gruyter, forthcoming 2023.

Luhmann, Niklas. *Die Gesellschaft der Gesellschaft.* Suhrkamp, 1997.

---. *The Reality of the Mass Media.* Polity Press, 2000.

Lussier, Germain. "After Avengers: Infinity War, We're Dying to Have These Questions Answered." *io9*, April 30, 2018, io9.gizmodo.com/after-avengers-infinity-war-were-dying-to-have-these-1825580661.

---. "A Major Shake Up Just Changed the Game for DC Films." *io9*, May 18, 2016, io9.gizmodo.com/a-major-shake-up-just-changed-the-game-for-dc-films-1777328048.

---. "DC Did Something Pretty Radical to Distance Itself from Marvel, and You've Already Seen It." *io9*, June 25, 2016, io9.gizmodo.com/dc-did-something-pretty-radical-to-distance-themselves-1782609074.

---. "Logan Is Beautiful, Sophisticated, and Still a Kick-Ass Superhero Film." *io9*, February 17, 2017, io9.gizmodo.com/logan-is-beautiful-sophisticated-and-still-a-kick-ass-1792467103.

---. "Mark Ruffalo and Tom Holland Sure Did Their Best to Spoil Infinity War." *io9*, May 3, 2018, io9.gizmodo.com/mark-ruffalo-and-tom-holland-did-their-best-to-spoil-in-1825719864.

---. "Movie Review: Suicide Squad Is Chaotic, Manic, and a Total Mess." *io9*, August 2, 2016, io9.gizmodo.com/movie-review-suicide-squad-is-as-messy-and-weird-as-th-1784666704.

---. "Thanks to Infinity War, Marvel May Need a New Strategy to Promote Its Upcoming Releases." *io9*, May 7, 2018, io9.gizmodo.com/thanks-to-infinity-war-marvel-may-need-a-new-strategy-1825787133.
---. "The Unlikely Origins of Deadpool, The X-Men Character Who Conquered All Media." *io9*, February 8, 2016, io9.gizmodo.com/the-unlikely-origins-of-deadpool-the-x-men-character-w-1757814457.
Macksay, Richard. "Foreword: Pausing on the Threshold." In: Gerard Genette, *Paratexts: Thresholds of Interpretation*. Cambridge University Press, 1997, pp. xi–xxii.
Malik, Kenan. "Black Panther Has a Burden That No Superhero Is Strong Enough to Carry." *The Guardian*, February 18, 2018, www.theguardian.com/commentisfree/2018/feb/18/black-panther-has-burden-no-superhero-strong-enough-to-carry.
Maltby, Richard. *Hollywood Cinema*. Blackwell, 1996.
Manovich, Lev. "What is Digital Cinema?" *The Visual Culture Reader*, 2nd edition. Edited by Nicholas Mirzoeff. Routledge, 2002, pp. 405–16.
Marco, Derilene. "Vibing with Blackness: Critical Considerations of *Black Panther* and Exceptional Black Positionings." *Arts*, vol. 7, no. 4, 2018, https://www.mdpi.com/2076-0752/7/4/85.
Marshall, Rick. "Deadpool and Gambit: The Long Road to 'X-Men Origins: Wolverine' . . . And Beyond?" *MTV News*, December 11, 2008, www.mtv.com/news/2593264/deadpool-and-gambit-the-long-road-to-x-men-origins-wolverine-and-beyond.
Marx, Karl. *Capital: A Critique of Political Economy, Volume One: The Process of Production of Capital*. Translated by Ben Fowkes. Penguin, 1976.
---. *Grundrisse der Kritik der Politischen Ökonomie, 1857–1858*. Europäische Verlagsanstalt, 1970.
Massumi, Brian. "Notes on the Translation and Acknowledgements." In: Gilles Deleuze and Félix Guattari, *A Thousand Plateaus: Capitalism and Schizophrenia*. University of Minnesota Press, 1987, pp. xvi–ixx.
Masters, Kim. "Superman vs. Batman? DC's Real Battle is How to Create Its Superhero Universe." *Hollywood Reporter*, April 29, 2015, www.hollywoodreporter.com/news/general-news/superman-batman-dcs-real-battle-792190/.
Mayer, Ruth. *Serial Fu Manchu: The Chinese Supervillain and the Spread of Yellow Peril Ideology*. Temple University Press, 2014.
McCarthy, Tyler. "Will 'Batman v Superman: Dawn of Justice' Poor Performance Affect Other DC Movies?" *International Business Times*, April 6, 2016, www.ibtimes.com/will-batman-v-superman-dawn-justice-poor-performance-affect-other-dc-movies-2349387.
McClintock, Pamela. "Disney's 'Black Panther' Playbook: A Peek at the Marketing of a Phenomenon." *Hollywood Reporter*, February 21, 2018, www.hollywoodreporter.com/heat-vision/black-panther-how-disney-created-a-phenomenon-1086820.
McCloud, Scott. *Understanding Comics: The Invisible Art*. HarperPerennial, 2006.
McGuigan, Jim. *Cool Capitalism*. Pluto Press, 2009.
McLuhan, Marshall. *Understanding Media: The Extensions of Man*. Routledge, 2001.
McMillan, Graeme. "Hugh Jackman Explains Why Jerry Seinfeld Is Behind the End of Wolverine." *The Hollywood Reporter*, June 9, 2015, www.hollywoodreporter.com/heat-vision/hugh-jackman-explains-why-jerry-801353.
---. "Why the 'Deadpool' Trailer Was the Best Received at Comic-Con." *The Hollywood Reporter*, July 11, 2015, www.hollywoodreporter.com/heat-vision/comic-con-deadpool-trailer-was-808196.
McNary, Dave. "Warner Bros. Sets Up 'Suicide Squad.'" *Variety*, February 25, 2009, variety.com/2009/film/features/warner-bros-sets-up-suicide-squad-1118000590/.

---. "'Black Panther' Becomes Fandango's Top Early Pre-Seller Among Marvel Movies." *Variety*, January 10, 2018, variety.com/2018/film/news/black-panther-advance-ticket-sales-record-1202659579/.

Meehan, Eileen R. "Holy Commodity Fetish, Batman! The Political Economy of a Commercial Intertext." *Many More Lives of Batman*. Edited by Roberta Pearson, William Urrichio, and Will Brooker. BFI/Palgrave, 2015, pp. 69–87.

Meier, Stefan. *Superman Transmedial: Eine Pop-Ikone im Spannungsfeld von Medienwandel und Serialität*. Transcript, 2015.

Melrose, Kevin. "'Suicide Squad's Jared Leto Channels 'The Killing Joke' in Latest Photo." *CBR*, August 10, 2016, www.cbr.com/suicide-squads-jared-leto-channels-the-killing-joke-in-latest-photo.

Michelinie, David, and John Romita Jr. "The Old Man and the Sea Prince!" *Iron Man*, vol. 1, no. 120, Marvel Comics, 1979.

---. "Demon in a Bottle!" *Iron Man*, vol. 1, no. 128, Marvel Comics, 1979.

Miller, Frank, and Klaus Janson. "Last Hand." *Daredevil*, vol. 1, no. 181, Marvel Comics, 1982.

Mittell, Jason. *Complex TV: The Poetics of Contemporary Television Storytelling*. New York University Press, 2015. Kindle e-book.

---. "Narrative Complexity in Contemporary American Television." *The Velvet Light Trap*, vol. 58, 2006, pp. 29–40.

Morton, Drew. *Panel to the Screen: Style, American Film, and Comic Books During the Blockbuster Era*. University Press of Mississippi, 2017.

Mudde, Cas, and Cristóbal Rovira Kaltwasser. *Populism: A Very Short Introduction*. Oxford University Press, 2017.

Muncy, Julie. "The Russo Brothers Reveal the Post-Infinity War Fates of a Few More MCU Characters." *io9*, May 13, 2018, io9.gizmodo.com/the-russo-brothers-reveal-the-post-infinity-war-fates-o-s1825992323.

---. "These Activists Are Registering Voters at Black Panther Showings." *io9*, February 18, 2018, io9.gizmodo.com/these-activists-are-registering-voters-at-black-panther-1823116870.

---. "Twitter Trolls Are Posting About Fake Assaults at Black Panther Screenings." *io9*, February 17, 2018, io9.gizmodo.com/twitter-trolls-are-posting-about-fake-assaults-at-black-1823103060.

Naremore, James, and Patrick Brantlinger. "Introduction: Six Artistic Cultures." *Modernity and Mass Culture*. Edited by James Naremore and Patrick Brantlinger. Indiana University Press, 1991, pp. 1–21.

Newkirk, Vann R. II. "The Provocation and Power of *Black Panther*." *The Atlantic*, February 14, 2018, www.theatlantic.com/entertainment/archive/2018/02/the-provocation-and-power-of-black-panther/553226.

Newman, Michael Z. "From Beats to Arcs: Toward a Poetics of Television Narrative." *The Velvet Light Trap*, vol. 58, no. 1, 2006, pp. 16–28.

Nightingale, Victoria. "Improvising Elvis, Marilyn, and Mickey Mouse." *Australian Journal of Communication*, vol. 21, no. 1, 1994, pp. 1–20.

Nolte, John. "'Black Panther' Review: The Movie's Hero Is Trump, the Villain Is Black Lives Matter." *Breitbart*, February 16, 2018, www.breitbart.com/big-hollywood/2018/02/16/black-panther-review-great-actors-make-failure-launch/.

---. "Hollywood Turns Against Obama with 'Captain America: The Winter Solider.'" *Breitbart*, April 7, 2014, www.breitbart.com/california/2014/04/06/hollywood-turns-against-obama-with-captain-america-winter-soldier-2.

North, Dan. *Performing Illusions: Cinema, Special Effects, and the Virtual Actor*. Wallflower, 2008.

Nyberg, Amy Kiste. "William Gaines and the Battle over EC Comics." *A Comics Studies Reader*. Edited by Jeet Heer and Kent Worcester.s University of Mississippi Press, 2009, pp. 58–68.
O'Brien, Lucy. "Suicide Squad: Here's a Green-Haired Jared Leto Striking the Killing Joke Pose." *IGN*, April 10, 2015, www.ign.com/articles/2015/04/10/suicide-squad-heres-a-green-haired-jared-leto-striking-the-killing-joke-pose.
O'Neil, Denny, and Herb Trimpe. "And One of Them Must Die!" *Iron Man*, vol. 1, no. 199, Marvel Comics, 1985.
O'Neil, Denny, and Luke McDonnell. "And Who Shall Clothe Himself in Iron?" *Iron Man*, vol. 1, no. 170, Marvel Comics, 1983.
O'Neil, Denny, and Mark Bright. "Resolutions!" *Iron Man*, vol. 1, no. 200, Marvel Comics, 1985.
Oldham, Stuart. "Ryan Reynolds Gets Redemption as 'Deadpool' Trailer Wows Comic-Con." *Variety*, July 12, 2015, variety.com/2015/film/news/deadpool-trailer-comic-con-ryan-reynolds-1201538560.
Oliver, Glen. "Watch Quickly!! Some Test Footage from Tim Miller and Ryan Reynolds' DEADPOOL Movie!!" *Aint It Cool News*, July 28, 2014, www.aintitcool.com/node/68191.
Opam, Kwame. "What Hugh Jackman Leaving the X-Men Franchise Means for the Superhero Genre." *The Verge*, March 3, 2017, www.theverge.com/2017/3/3/14803518/logan-hugh-jackman-x-men-wolverine-final-movie.
Owczarski, Kimberly Ann. "Batman, Time Warner, and Franchise Filmmaking in the Conglomerate Era." Unpublished Diss. The University of Texas at Austin, 2008, repositories.lib.utexas.edu/handle/2152/17995.
Packard, Stephen. "Whose Side Are You on? Zur Allegorisierung von 9/11 in Marvel's *Civil War*-Comics." *9/11 als kulturelle Zäsur: Repräsentation des 11. September 2001 in kulturellen Diskursen, Literatur und visuellen Medien*. Edited by Sandra Poppe, Thorsten Schüller, and Sascha Seiler. Transcript, 2009, pp. 317–36.
Palmer, Frank. "Deadpool 2 Reportedly Having Disastrous Test Screenings; FOX Shocked." *ScreenGeek*, March 12, 2018, www.screengeek.net/2018/03/11/deadpool-2-poor-test-screenings-fox-shocked/.
Pao, Migz. "Wolverine 3 Release Date Set on March 2017 as Liev Schreiber Returns as Sabretooth in the Movie; 'Old Man Logan' Storyline to Be Used in the Third Film?" *KDramaStars*, September 16, 2014., www.kdramastars.com/articles/37764/20140916/wolverine-3-release-date.htm?utm_source=feedburner&utm_medium=email&utm_campaign=Feed%3A+KdramastarsTopNews+%28fKDramaStars+%3A+Top+News%29.
Parker, Ryan. "Twitter Trolls Post Fake Claims of Racially Motivated Assaults at 'Black Panther' Showings." *The Hollywood Reporter*, September 16, 2018, www.hollywoodreporter.com/heat-vision/twitter-trolls-post-fake-claims-racially-motivated-assaults-at-black-panther-showings-1085843?utm_source=twitter&.
Parody, Claire. "Franchising/Adaptation." *Adaptation*, vol 4, no. 2, 2011, pp. 210–18.
Peil, Dietmar. "Allegorie." *Metzler Lexikon Literatur- und Kulturtheorie*, 4th edition. Edited by Ansgar Nünning. Metzler, 2008, p. 12.
Peris, Sebastian. "'Black Panther' & 'Avengers: Infinity War' Top Most Tweeted Movies List." *Heroic Hollywood*, December 5, 2018, heroichollywood.com/black-panther-avengers-infinity-war-top-tweeted/.
Perry, Spencer. "Hugh Jackman Teases 'One Last Time' as Wolverine." *SuperHeroHype*, March 28, 2015, https://www.superherohype.com/news/334957-hugh-jackman-teases-one-last-time-as-wolverine.
---. "Update: Test Footage for Deadpool Feature Film Online." *SuperHeroHype*, July 28, 2014, www.superherohype.com/news/310869-test-footage-for-deadpool-feature-film-online.

Phillips, Andrea. *A Creator's Guide to Transmedia Storytelling: How to Captivate and Engage Audiences Across Multiple Platforms*. McGraw Hill, 2012.

Pimentel, Julia. "New Petition Wants 25 Percent of 'Black Panther' Profits to Be Invested in Black Communities." *Complex*, June 1, 2018, www.complex.com/pop-culture/2018/02/petition-demands-black-panther-profits-invested-black-community.

Pollard, Andrew. "Ryan Reynolds Set to Sign on for DEADPOOL Ahead of March Start." *Starburst Magazine*, December 5, 2014, www.starburstmagazine.com/ryan-reynolds-set-to-sign-on-for-deadpool-ahead-of-march-start.

Prokopny, Steve. "Capone Endures the Cut-and-Paste Action Antics of SUICIDE SQUAD." *Aint It Cool News*, August 5, 2016, www.aintitcool.com/node/75909.

Pulliam-Moore, Charles. "Report: Joe Russo Gave the Infinity War Answers You've Been Waiting for. . . to a Bunch of Teens." *io9*, May 4, 2018, io9.gizmodo.com/joe-russo-gave-the-infinity-war-answers-youve-been-wait-1825776831.

---. "Why Do You Hurt Us Like This, James Gunn?" *io9*, May 7, 2018, io9.gizmodo.com/why-do-you-hurt-us-like-this-james-gunn-1825821196.

Pustz, Matthew. "Comics and Fandom." *The Routledge Companion to Comics*. Edited by Frank Bramlett, Roy T. Cook, and Aaron Meskin. Routledge, 2020, pp. 264–74.

---. *Comic Book Culture: Fanboys and True Believers*. University Press of Mississippi, 1999.

Rasmus, Daniel. "'Captain America: Civil War' Reflects Current Global Issues in a Surprisingly Personal Way." *Pop Matters*, May 18, 2016, www.popmatters.com/captain-america-civil-war-2495433973.html.

Raunig, Gerald. *A Thousand Machines: A Concise Philosophy of the Machine as Social Movement*. Translated by Aileen Derieg. Semiotext(e), 2010.

---. "Einige Fragmente über Maschinen." *Grundrisse*, vol. 17, 2005, pp. 41–49.

Rauscher, Andreas. "Avengers Assemblage: Genre Settings und Worldbuilding in den Marvel-Filmen." *RabbitEye – Zeitschrift für Filmforschung*, vol. 6, 2014, pp. 68–83.

---. "The Marvel Universe on Screen: A New Wave of Superhero Movies?" *Comics as a Nexus of Cultures: Essays on the Interplay of Media, Disciplines, and International Perspectives*. Edited by Mark Berninger, Jochen Ecke, and Gideon Haberkorn. McFarland, 2010, pp. 21–32.

Raya Bravo, Irene. "La Recuela: Entre el Remake y la Secuela: El Caso de Jurassic World." *Fonseca: Journal of Communication*, vol. 14, 2017, pp. 45–57.

Reese, Rhett, and Paul Wernick. *Deadpool*. (Screenplay Draft). 2010. *The Internet Archive*, January 1, 2014, archive.org/stream/pdfy-1CeJQ_gog6XPXRwe/Deadpool%20Movie%20Leaked%20Script_djvu.txt.

Reeves, Jimmie L., Marc C. Rodgers, and Michael Epstein. "Rewriting Popularity: The Cult Files." *Deny All Knowledge: Reading the X-Files*. Edited by David Lavery, Angela Hague, and Marla Cartwright. Syracruse University Press, 1996, pp. 22–35.

Reynolds, Richard. "Masked Heroes." *The Superhero Reader*. Edited by Charles Hatfield, Jeet Heer, and Kent Worcester. University of Mississippi Press, 2013, pp. 99–115.

Rickford, Russell. "I Have a Problem with Black Panther." *Africa Is a Country*, February 2018, africasacountry.com/2018/02/i-have-a-problem-with-black-panther.

Rivera, Joshua. "Ryan Reynolds' Raunchy 'Deadpool' Crushed Comic-Con for One Simple Reason – It Looks like They Nailed It." *Business Insider*, July 13, 2015, https://www.businessinsider.in/Ryan-Reynolds-raunchy-Deadpool-crushed-Comic-Con-for-one-simple-reason-it-looks-like-they-nailed-it/articleshow/48062340.cms.

Romano, Aja. "Ryan Reynolds Plays Deadpool in This 2012 Test Footage." *The Daily Dot*, July 28, 2014, www.dailydot.com/parsec/new-deadpool-test-footage-leaks/.

Rosenberg, Alyssa. "What 'Captain America: The Winter Soldier' Gets Very Wrong." *The Washington Post*, April 10, 2014, www.washingtonpost.com/news/act-four/wp/2014/04/10/what-captain-america-the-winter-soldier-gets-very-wrong/?utm_term=.e15662479164.

Roxborough, Scott. "Berlin: Hugh Jackman Calls 'Logan' a 'Love Letter to Wolverine Fans.'" *The Hollywood Reporter*, February 17, 2017, www.hollywoodreporter.com/heat-vision/hugh-jackman-logan-is-a-love-letter-wolverine-fans-berlin-film-festival-977218.

Ryan, Marie-Laure. "Story/Worlds/Media: Tuning the Instruments of a Media-Conscious Narratology." *Storyworlds across Media: Toward a Media-Conscious Narratology*. Edited by Marie-Laure Ryan and Jan-Noël Thon. University of Nebraska Press, 2014, [n. p.]. Kindle e-book.

"Ryan Reynolds Is Deadpool." *Just Jared*, February 18, 2008, web.archive.org/web/20080225173642/http://justjared.buzznet.com:80/2008/02/18/ryan-reynolds-deadpool/.

Ryzik, Melena. "The Afrofuturistic Designs of 'Black Panther.'" *The New York Times*, February 23, 2018, www.nytimes.com/2018/02/23/movies/black-panther-afrofuturism-costumes-ruth-carter.html.

Scahill, Andrew. "Serialized Killers: Prebooting Horror in *Bates Motel* and *Hannibal*." *Cycles, Sequels, Spin-offs, Remakes, and Reboots: Multiplicities in Film and Television*. Edited by Amanda Ann Klein and R. Barton Palmer. University of Texas Press, 2016, pos. 6017–6371. Kindle ebook.

Schaefer, Sandy. "'Wolverine 3', 'Fantastic Four 2', 'Taken 3' and More Get Release Dates." *Screen Rant*, July 27, 2016, screenrant.com/wolverine-3-taken-3-fantastic-four-2-release-date.

Schager, Nick. "The Politics of 'Captain America: Civil War': A Conservative Manifesto." *Daily Beast*, August 5, 2016, www.thedailybeast.com/the-politics-of-captain-america-civil-war-a-conservative-manifesto.

Schatz, Tom. "The Studio System and Conglomerate Hollywood." *The Contemporary Hollywood Film Industry*. Edited by Paul McDonald and Janet Wasko. Blackwell, 2008, pp. 13–42.

Schwerdtfeger, Conner. "How the DCEU Will Move Forward Following the Batman V Superman Debacle." *Cinemablend*, April 10, 2016, www.cinemablend.com/new/How-DCEU-Move-Forward-Following-Batman-V-Superman-Debacle-123707.html.

Sconce, Jeffrey. "What If? Charting Television's New Textual Boundaries." *Television after TV: Essays on a Medium in Transition*. Edited by Lynn Spigel and Jan Olsson. Duke University Press, 2004, pp. 93–112.

Scott, A. O. "Review: In 'Captain America: Civil War,' Super-Bro Against Super-Bro." *The New York Times*, May 5, 2016, www.nytimes.com/2016/05/06/movies/captain-america-civil-war-review-chris-evans.html.

Scott, Suzanne. "Dawn of the Undead Author: Fanboy Auteurism and Zack Snyder's 'Vision.'" *A Companion to Media Authorship*. Edited by Jonathan Gray and Derek Johnson. John Wiley & Sons, 2013, pp. 440–59.

---. "*Textual Poachers*, Twenty Years Later: A Conversation between Henry Jenkins and Suzanne Scott." In: Henry Jenkins, *Textual Poachers: Television Fans and Participatory Culture*, Updated Twentieth Anniversary Edition, Routledge, 2013, pp. xii-l.

Shaviro, Steven. "Post-Continuity: An Introduction." *Post-Cinema: Theorizing 21st Century Film*. Edited by Shane Denson and Julia Leyda. Reframe Books, 2016, [n. p.].

Shirey, Paul. "Exclusive Update: Ryan Reynolds Reacts to the Deadpool PG-13 Rating." *JoBlo.com*, April 1, 2015, www.joblo.com/movie-news/exclusive-update-ryan-reynolds-reacts-to-the-deadpool-pg-13-rating-280.

Shone, Tom. *Blockbuster: How Hollywood Learned to Stop Worrying and Love the Summer.* Free Press, 2004.

Shouse, Eric. "Feeling, Emotion, Affect." *M/C Journal*, vol. 8, no. 6, 2005, journal.media-culture.org.au/mcjournal/article/view/2443.

Siegel, Lucas. "Marvel Announces BLACK PANTHER, CAPTAIN MARVEL, INHUMANS, AVENGERS: INFINITY WAR Films, CAP & THOR 3 Subtitles." *Newsarama*, October 28, 2014, www.newsarama.com/22573-marvel-announces-black-panther-captain-marvel-inhumans-avengers-infinity-war-films-cap-thor-3-subtitles.html.

Simonpillai, Radheyan. "In Defense of 'Superman Returns.'" *Complex*, June 13, 2013, www.complex.com/pop-culture/2013/06/in-defense-of-superman-returns.

Singer, Marc. "The Myth of Eco." *Studies in Comics*, vol. 4, no. 2, 2013, pp. 355–66.

Smith, Jamil. "The Revolutionary Power of *Black Panther*." *Time.com*, February 19, 2018, time.com/black-panther.

Smith, Kevin, and Joe Quesada. *Daredevil: Guardian Devil.* Marvel Comics, 2010.

Smith, Murray. "Theses on the Philosophy of Hollywood History." *Contemporary Hollywood Cinema.* Edited by Steve Neale and Murray Smith. Routledge, 1998, pp. 3–20.

Sneider, Jeff. "Jared Leto Eyed to Play the Joker in WB's 'Suicide Squad' (Exclusive)." *TheWrap*, November 7, 2014, www.thewrap.com/jared-leto-eyed-to-play-the-joker-in-wbs-suicide-squad-exclusive.

Sobchack, Vivian. *Screening Space: The American Science Fiction Film.* Ungar, 1987.

Sonçul, S. Yiğit. "From Screens to Streets: The Dissemination of Guy Fawkes' Image in Physical and Living Media." *Between*, vol. 4, no. 7, 2014, pp. 1–9.

Springer, Simon. "Neoliberalism." *The Ashgate Companion to Critical Geopolitics.* Ashgate, 2013, pp. 147–64.

Stanfill, Mel. *Exploiting Fandom: How the Media Industry Seeks to Manipulate Fans.* University of Iowa Press, 2019.

Stanford, Jason. "Dreams of Superman's Fathers." *The Huffington Post*, December 7, 2017, www.huffingtonpost.com/jason-stanford/dreams-of-supermans-fathe_b_3405590.html?guccounter=1.

Staff, StarTrek.com. "Everything You Need to Know for SDCC 2019." *Star Trek*, July 12, 2019, intl.startrek.com/news/star-trek-sdcc-guide-patrick-stewart.

Staskiewicz, Keith. "'Batman v Superman': First Look at EW's Super Cover." *EW.com*, July 1, 2015, ew.com/article/2015/07/01/first-look-batman-v-superman-dawn-justice-ews-cover.

Statzel, Sophie R. "Cybersupremacy: The New Face and Form of White Supremacist Activism." *Digital Media and Democracy: Tactics in Hard Times.* Edited by Megan Boler. MIT Press, 2008, pp. 403–28.

St. Félix, Doreen. "On Killmonger, the American Villain of 'Black Panther.'" *The New Yorker*, February 20, 2018, www.newyorker.com/culture/culture-desk/on-killmonger-black-panther-s-american-villain.

---. "Ruth E. Carter's Threads of History." *The New Yorker*, September 10, 2018, www.newyorker.com/magazine/2018/09/10/ruth-e-carters-threads-of-history.

Stein, Daniel. "Popular Seriality, Authorship, Superhero Comics." *Media Economies: Perspectives on American Cultural Practices.* Edited by Marcel Hartwig, Evelyne Keitel, and Gunter Süß. WVT, 2014, pp. 133–57.

Steinert, Heinz. *Culture Industry.* Polity Press, 2003.

Stevens, Dana. "Iron Man: What if Oscar Wilde Were a Superhero?" *Slate Magazine*, May 1, 2008, slate.com/culture/2008/05/iron-man-reviewed.html.

---. "The Dark Knight, Reviewed." *Slate Magazine*, July 17, 2008, slate.com/culture/2008/07/the-dark-knight-reviewed.html.

Stewart, Felicia. "Cross My Heart and Hope to Die in Wakanda: Expressions of Solidarity in *Black Panther*." *Why Wakanda Matters: What Black Panther Reveals About Psychology, Identity, and Communication*. SmartPop, 2020, pp. 2–16.
Straume, Ingerid S. "The Political Imaginary of Global Capitalism." *Depoliticization: The Political Imaginary of Global Capitalism*. Edited by Ingerid S. Straume and J. F. Humphrey. NSU Press, 2011, pp. 27–50.
Stringer, Julian, editor. *Movie Blockbusters*. Routledge, 2003. Kindle e-book.
Suebsaeng, Asawin. "Like Most Libertarians, Iron Man Grows Up and Moves On." Rev. of *Iron Man 3*, *Mother Jones*, May 3, 2013, www.motherjones.com/politics/2013/05/film-review-iron-man-3-politics.
"Suicide Squad (2016) – User Ratings." *IMDb*, www.imdb.com/title/tt1386697/ratings.
"Suicide Squad – Customer Reviews." *Amazon.com*, www.amazon.com/Suicide-Squad-Will-Smith/dp/B01J7YLPGM/ref=sr_1_1?ie=UTF8&qid=1540459967&sr=8-1&keywords=suicide+squad.
"Suicide Squad." *Metacritic*, August 5, 2016, www.metacritic.com/movie/suicide-squad.
"Suicide Squad." *Rotten Tomatoes*, August 22, 2017, www.rottentomatoes.com/m/suicide_squad_2016.
Tasker, Yvonne. "Introduction: Action and Adventure Cinema." *The Action and Adventure Cinema*. Edited by Yvonne Tasker. Routledge, 2004, pp. 1–13.
Taylor, Aaron. "Avengers Dissemble! Transmedia Superhero Franchises and Cultic Management." *Journal of Adaptation in Film & Performance*, vol. 7, no. 2, 2014, pp. 181–94.
---. "How to See Things Differently: Tim Burton's Reimaginings." *The Works of Tim Burton: Margins to Mainstream*. Edited by Jeffrey Andrew Weinstock. Palgrave Macmillan, 2013, pp. 99–116. Kindle ebook.
Terranova, Tiziana. "Free Labour." *Network Culture: Politics for the Information Age*. Pluto Press, 2004, pp. 73–97.
Thompson, Kristin. *Storytelling in Film and Television*. Harvard University Press, 2003.
Thompson, Luke Y. "Review: DEADPOOL Is a Heartfelt Valentine to Your Inner Adolescent." *Nerdist*, February 6, 2016, nerdist.com/review-deadpool-is-a-heartfelt-valentine-to-your-inner-adolescent.
Tomasovic, Dick. "The Hollywood Cobweb: New Laws of Attraction." *The Cinema of Attractions Reloaded: Film Culture in Transition*. Edited by Wanda Strauven. Amsterdam University Press, 2006, pp. 309–20.
Tracey, Janey. "Jared Leto Teases a Reference to The Killing Joke in Suicide Squad." *Outer Places*, November 5, 2015, www.outerplaces.com/science-fiction/item/9542-jared-leto-teases-a-reference-to-the-killing-joke-in-suicide-squad.
Trendacosta, Katharine. "Finally a Look at Jared Leto's Suicide Squad Joker Hair." *io9*, April 9, 2015, io9.gizmodo.com/finally-a-look-at-jared-letos-suicide-squad-joker-hair-1696913327.
---. "Just How Insane a Body Count Does the Joker Rack Up in Suicide Squad?" *io9*, January 21, 2015, io9.gizmodo.com/just-how-insane-a-body-count-does-the-joker-rack-up-in-1680816778.
---. "Warner Bros. Needs to Stop Whining About All the Money Its DC Movies Made." *io9*, November 8, 2016, io9.gizmodo.com/warner-bros-needs-to-stop-whining-about-all-the-money-1788718682.
---. "What Warner Bros. Needs to Do to Save the DC Extended Universe from Its Biggest Enemy, Warner Bros." *io9*, September 1, 2016, io9.gizmodo.com/what-warner-bros-needs-to-do-to-save-the-dc-extended-u-1786059387.

Truitt, Brian. "Hugh Jackman Remembers Two Decades of Wolverine." *USA Today*, March 1, 2017.

Turan, Kenneth. "In 'Logan,' an Authentic Drama between Scenes of Brutal Violence to Feed the Comic-Book Beast." *Los Angeles Times*, March 2, 2017, www.latimes.com/.../la-et-mn-logan-review-20170302-story.html.

Uricchio, William, and Roberta Pearson. "I'm Not Fooled by That Cheap Disguise." *Many More Lives of Batman*. Edited by Roberta Pearson, William Urrichio, and Will Brooker. BFI/Palgrave, 2015, pp. 204–36.

van Winkle, Dan. "Absurd Trolls Try to Tank *Blank Panther* User Ratings: 'Minorities ... Should Stay That Way.'" *The Mary Sue*, February 1, 2018, www.themarysue.com/black-panther-rating-trolls.

---. "Deadpool Animation Is Maybe Leaked Deadpool Movie Test Footage, Is Definitely Awesome." *The Mary Sue*, July 28, 2014, www.themarysue.com/deadpool-test-footage.

Venable, Nick. "Deadpool Movie Update from Ryan Reynolds Promises It's Still Alive." *Cinemablend*, March 18, 2014, www.cinemablend.com/new/Deadpool-Movie-Update-From-Ryan-Reynolds-Promises-It-Still-Alive-38384.html.

Vercellone, Carlo. "From Formal Subsumption to General Intellect: Elements for a Marxist Reading of the Thesis of Cognitive Capitalism." *Historical Materialism*, vol. 15, 2007, pp. 13–36.

Verevis, Constantine. "New Millennial Remakes." *Media of Serial Narrative*. Edited by Frank Kelleter. Ohio State University Press, 2017, pp. 148–66.

Vespe, Eric. "Quint Reviews SUICIDE SQUAD!!!" *Aint It Cool News*, August 3, 2016, http://www.aintitcool.com/node/75891.

Vignold, Peter. *Das Marvel Cinematic Universe: Anatomie einer Hyperserie*. Schüren, 2017.

Virno, Paolo. "Notes on the 'General Intellect.'" *Marxism Beyond Marxism*. Edited by Saree Makdisi, Cesare Casarino, and Rebecca Karl. Routledge, 1996, [n. p.]. Kindle e-book.

Watercutter, Angela. "'*Captain America: Civil War* Is Fantastic, But Not Because of Captain America." *Wired*, May 18, 2016, www.wired.com/2016/05/captain-america-civil-war-review/.

Weintraub, Steve. "Hugh Jackman on Why He Kept Playing Wolverine All These Years." *Collider*, March 3, 2017, collider.com/hugh-jackman-logan-wolverine-interview.

Whitbrook, James. "Report: Warner Bros. Turned Suicide Squad into a Mess in Its Panic Over BvS Criticism." *io9*, August 3, 2016, io9.gizmodo.com/report-warner-bros-turned-suicide-squad-into-a-mess-i-1784760580.

White, Adam. "'The Bloody, Primal Wolverine Movie Fans Always Wanted': First Footage of New X-Men Movie Logan Gets Rapturous Response." *The Telegraph*, December 9, 2016, www.telegraph.co.uk/films/2016/12/09/bloody-primal-wolverine-movie-fans-always-wanted-first-footage/.

Wickman, Forrest, and David Canfield. "Here's What Critics Have to Say About Suicide Squad." *Slate Magazine*, August 2, 2016, www.slate.com/blogs/browbeat/2016/08/02/suicide_squad_review_roundup.html.

Williams, Raymond. *Television: Technology and Cultural Form*. Routledge Classics, 2003.

Willmore, Alison. "'Captain America' and the Age of Snowden." Rev. of *Captain America: The Winter Soldier*. *BuzzFeed*, April 8, 2014, www.buzzfeed.com/alisonwillmore/captain-america-and-the-age-of-snowden.

Woerner, Meredith. "WB Announces a Ton of New DC Movies, Including Who's Playing The Flash." *io9*, October 15, 2014, io9.gizmodo.com/wb-announces-a-ton-of-new-dc-movies-including-whos-pla-1646664939.

Wolf, Mark J. P. *Building Imaginary Worlds: The Theory and History of Subcreation*. Routledge, 2012. Kindle ebook.
Wyatt, Justin. *High Concept: Movies and Marketing in Hollywood*. University of Texas Press, 1994. Kindle ebook.
Wylie, Philip. "Gladiator." *The Superhero Reader*. Edited by Charles Hatfield, Jeet Heer, and Kent Worcester. University of Mississippi Press, 2013, pp. 23–29.
Yockey, Matt. "Introduction. Excelsior! Or, Everything That Rises Must Converge." *Make Ours Marvel: Media Convergence and a Comics Universe*. Edited by Matt Yockey. University of Texas Press, 2017, pp. 1–37.
---, editor. *Make Ours Marvel. Media Convergence and a Comics Universe*. University of Texas Press, 2017.
---. "Somewhere in Time: Utopia and the Return of Superman." *The Velvet Light Trap*, vol. 61, 2008, pp. 26–37.
Zuboff, Shoshanna. *The Age of Surveillance Capitalism: The Fight for the Future at the New Frontier of Power*. Profile Books, 2019.

FILMOGRAPHY

Feature Films (Titles in Alphabetical Order)

Ant-Man. Dir. Peyton Reed. Perf. Paul Rudd, Evangeline Lilly, Corey Stoll, Michael Peña, and Michael Douglas. Walt Disney Pictures, 2015. Blu-Ray.
Ant-Man and the Wasp. Dir. Peyton Reed. Perf. Paul Rudd, Evangeline Lilly, Michael Douglas, Michelle Pfeiffer, and Michael Peña. Walt Disney Pictures, 2018. Film.
Aquaman. Dir. James Wan. Perf. Jason Momoa, Amber Heard, Willem Dafoe, Patrick Wilson, and Dolph Lundgren. Warner Bros., DC Entertainment, 2018. Film.
Avengers: Age of Ultron. Dir. Joss Whedon. Perf. Robert Downey Jr., Chris Evans, Chris Hemsworth, Scarlett Johansson, and Jeremy Renner. Walt Disney Pictures, 2015. Blu-Ray.
Avengers: Endgame. Dir. Anthony and Joe Russo. Perf. Robert Downey Jr., Chris Evans, Chris Hemsworth, Scarlett Johansson, and Tom Holland. Walt Disney Pictures, 2019. Amazon Video.
Avengers: Infinity War. Dir. Anthony and Joe Russo. Perf. Robert Downey Jr., Chris Evans, Chris Hemsworth, Scarlett Johansson, and Tom Holland. Walt Disney Pictures, 2018. Amazon Video.
Batman. Dir. Tim Burton. Perf. Michael Keaton, Jack Nicholson, Kim Basinger, Billy Dee Williams, and Jack Palance. Warner Bros., 1989. Amazon Video.
Batman Begins. Dir. Christopher Nolan. Perf. Christian Bale, Michael Caine, Liam Neeson, and Katie Holmes. Warner Bros., 2005. Amazon Video.
Batman Forever. Dir. Joel Schumacher. Perf. Val Kilmer, Jim Carrey, Tommy Lee Jones, Chris O'Donnell, and Nicole Kidman. Warner Bros., 1995. Amazon Video.
Batman Returns. Dir. Tim Burton. Perf. Michael Keaton, Danny DeVito, Christopher Walken, Michelle Pfeiffer, and Michael Gough. Warner Bros., 1992. Amazon Video.
Batman & Robin. Dir. Joel Schumacher. Perf. George Clooney, Chris O'Donnell, Alicia Silverstone, Uma Thurman, and Arnold Schwarzenegger. Warner Bros., 1997. Amazon Video.

Batman V. Superman: Dawn of Justice. Dir. Zack Snyder. Perf. Ben Affleck, Henry Cavill, Amy Adams, Gal Gadot, and Jesse Eisenberg. Warner Bros., 2016. Blu-Ray.

Birds of Prey and the Fantabulous Emancipation of One Harley Quinn. Dir. Cathy Tan. Perf. Margot Robbie, Mary Elizabeth Winstead, Jurnee Smollett-Bell, Rosie Perez, and Ewan McGregor. Warner Bros. Pictures, 2020. Amazon Video.

Black Panther. Dir. Ryan Coogler. Perf. Chadwick Boseman, Michael B. Jordan, Lupita Nyong'o, Danai Gurira, and Martin Freeman. Walt Disney Pictures, 2018. Amazon Video.

Black Widow. Dir. Cate Shortland. Perf. Scarlett Johansson, Florence Pugh, David Harbour, Rachel Weisz, and Ray Winstone. Walt Disney Pictures, 2021. Disney+.

Blade. Dir. Stephen Norrington. Perf. Wesley Snipes, N'Bushe Wright, Kris Kristofferson, Donal Logue, and Udo Kier. New Line Cinema, 1998. DVD.

Blade II. Dir. Guillermo Del Toro. Perf. Wesley Snipes, Kris Kristofferson, Ron Perlman, Leonor Varela, and Norman Reedus. New Line Cinema, 2002. Amazon Video.

Blade: Trinity. Dir. David Goyer. Perf. Wesley Snipes, Kris Kristofferson, Jessica Biel, Dominic Purcell, and Ryan Reynolds. New Line Cinema, 2004. Amazon Video.

Captain America: The First Avenger. Dir. Joe Johnston. Perf. Chris Evans, Hugo Weaving, Tommy Lee Jones, Hayley Atwell, and Samuel L. Jackson. Paramount Pictures, 2011. Film.

Captain America: The Winter Soldier [German Title: *The Return of the First Avenger*]. Dir. Anthony Russo and Joe Russo. Perf. Chris Evans, Robert Redford, Samuel L. Jackson, Scarlett Johansson, and Anthony Mackie. Walt Disney Pictures, 2014. Amazon Video.

Captain America: Civil War. Dir. Anthony Russo and Joe Russo. Perf. Chris Evans, Robert Downey Jr., Scarlett Johansson, Jeremy Renner, and Sebastian Stan. Walt Disney Pictures, 2016. Film.

Captain Marvel. Dir. Anna Boden and Ryan Fleck. Perf. Brie Larson, Samuel L. Jackson, Ben Mendelsohn, Djimon Hounsou, and Lee Pace. Walt Disney Pictures, 2019. Amazon Video.

Constantine. Dir. Francis Lawrence. Perf. Keanu Reeves, Rachel Weisz, Djimon Honsou, Shia LaBeouf, and Tilda Swinton. Warner Bros., 2005. DVD.

Daredevil. Dir. Mark Steven Johnson. Perf. Ben Affleck, Jennifer Garner, Colin Farrell, Jon Favreau, and Michael Clarke Duncan. 20th Century Fox, 2003. Amazon Video.

Dark Phoenix. Dir. Simon Kinberg. Perf. James McAvoy, Michael Fassbender, Jennifer Lawrence, Nicholas Hoult, and Sophie Turner. 20th Century Fox, 2019. Amazon Video.

Deadpool. Dir. Tim Miller. Perf. Ryan Reynolds, Morena Baccarin, Ed Skrein, T. J. Miller, and Gina Carano. 20th Century Fox, 2016. Blu-Ray.

Deadpool 2. Dir. David Leitch. Perf. Ryan Reynolds, Morena Baccarin, Josh Brolin, T. J. Miller, and Brianna Hildebrandt. 20th Century Fox, 2018. Amazon Video.

Doctor Strange. Dir. Scott Derrickson. Perf. Benedict Cumberbatch, Chiwetel Ejiofor, Rachel McAdams, Benedict Wong, and Mads Mikkelsen. Walt Disney Pictures, 2016. Amazon Video.

Fantastic Four. Dir. Tim Story. Perf. Ioan Gruffudd, Jessica Alba, Michael Chiklis, Chris Evans, and Julian McMahon. 20th Century Fox, 2005. DVD.

Guardians of the Galaxy. Dir. James Gunn. Perf. Chris Pratt, Zoe Saldana, Dave Bautista, Bradley Cooper, and Vin Diesel. Walt Disney Pictures, 2014. DVD.

Guardians of the Galaxy Vol. 2. Dir. James Gunn. Perf. Chris Pratt, Zoe Saldana, Dave Bautista, Bradley Cooper, and Vin Diesel. Walt Disney Pictures, 2017. Amazon Video.

Hulk. Dir. Ang Lee. Perf. Eric Bana, Nick Nolte, Jennifer Connelly, Sam Elliot, and Josh Lucas. Universal Studios, 2003. DVD.

Iron Man. Dir. Jon Favreau. Perf. Robert Downey Jr., Gwyneth Paltrow, Jeff Bridges, Terrence Howard, and Jon Favreau. Paramount, 2008. DVD.

Iron Man 2. Dir. Jon Favreau. Perf. Robert Downey Jr., Gwyneth Paltrow, Don Cheadle, Mickey Rourke, and Sam Rockwell. Walt Disney Pictures, 2010. DVD.

Iron Man 3. Dir. Shane Black. Perf. Robert Downey Jr., Gwyneth Paltrow, Don Cheadle, Guy Pearce, and Rebecca Hall. Walt Disney Pictures, 2013. Amazon Video.
Joker. Dir. Todd Phillips. Perf. Joaquin Phoenix, Robert De Niro, Zazie Beetz, Frances Conroy, and Marc Maron. Warner Bros. Pictures, 2019. Amazon Video.
Justice League. Dir. Zack Snyder and Joss Whedon. Perf. Ben Affleck, Henry Cavill, Ezra Miller, Gal Gadot, and Jason Momoa. Warner Bros., 2017. Amazon Video.
Logan. Dir. James Mangold. Perf. Hugh Jackman, Patrick Stewart, Dafne Keen, Boyd Holbrook, and Richard E. Grant. 20th Century Fox, 2017. Blu-Ray.
Man of Steel. Dir. Zack Snyder. Perf. Henry Cavill, Amy Adams, Michael Shannon, Kevin Costner, and Diane Lane. Warner Bros. 2013. DVD.
Marvel's The Avengers. Dir. Joss Whedon. Perf. Robert Downey Jr., Chris Evans, Chris Hemsworth, Scarlett Johansson, and Jeremy Renner. Walt Disney Pictures, 2012. DVD.
New Mutants. Dir. Josh Boone. Perf. Maisie Williams, Anna Taylor-Joy, Charlie Heaton, Alice Braga, and Blu Hunt. Walt Disney Pictures, 2020. Amazon Video.
Shazam! Dir. David F. Sandberg. Perf. Zachary Levi, Mark Strong, Asher Angel, Jack Dylan Grazer, and Djimon Hounsou. Warner Bros. Pictures, 2019. Amazon Video.
Suicide Squad. Dir. David Ayer. Perf. Jared Leto, Will Smith, Margot Robbie, Jai Courtney, and Viola Davis. Warner Bros., 2016. Blu-Ray.
Supergirl. Dir. Jeannot Szwarc. Perf. Helen Slater, Faye Dunaway, Peter O'Toole, Hart Bochner, and Mia Farrow. Tri-Star, 1984. DVD.
Superman. Dir. Richard Donner. Perf. Christopher Reeve, Margot Kidder, Marlon Brando, Gene Hackman, and Valerie Perrine. Warner Bros., 1978. DVD.
Superman II. Dir. Richard Lester. Perf. Christopher Reeve, Margot Kidder, Gene Hackman, Terrence Stamp, and Ned Beatty. Warner Bros., 1980. DVD.
Superman III. Dir. Richard Lester. Perf. Christopher Reeve, Richard Pryor, Robert Vaughn, Margot Kidder, and Annette O'Toole. Warner Bros., 1983. DVD.
Superman IV: The Quest for Peace. Dir. Sidney J. Furie. Perf. Christopher Reeve, Margot Kidder, Gene Hackman, Jackie Cooper, and Marc McClure. Cannon Films, 1987. DVD.
Superman Returns. Dir. Bryan Singer. Perf. Brandon Routh, Kate Bosworth, Kevin Spacey, James Marsden, and Parker Posey. Warner Bros., 2006. DVD.
Spider-Man. Dir. Sam Raimi. Perf. Tobey Maguire, Kirsten Dunst, James Franco, Willem Dafoe, and Rosemary Harris. Columbia Pictures, 2002. Amazon Video.
Spider-Man 2. Dir. Sam Raimi. Perf. Tobey Maguire, Kirsten Dunst, James Franco, Alfred Molina, and Rosemary Harris. Columbia Pictures, 2004. Amazon Video.
Spider-Man 3. Dir. Sam Raimi. Perf. Tobey Maguire, Kirsten Dunst, James Franco, Thomas Haden Church, and Topher Grace. Columbia Pictures, 2007. Amazon Video.
Spider-Man: Far from Home. Dir. Jon Watts. Perf. Tom Holland, Jake Gyllenhall, Jon Favreau, Samuel L. Jackson, and Zendaya. Columbia Pictures, 2019. Amazon Video.
Spider-Man: Homecoming. Dir. Jon Watts. Perf. Tom Holland, Robert Downey Jr., Donald Glover, Michael Keaton, and Zendaya. Columbia Pictures, 2017. Blu-Ray.
The Dark Knight. Dir. Christopher Nolan. Perf. Christian Bale, Michael Caine, Heath Ledger, and Maggie Gyllenhall. Warner Bros., 2008. DVD.
The Dark Knight Rises. Dir. Christopher Nolan. Perf. Christian Bale, Michael Caine, Gary Oldman, Anne Hathaway, and Tom Hardy. Warner Bros., 2012. Amazon Video.
The Incredible Hulk. Dir. Louis Leterrier. Perf. Edward Norton, Liv Tyler, Tim Roth, Tim Blake Nelson, and William Hurt. Universal Studios, 2008. DVD.
The Punisher. Dir. Jonathan Hensleigh. Perf. Thomas Jane, John Travolta, Will Patton, Roy Scheider, and Laura Harring. Lionsgate, 2004. Amazon Video.

The Suicide Squad. Dir. James Gunn. Perf. Idris Elba, Margot Robbie, Viola Davis, Joel Kinnaman, and John Cena. Warner Bros., 2021. Film.

The Wolverine. Dir. James Mangold. Perf. Hugh Jackman, Hiroyuki Sanada, Tao Okamoto, Rila Fukushima, and Famke Janssen. 20th Century Fox. Amazon Video.

Thor. Dir. Kenneth Brannagh. Perf. Chris Hemsworth, Natalie Portman, Tom Hiddleston, Anthony Hopkins, and Clark Gregg. Walt Disney Pictures, 2011. DVD.

Thor: The Dark World. Dir. Alan Taylor. Perf. Chris Hemsworth, Natalie Portman, Tom Hiddleston, Anthony Hopkins, and Idris Elba. Walt Disney Pictures, 2014. Blu-Ray.

Thor: Ragnarok. Dir. Taika Waititi. Perf. Chris Hemsworth, Tom Hiddleston, Idris Elba, Anthony Hopkins, and Cate Blanchett. Walt Disney Pictures, 2017. Amazon Video.

Wonder Woman. Dir. Patty Jenkins. Perf. Gal Gadot, Chris Pine, Connie Nielsen, Robin Wright, and Lucy Davis. Warner Bros., 2017. Amazon Video.

Wonder Woman 1984. Dir. Patty Jenkins. Perf. Gal Gadot, Chris Pine, Pedro Pascal, Kirsten Wiig, and Robin Wright. Warner Bros., 2020. HBO Max Video.

Venom. Dir. Ruben Fleischer. Perf. Tom Hardy, Vanessa Williams, Riz Ahmed, Scott Haze, and Jenny Slate. Sony Pictures, 2018. Amazon Video.

V for Vendetta. Dir. James McTeigue. Perf. Hugo Weaving, Natalie Portman, John Hurt, Stephen Rea, and Stephen Fry. Warner Bros., 2006. Amazon Video.

X2: X-Men United. Dir. Bryan Singer. Perf. Patrick Stewart, Ian McKellen, Hugh Jackman, Halle Berry, and Famke Janssen. 20th Century Fox, 2003. DVD.

X-Men. Dir. Bryan Singer. Perf. Patrick Stewart, Ian McKellen, Hugh Jackman, Halle Berry, and Famke Janssen. 20th Century Fox, 2000. DVD.

X-Men: Apocalypse. Dir. Bryan Singer. Perf. James McAvoy, Michael Fassbender, Jennifer Lawrence, Hugh Jackman, and Olivia Munn. 20th Century Fox, 2016. Film.

X-Men: Days of Future Past. Dir. Bryan Singer. Perf. James McAvoy, Michael Fassbender, Jennifer Lawrence, Hugh Jackman, and Peter Dinklage. 20th Century Fox, 2014. Blu-Ray.

X-Men: First Class. Dir. Matthew Vaughn. Perf. James McAvoy, Michael Fassbender, Jennifer Lawrence, Rose Byrne, and January Jones. 20th Century Fox, 2011. DVD.

X-Men Origins: Wolverine. Dir. Gavin Hood. Perf. Hugh Jackman, Liev Schreiber, Ryan Reynolds, Dominic Monaghan, and Danny Huston. 20th Century Fox, 2009. DVD.

X-Men: The Last Stand. Dir. Brett Ratner. Perf. Patrick Stewart, Ian McKellen, Hugh Jackman, Halle Berry, and Famke Janssen. 20th Century Fox, 2003. DVD.

Zack Snyder's Justice League. Dir. Zack Snyder. Perf. Ben Affleck, Henry Cavill, Ezra Miller, Gal Gadot, and Jason Momoa. Warner Bros., 2021. HBO Max Video.

Television (Titles in Alphabetical Order)

Arrow. Created by Greg Berlanti, Marc Guggenheim, and Andrew Kreisberg. Berlanti Productions, DC Entertainment, and Warner Bros. Television, 2012–20.

Constantine. Created by Daniel Cerone and David S. Goyer. Ever After Productions, DC Entertainment, and Warner Bros. Television, 2014–15.

Gotham. Created by Bruno Heller. Primrose Hill Productions, DC Entertainment, and Warner Bros. Television, 2014–19.

Helstrom. Created by Paul Zbyszewski. Marvel Television, Lone Lemon Entertainment, and ABC Signature Studios, 2020.

Krypton. Created by David Goyer. Phantom Four Films, DC Entertainment, and Warner Bros. Television, 2018–19.

Legion. Created by Noah Hawley. 26 Keys Production, The Donners' Company, Bad Hat Harry Productions, Kinberg Genre, Marvel Television, and FXP, 2017–19.

WORKS CITED

Loki. Created by Michael Waldron. Marvel Studios, Disney Platform Distribution, 2021.
Marvel's Agent Carter. Created by Christopher Marcus and Stephen McFeely. ABC Studios, Marvel Television, and F&B Fazekas & Butters, 2015–16.
Marvel's Agents of S.H.I.E.L.D. Created by Joss Whedon, Jed Whedon, and Maurissa Tancharoen.
"Beginning of the End," season 1, episode 22, NBC, April 18, 2015. *Disney+*, www.disneyplus.com/de-de/video/41135551-8a41-4363-85a0-f4897418182a
"End of the Beginning," season 1, episode 16, NBC, March 28, 2015. *Disney+*, www.disneyplus.com/de-de/video/172ea523-d517-49cd-b318-
"Nothing Personal," season 1, episode 20, NBC, April 11, 2015. *Disney+*, www.disneyplus.com/de-de/video/ffd65c3e-bc8b-473e-b293-c569ae1e8138
"Pilot," season 1, episode 1, NBC, September 24, 2013. *Disney+*, www.disneyplus.com/de-de/video/aa5aa0af-84a7-42d1-81fc-1c903c1ed203
"Providence," season 1, episode 18, NBC, April 4, 2015. *Disney+*, www.disneyplus.com/de-de/video/690a8eca-f9c4-4d67-aa1f-eed97d54070a
"Ragtag," season 1, episode 21, NBC, April 18, 2015. *Disney+*, www.disneyplus.com/de-de/video/dc51b05f-435d-42db-a142-92a57b8de6a6
"Repairs," season 1, episode 9, NBC, March 7, 2015. *Disney+*, www.disneyplus.com/de-de/video/ef8e33d5-dabb-481a-9326-9d2d160c13ef
"T.A.H.I.T.I.," season 1, episode 14, NBC, March 21, 2015. *Disney+*, www.disneyplus.com/de-de/video/3859100e-2136-4c9c-88dc-4f92c0c09546
"The Only Light in the Darkness," season 1, episode 19, NBC, April 11, 2015. *Disney+*, www.disneyplus.com/de-de/video/7c8b7b24-567a-46a3-acdb-56f454ac4f98
"The Well," season 1, episode 8, NBC, November 19, 2013. *Disney+*, www.disneyplus.com/de-de/video/bdc0aaa1-8ad7-4757-893a-a7c02f80ad00
"Turn, Turn, Turn," season 1, episode 18, NBC, April 8, 2013. *Disney+*, www.disneyplus.com/de-de/video/4d41464b-f7bc-42ab-b023-84481084f5fa
"Yes Men," season 1, episode 15, NBC, March 28, 2015. *Disney+*, www.disneyplus.com/de-de/video/74669a7b-e42c-4f12-8e1c-0e516110cebb
Marvel's Cloak and Dagger. Created by Joe Pokaski. Wandering Rocks Productions, ABC Signature Studios, and Marvel Television, 2018–19.
Marvel's Daredevil. Created by Drew Goddard. Marvel Television, ABC Studios, DeKnight Productions, and Goddard Textiles, 2015–18.
Marvel's Inhumans. Created by Scott Buck. ABC Studios, Marvel Television, and Devilina Productions, 2017.
Marvel's Iron Fist. Created by Scott Buck. ABC Studios and Marvel Television, 2017–18.
Marvel's Jessica Jones. Created by Melissa Rosenberg. Tall Girls Productions, Marvel Television, and ABC Studios, 2015–19.
Marvel's Luke Cage. Created by Cheo Hodari Choker. Marvel Television and ABC Studios, 2016–18.
Marvel's Runaways. Created by Josh Schwarz and Stephanie Savage. Marvel Television, ABC Signature Studios, and Fake Empire Productions, 2017–19.
Marvel's The Defenders. Created by Douglas Petrie and Marco Ramirez. Marvel Television, ABC Studios, Goddard Textiles, and Nine and a Half Fingers, Inc., 2017.
Marvel's The Punisher. Created by Steve Lightfoot. Marvel Television, ABC Studios, and Bohemian Risk Productions, 2017–19.
Powerless. Created by Ben Queen. Ehsugadee Productions, DC Entertainment, and Warner Bros. Television, 2017.
Stephen Colbert's Election Night 2020: Democracy's Last Stand: Building Back America Great Again Better 2020. Written by Felipe Torres Medina, Showtime Networks, 3 November 2020.

The Falcon and the Winter Soldier. Created by Malcolm Spellman. Marvel Studios, Disney Platform Distribution, 2021.

The Flash. Created by Greg Berlanti, Andrew Kreisberg, and Geoff Johns. Berlanti Productions, DC Entertainment, and Warner Bros. Television, since 2014.

The Gifted. Created by Matt Nix. Flying Glass of Milk Productions, The Donners' Company, Bad Hat Harry Productions, Kinberg Genre, Marvel Television, and 20th Century Fox Television, 2017–19.

The Incredible Hulk. Created by Kenneth Johnson. Marvel Comics and Universal Television, 1978–82.

The Late Show with Stephen Colbert. Created by Stephen Colbert. Spartina Productions and CBS Studios, since 2015.

WandaVision. Created by Jac Schaeffer. Marvel Studios, Disney Platform Distribution, 2021.

Online Video Clips and Promotional Video Materials (Titles in Alphabetical Order)

"America: Endgame." *YouTube*, August 18, 2020, youtu.be/26XPaQ3YpK4.

"America: Endgame (RNC Edition)." *YouTube*, August 25, 2020, youtu.be/4RekBeoyA7E.

"Deadpool 2 Official Teaser Trailer #4 (2018) Ryan Reynolds Marvel Movie HD." *YouTube*, February 7, 2018, www.youtube.com/watch?v=xjMsqpH_x-8.

"Deadpool – Gentlemen, Touch Yourself Tonight | 2016." *YouTube*, January 28, 2016, www.youtube.com /watch?v=KsdD1MJXOpk.

"Deadpool Leaked Footage." *Metatube*, August 7, 2014, www.metatube.com/en/videos/247219/ Deadpool-Leaked-Footage.

"Deadpool | Official HD Trailer #1 | 2016." *YouTube*, August 4, 2015, www.youtube.com/watch?v=Xithigfg7dA.

"Deadpool | Red Band Trailer [HD] | 20th Century FOX." *YouTube*, August 4, 2015, www.youtube.com/watch?v=FyKWUTwSYAs.

"Deadpool | Trailer Trailer." *YouTube*, August 3, 2015, www.youtube.com/watch?v=QPZHBjyUGhQ.

"How Deadpool Spent Halloween." *YouTube*, November 3, 2015, www.youtube.com/watch?v=1Nvg0LwWeTU&t=3s.

"Is Deadpool Going to be PG-13? Ryan Reynolds Weighs In." *YouTube*, April 1, 2015, www.youtube.com/watch?v=Z5TB0pKLj0Y.

"Logan | Official Trailer [HD] | 20th Century FOX." *YouTube*, October 20, 2016, www.youtube.com/ watch?v=Div0iP65aZo.s

"'Logan' Final Official Red Band Trailer (2017)." *YouTube*, January 19, 2017, www.youtube.com/ watch?v=g8nNfNaB18M.

"Marvel Studios' Black Panther – Official Trailer." *YouTube*, October 16, 2017, www.youtube.com/ watch?v=xjDjIWPwcPU.

"Team Biden." *YouTube*, July 17, 2020, https://youtu.be/678wgwQLpa4.

Index

References to notes are indicated by n; references to images are in *italics*.

9/11 attacks, 75, 151
20th Century Fox, 7, 101, 114; see also
    X-Men (film series)
2020 US election, 149–50

Action Comics (comic book), 28
action sequences, 5, 13, 93, 95, 157–8
activism, 174–6, 184
Actor-Network-Theory (ANT), 14–15
Adorno, Theodor W., 18, 44, 49, 186
    "Culture Industry Reconsidered", 34
    Dialectic of Enlightenment, 24, 26–7,
        29–30, 35, 53
    "Free Time", 30–1, 32–4, 37, 51
Adventures of Superman, The (novel), 28
Affleck, Ben, 7
African-Americans *see* race
agency, 11–18, 32–3, 38, 70, 73
Agent Carter (2013), 104
Agents of S.H.I.E.L.D. (TV series), 101,
    102–3, 104, 105
Ain't It Cool News (*AICN*) (website), 97,
    98–9, 118n22, 126–7, 130
    and *Suicide Squad*, 138, 143–4
Alias (2001–3), 74
allegory, 13, 69, 72, 178n2–3
    and *Black Panther*, 173, 176

and perseverance, 73, 74–5
and politics, 151, 153, 158–9, 160, 165–7
Alyn, Kirk, 28
Amazing Spider-Man, The (2012/14), 7,
    101
Amazon Video, 51, 106, 115, 182
ambivalence, 171–6
amusement parks, 6
analepses, 140, 141–2
Andrejevic, Mark, 48
Ant-Man (2015), 108
Aquaman (2018), 107
Aquaman (character), 109
Askwith, Ivan, 11
Assange, Julian, 163
audience *see* politics of engagement
Avengers, The (2012), 102, *103*, 109
Avengers: Age of Ultron (2015), 104, 110,
    111
Avengers: Endgame (2019), 1, 83, 112, 113,
    149–50
Avengers: Infinity War (2018), 111–13
Ayer, David, 137–9

Backman, Russell, 66
Bale, Christian, 7
Barla, Josef, 15

Batman (1989), 5, 7, 9–10, 89, 110
  and hyper-referentiality, 85, 86–7
  and reboots, 101
Batman (character), 23, 29, 55, 66
  and politics, 69, 149
Batman, The (2022), 7
Batman & Robin (1997), 7, 85, 87, 89, 90, 97
Batman Begins (2005), 91, 110
Batman Forever (1995), 7, 85, 87, *88*, 89, 110
Batman Returns (1992), 7, 85, 87, *88*, 89
Batman V. Superman: Dawn of Justice (2016), 107, 109, 110–11, 139
Batman: Year One (1987), 110–11
Battlestar Galactica (TV series), 20n4
Bell, Josh, 160
Bendis, Brian Michael, 96
Berger, Richard, 66
Biden, Joe, 149, 150
Birdman (2014), 23
Birds of Prey: The Emancipation of Harley Quinn (2020), 107, 113, 145
Black Lives Matter, 170, 171
Black Panther (2018), 19
  and populism, 152–3, 154, 158, 169–76, 177, 184
Black radicalism *see* race
Black Widow (2021), 108, 114
Blade (film series), 5, 93, 136
Bolin, Göran, 40
Boltanski, Luc, 18, 38, 41–3, 115
  The New Spirit of Capitalism, 49
Bond, James (character), 20n4, 23, 58n30
Bonikowski, Bart, 155–6
Booth, Paul, 106
Bordwell, David, 83, 153–4
Boseman, Chadwick, 158
Boutang, Yann Moulier, 47, 57n25, 187
  Cognitive Capitalism, 48–9
Boys, The (TV series), 71
Brando, Marlon, 64
Brooker, Will, 65–6
Burke, Liam, 75, 86–7, 93–4, 96, 97–8
Burton, Tim, 85, 86–7

camera angles, 94
Canby, Vincent, 86
capitalism, 2, 3, 10, 181–2
  and culture, 30–1, 32, 36–7
  and digital-era, 18, 38–52, 187–8
  and film waves, 115–17
  and industrial, 72, 74
  and mass culture, 26–7
  and reproduction, 11–18
  and seriality, 24
Captain America (character), 29, 53, 55, 104
Captain America: Civil War (2016), 19, 109, 152–3, 158, 164–9, 177
Captain America: The First Avenger (2011), 100, 102, 159–60, 163
Captain America: The Winter Soldier (2014), 19, 102, 103
  and populism, 152–3, 158, 159–64, 177
Captain Marvel (character), 29
Carter, Agent Peggy (character), 104
Cartoon Network, 136
cartoons, 6
Castoriadis, Cornelius, 68
Catwoman (2002), 91
CGA (computer-generated animation), 158, 179n7
Chabon, Michael, 29
  The Amazing Adventures of Kavalier and Clay, 23
characters, 23–4, 53, 63, 64, 104–5; *see also* individual characters
Chiapello, Ève, 18, 38, 41–3, 115
  The New Spirit of Capitalism, 49
Christiansen, Steen, 158
Churchill, Winston, 163
cinematography, 82
cliffhangers, 12
Clooney, George, 7, 87
closure, 93
Colbert, Stephen, 149
collectivism, 31
Columbia Pictures, 101
comic books, 1, 2
  and approximations, 117n4
  and fandom, 35, 50, 125
  and navigation, 95
  and non-linear seriality, 96
  see also DC Comics; Marvel Comics
comicbookmovie (website), 126–7
ComicBookResources (website), 126–7
Comics Code, 35
commodities, 15–16, 26–7, 30–5, 50

competition, 109–10
conspiracist ideology, 153, 159–64
Constantine (2005), 91
continuity, 64, 76n9, 91–3
Convergence Culture (Jenkins), 38, 39, 40, 42, 49–50
Coogler, Ryan, 169, 173
cover identity, 29
COVID-19 pandemic, 6, 19, 108, 182, 190
 and streaming, 84, 115
Crary, Jonathan
 24/7, 44–5, 182–3
Cucco, Mario, 89
culture, 2–3, 10, 17–18
 and digital era, 38–44
 and engagement, 11–12
 and externalities, 44–52, 84–5
 and industry, 24, 25–37
Cyborg (character), 109

Daily Dot, The (website), 130
Daniels, Les
 Complete History of Superman, 28
Daredevil (TV series), 96, 114
Dark Knight, The (2008), 1, 75, 101, 153
 and trilogy, 7, 66
Dark Knight Rises, The (2012), 69, 101
Dark Phoenix (2019), 6, 107
Dath, Dietmar, 72
Daum, Timo, 48, 57n26
DC Comics, 4, 5, 6, 25, 91
 and Batman, 86, 87
 and *Database*, 106
 and fan clubs, 56n10
 and hyper-referentiality, 82–3
 and media franchising, 88–9
 and serial proliferation, 53–5
 and Warners, 118n12
 see also Superman (character)
DC Extended Universe (DCEU), 107, 114, 138–40, 143, 186, 187
De Kosnik, Abigail, 34–5, 41
Deadpool (2016), 6, 19, 107, 108, 124–5
 and fandom, 130–7, 144
 and politics, 71
 and reviewers, 142–3
Deadpool 2 (2018), 107, 144–5
Defenders, The (TV series), 114
demographics, 105

Denson, Shane, 10, 19, 62–3, 65
detective fiction, 7–8
digital era, 3, 11, 18–19, 24–5, 116
 and capitalism, 16, 44–52, 186–8
 and Jenkins, 37–44
 and second-wave films, 93–4
 and technology, 84
 see also social media
DiPaolo, Marc, 70
Disney, 100, 108; see also *Marvel Cinematic Universe (MCU)*
Disney+, 51, 114–15, 182, 189
Dittmer, Jason, 152
Doctor Who (TV series), 125
Donner, Richard see *Superman* (1978)
Doom Patrol (TV series), 114
Doyle, Arthur Conan, 7–8, 29
Dracula (character), 23, 65

Ebert, Roger, 86, 90
Eco, Umberto, 7–8, 19
 "Repetition and Innovation", 24, 25
 "The Myth of Superman", 26–7, 59–61, 72
economics, 5–6
Edwards, Jason, 15, 31
Electoral Justice Project, 175
elites, 19, 152, 155, 156–7
engagement *see* politics of engagement
Esposito, Elena, 53–4, 73, 177–8
Evans, Chris, 158
Evans, Elizabeth, 11
exhaustion, 121
externalities, 48–9, 50–2, 84–5

Facebook, 47, 48, 106, 174–5
Falcon and the Winter Soldier, The (TV series), 115
fanboys, 96–8
fandom, 1, 2, 3, 116
 and activities, 14
 and attachment, 34–5
 and *Avengers: Infinity War*, 112–13
 and *Black Panther*, 169
 and comics, 56n10
 and *Deadpool*, 130–7
 and digital era, 41
 and franchises, 45–6
 and hyper-referentiality, 83–4

and industry, 50–1
and *Logan*, 122–4
and management, 13, 19, 125–30, 144–6, 188
and online, 97–100, 101–2, 106–7
and second-wave films, 96–7
and social media, 185–6
and *Suicide Squad*, 137–44
and third-wave films, 104–5
Fantastic Beasts franchise, 6, 189
Fantastic Four (2005/15), 1, 91, 107
far-right, 40, 174–5, 184
fascism, 69, 184
Fast and Furious franchise, 6, 189
Feige, Kevin, 97
Felski, Rita, 14–15
feminism, 151
Fenster, Mark
   Conspiracy Theories, 162, 163
financial crisis, 151
first-wave films, 85–90, 115
Flash Gordon (character), 28, 29, 109
flashbacks, 93, 140–1
Ford, Sam, 11–12
   Spreadable Media, 39–40
Fordism, 18, 30, 31, 32, 44; *see also* post-Fordism
fourth-wave films, 107–15, 116–17
Fox *see* 20th Century Fox
franchises, 6–7, 9–10, 87–90, 182–3
   and fandom, 45–6
   and streaming, 187
   and television, 189
   see also *Marvel Cinematic Universe (MCU)*
Franich, Darren, 163–4
Frankenstein's Monster (character), 23, 65
Fu Manchu (character), 14, 23
Fuchs, Christian, 40

Gaddafi, Muammar, 163
Gallio, Niccolò, 124
Game of Thrones (TV series), 45
games, 189
Gardner, Jared, 97
Garfield, Andrew, 7, *8*
gender, 151
geopolitics, 153, 164–9
Gidron, Noam, 155–6

Gifted, The (TV series), 107, 114
globalization, 44, 45
Godzilla series, 189
good-versus-evil conflict, 72, 75, 152
Google, 47, 48
Gotham City, 87
Graeber, David, 69
Gray, Jonathan, 98
Green, Joshua, 11–12
   Spreadable Media, 39–40
Green Lantern (2011), 101, 130, 136
GTA 5 (game), 189
Guardians of the Galaxy (2014), 108

Hagedorn, Roger, 63
Hardt, Michael, 45
Harry Potter franchise, 6, 58n30, 189
Harvey, David, 116–17
Hassler-Forest, Dan, 1, 4, 72, 75
   and politics, 70, 151
   Science Fiction, Fantasy, and Politics, 45–6, 47
Hatfield, Charles, 69–70
HBO Max, 114, 115, 182
Heer, Jeet, 69–70
Hills, Matt, 19
   Fan Cultures, 125–6, 127–8
Hobbit, The (franchise), 6
Hofstadter, Richard, 156
Holland, Tom, 7, *8*
Holmes, Sherlock (character), 7–8, 29
Horkheimer, Max, 18
   Dialectic of Enlightenment, 24, 26–7, 29–30, 32, 34, 35, 53
Hugo Hercules (comic strip), 28
Hulk (2003), 7, 91
HYDRA, 103, 110, 159–60, 162, 163
hyper-referentiality, 19, 81–5, 115–16, 182–3
   and *Batman* series, 86–7
   and *Deadpool*, 136
   and fourth-wave films, 108–9, 110–11
   and second-wave films, 96–7
   and *Superman* series, 85–6
   and third-wave films, 101, 104–5
hypertext, 105–6

ideology, 32, 33, 37, 41–2
   and conspiracist, 153

and populism, 155–6
see also politics
immaterial labor, 44–52
Incredible Hulk (character), 109
Incredible Hulk, The (2008), 7, 81–2, 100, 102, 104
Incredible Hulk, The (TV series), 81
innovation, 25–6
intellectual property, 9, 10, 54, 62, 84, 100
Internet, 11, 186; *see also* digital era; websites
intertextuality, 82, 83, 117n3, 149
Invincible Iron Man, The (comic series), 73
io9.com (website), 127, 130, 132, 136, 164
 and *Suicide Squad*, 138, 139–40, 142, 143–4
Iron Fist (TV series), 114
Iron Man (character), 73
 and Captain America, 165, 167, *168*
 and Spider-Man, 109
Iron Man (2008), 75, 100, 102, 104
 and politics, 153, 158
Iron Man 2 (2010), 100, 102
Iron Man 3 (2013), 1, 100, 102, 103
iTunes, 106

Jackman, Hugh, 7, 122–3, 124
Jahn-Sudmann, Andreas, 109–10
Jameson, Fredric, 165
Jaws (1975), 5
Jenkins, Henry, 11–12, 18, 24–5, 126
 Convergence Culture, 3
 and digital era, 37–44, 45, 49–50, 98
Jessica Jones (comic series), 74
Jessica Jones (TV series), 114
Johnson, Derek, 9, 88
Joker (character), 86, 139
Joker (2019), 107–8, 145
Jonah Hex (2010), 101
Jones, Jessica (character), 74
justice, 29, 70
Justice League (2017), 83, 107, 109, 183

Kahen-Kashi, David, 160, 161
Kaltwasser, Cristóbal Rovira, 151–2, 154–5, 156
Keaton, Michael, 7, 86, 87, *88*
Kelleter, Frank, 7, 8–9, 14, 15, 109–10
 and fandom, 128, 129, 140

and seriality, 62, 63–4, 65
Kent, Clark (character), 28, 59, 87
Killmonger (character), 170–3
Kilmer, Val, 7, 87, *88*
Kirby, Jack, 96
Klock, Geoff, 71
Kobek, Jarett
 I Hate the Internet, 181, 182, 185
Kozinets, Robert, 50

Laclau, Ernesto, 155
Lang, Fritz, 28
Late Show (TV show), 149
Latour, Bruno, 14, 15, 20n7–8
Lazzarato, Maurizio, 47, 49, 57n24
Lee, Ang, 7
Legion (TV series), 107, 114
leisure *see* recreation
Leterrier, Louis, 7, 81–2
Leto, Jared, 139, 145
Lévy, Pierre, 40, 44
licensing, 100
Liefeld, Rob, 131, 134, 146n7
linear seriality, 62–5, 67, 82–3
 and second-wave films, 91–3
 and third-wave films, 100–1, 102, 105–6
Logan (2017), 73, 107, 108, 121–5
 and fandom, 127, 144
logos, 89
Loki (TV series), 115
Loock, Kathleen, 62
Lord of the Rings franchise, 6, 58n30
Lost (TV series), 11
"lost parents", 29
Lucas, George, 6
Luhmann, Niklas, 58n29, 77n19, 150
 The Reality of Mass Media, 177
Luke Cage (TV series), 114

McAvoy, James, 7
Mack, David, 96
McLuhan, Marshall, 94–5
Maguire, Tobey, 7, *8*
Maltby, Richard, 153
Man of Steel (2013), 7, 101, 107, 139
Mangold, James *see Logan*
Manichean conflict, 70, 150, 159
Mark of Zorro, The (1920), 28

marketing, 5, 13, 19, 89, 124
  and *Black Panther*, 169, 180n14
  and *Deadpool*, 132–4
  and *Deadpool 2*, 144–5
  and *Logan*, 127
  see also media
Marvel Cinematic Universe (MCU), 7, 65, 106–7, 186, 187
  and fourth-wave films, 107, 110, 112
  and *One Shots*, 103–4, 119n29
  and television, 102–3, 114–15
  and third-wave films, 100–2, 104–6
  see also Captain America
Marvel Comics, 4, 5, 6, 25
  and *Deadpool*, 135
  and fan clubs, 56n10
  and hyper-referentiality, 82–3
  and *The Incredible Hulk*, 81–2
  and *Invincible Iron Man* series, 73
  and Jones, Jessica, 74
  and linear seriality, 65
  and politics, 153
  and second-wave films, 90, 91
  and serial proliferation, 53–5
  see also X-Men (characters)
Marvel Database, 106
Marvel's Spider-Man (game), 189
Marvel's The Avengers (2012), 100
Marx, Karl, 27, 30
Marxism, 15–16
Mary Sue, The (website), 127, 132, 136
Matrix trilogy (1999–2003), 84
Mayer, Ruth, 14, 23–4, 102
media, 1, 2, 3, 16–17
  and *Black Panther*, 169–70, 171
  and collectivism, 31
  and cross-proliferation, 27–9
  and events, 127–8
  and franchising, 9, 10, 87–90
  and populism, 177–8
  see also digital era; social media
Meehan, Eileen, 9–10
Meier, Stefan, 86
merchandise, 5, 9, 23, 88–9, 125
Metacritic (website), 138, 139
Metropolis (1929), 28
Michael, George, 136
Miller, Frank, 96
Miller, Tim, 130, 132, 135, 137

mise-en-scène, 82, 87
Mittel, Jason, 103, 112
motifs, 29
Mudde, Cas, 151–2, 154–5, 156
music *see* soundtracks

narrative, 2, 7, 25
  and competition, 109–10
  and conspiracy, 162–4
  and continuity, 91–3
  and engagement, 13
  and evolving, 14
  and fourth-wave films, 108–9
  and fragmentation, 110–13
  and hypertext, 105–6
  and motifs, 29
  and perseverance, 73–5
  and political imaginary, 68–71
  and populism, 157
  and seriality, 8–9, 10, 62–4, 65, 67–8
  see also hyper-referentiality
nationalism, 152, 157
Nazi Germany, 160
Negri, Antonio, 45
neoliberalism, 44–5, 57n21, 75
Nerdist (website), 126–7, 136
Netflix, 51, 106, 114, 115, 182–3, 186
New Mutants, The (2020), 6, 107, 131
Nicieza, Fabian, 131
Nietzsche, Friedrich, 28
Nightcrawler (character), 94
Nightingale, Virginia, 125
N'Jobu (character), 170, 171–2
Nolan, Christopher, 7, 66, 69
Nolte, John, 160
non-linear seriality, 62, 65–7, 76n11, 95–6
  and *Deadpool*, 135–6
  and hyper-referentiality, 82–3, 85–90
  and *Suicide Squad*, 140–2
North, Dan, 158
NSA (National Security Agency), 160

Obama, Barack, 160
Ocasio-Cortez, Alexandria, 150

Palmiotti, Jimmy, 96
pandemic *see* COVID-19 pandemic
paratext, 106–7, 127–8
Parker, Peter (character), 73

partisan strife, 153, 159, 160, 164–9
Pattinson, Robert, 7
Pelosi, Nancy, 149
perseverance, 72–5
Phoenix, Joaquin, 145
Pirates of the Caribbean franchise, 6
politics, 60–1, 68–72, 74–5, 149–51
   and *Black Panther*, 169–76
   and *Captain America: Civil War*, 164–9
   and *Captain America: The Winter Soldier*, 159–64
   and *V for Vendetta*, 183–5
   see also capitalism; populism
politics of engagement, 2–3, 11–18, 83, 122–3
Popeye (comic strip), 28
popular culture *see* culture
populism, 2, 3, 13, 19, 151–9, 176–8
post-Fordism, 9, 44, 46, 57n21, 115
pre-boots, 62
pre-selling, 53–4
press *see* media
print, 31
production, 6, 34–6, 39–40, 41
professional consumers, 16–17
Professor X (character), 7, 73, 121
profit, 5–6, 10, 40, 51, 63
Pulse, The (2004–6), 74
Punisher, The (2004), 91
Punisher, The (TV series), 114

Quesada, Joe, 96

race, 151, 153, 154, 162, 169–76
radio, 28, 31
Raimi, Sam, 7, 73
reboots, 7–9, 10, 20n4, 101
recreation, 30–3, 34, 35–6, 37, 41, 44–5
Reese, Rhett, 130, 132
Reeve, Christopher, 5
regular people, 70, 71, 156–7
religion, 29
repetition, 25–7, 29–30, 53
requels, 62
retconning, 64
Reynolds, Richard, 29, 69
Reynolds, Ryan, 130, 131, 132, 133–4, 146n8

Robbie, Margot, 145
Rogers, Buck (character), 28
Romita, John, Sr., 96
Roosevelt, Franklin, 163
Rosenberg, Alyssa, 163–4
RottenTomatoes (website), 138, 139, 174
Russo, Anthony and Joe, 113, 159, 166

San Diego Comic Con, 100, 132
Sanders, Bernie, 150
Schiff, Adam, 149
Schumacher, Joel, 87
science, 29
Scott-Heron, Gil, 169
Scott, Suzanne, 97–8
second-wave films, 90–100, 115, 116
Seinfeld (TV show), 63
September 11 *see* 9/11 attacks
sequels, 2, 5, 6–7, 64
seriality, 10, 60–1, 188–9
   and agency, 11–18
   and characters, 23–4
   and culture industry, 33–7
   and fourth-wave films, 113
   and prehistory, 53–5
   and Superman, 59–60
   see also linear seriality; non-linear seriality
Shadow, The (magazine), 28
Shazam! (2019), 107, 113
S.H.I.E.L.D., 153, 159–62, 163
short films, 103–4, 105
Shuster, Joe, 27–8, 29
Siegel, Jerry, 27–8, 29
Singer, Bryan, 7
slavery, 171–2
Smith, Kevin, 96
Smith, Murray, 84
Snowden, Edward, 160
Snyder, Zack, 7, 71, 97, 108, 139
social imaginary significations, 68
social media, 122–3, 124, 126, 185–6, 189–90
   and *Deadpool*, 132, 133
   see also Facebook; Twitter; YouTube
Sony, 101, 108
soundtracks, 5, 142, 146n1, 169
special effects, 4, 13, 82, 93, 95, 157–8
Spider-Man (character), 23–4, 55, 62

Spider-Man (2002/2002/2007), 5, 7, *8*,
    91, 95–6
  and continuity, 92, 93
  and franchise, 101
  and perseverance, 73
  and politics, 70
Spider-Man: Homecoming (2018), 109
spin-offs, 2, 6–7, 100, 101
Stalin, Joseph, 163
Stanfill, Mel, 19, 41, 50–1
  Exploiting Fandom, 126, 137
Star Trek (film/TV series), 20n4, 45, 50,
    58n30
  and continuity, 76n9
  and franchise, 189
  and seriality, 63, 65
Star Wars (film series), 5, 6, 58n30, 84, 189
Stargirl (TV series), 114
Stark, Tony (character), 73, 82
state, the, 69, 70, 153, 157
Stein, Daniel, 14, 15, 67–8, 128, 129, 140
Steinert, Heinz, 29–30
Steinschaden, Fabian, 15
Stewart, Patrick, 7
storytelling *see* narrative
storyworld, 45, 63, 64–5, 70–1, 76n6, 101
  and television, 114
Straume, Ingerid, 41
streaming, 51–2, 84, 106, 114–15, 182–3,
    186–7
  and COVID-19 pandemic, 108
Stringer, Julian, 4
studios, 6, 20n2; *see also* individual studios
subplots, 92
Suicide Squad (2016), 19, 71, 107, 125
  and fandom, 137–44, 145, 188
Super Friends (TV series), 9
super-powers, 29, 59, 60
Supergirl (1984), 85
SuperHeroHype (website), 130
Superman (character), 1, 23–4, 27–9, 53,
    55n5
  and Eco, 26, 59–61, 72
  and politics, 69
  and reboots, 101
  and seriality, 63, 66
Superman (comic strip), 86
Superman (radio serial), 28
Superman (1978), 5, 6, 19

and franchise, 9, 89
and hyper-referentiality, 84, 85–6, 87, 183
and justice, 70
and seriality, 64
Superman II (1980), 5, 64, 85
Superman III (1983), 85
Superman IV: The Quest for Peace (1987), 85
Superman Returns (2006), 7, 91
surveillance, 153, 160, 162
Swamp Thing (TV series), 114

Taylor, Aaron, 31, 83, 96–8, 126
T'Challa (character), 170–1, 172–3
team-ups, 109–10
television, 11, 12–13, 31, 114–15, 182–3,
    188–9
  and *MCU*, 102–3, 105
  and seriality, 62, 63
Terranova, Tiziana, 40–1
terrorism, 103, 158, 159, 166; *see also* 9/11
    attacks
theatrical runs, 1, 89–90, 123, 126–7, 137
third-wave films, 100–7, 115
Thompson, Kristin, 12, 141, 143
Thor (2011), 100, 102
Thor: Ragnarok (2017), 109, 111
Thor: The Dark World (2013), 100, 102
Titans (TV series), 114
Tomasovic, Dick, 13
toys, 5, 6, 89
Transformers franchise, 6, 58n30
Trendacosta, Katharine, 140
Trump, Donald, 149–50, 170, 171, 173,
    182, 183
twists, 112–13
Twitter, 48, 106, 113, 149–50
  and *Black Panther*, 173–5, 176
  and *Suicide Squad*, 139

"Übermensch", 28
unfree symbolic commons, 53–4, 58n30

V for Vendetta (2005), 70, 91, 179n5, 183–5
Venom (2018), 1, 108
Vercellone, Carlo, 46–8, 54, 57n22–3, 187
Vignold, Peter, 188
villains, 69, 70, 71, 156–7, 177
violence, 69, 70, 71, 151, 162, 177
  and *Logan*, 121, 123

Walking Dead, The (TV series), 45
WandaVision (TV series), 115
War on Terror, 151
Warner Bros., 9, 91, 101, 107–8
  and television, 114, 115
  see also *DC Extended Universe (DCEU)*
Warner Communications (WCI), 9, 88–9
Watchmen (2008), 71, 101
Webb, Marc, 7
websites, 1, 98–9; *see also* individual sites
Wernick, Paul, 130, 132
Wessel, Ben, 150
Whedon, Josh, 97
Wilmore, Alison, 160, 161
Wolf, Mark J. P., 92
Wolverine (character), 6, 7, 73, 92
  and *Logan*, 121–3
  and spin-offs, 101
Wonder Woman (character), 1, 29, 53, 109
Wonder Woman (2017), 107
Wonder Woman 1984 (2020), 107, 108, 114

Worcester, Kent, 69–70
work, 30–1, 32, 34, 41, 44–5, 73–4; *see also* immaterial labor
world-building, 92–3
Wylie, Philip
  Gladiator, 28

X-Files, The (TV series), 11
X-Men (characters), 1, 23
X-Men (film series), 5, 6–7, 66–7, 101, 107
  and hyper-referentiality, 92–3, 94, *95*, 96
  see also *Deadpool*; *Logan*
X-Men: Apocalypse (2016), 107
X-Men Origins: Wolverine (2009), 130, 131–2

Yockey, Matt, 87, 153
YouTube, 48, 106, 150

Zuboff, Shoshanna, 48

EU representative:
Easy Access System Europe
Mustamäe tee 50, 10621 Tallinn, Estonia
Gpsr.requests@easproject.com

www.ingramcontent.com/pod-product-compliance
Lightning Source LLC
Chambersburg PA
CBHW070349240426
43671CB00013BA/2449